TRADE NAME ORIGINS

TRADE NAME ORIGINS

Adrian Room

Printed on recyclable paper

NTC *Publishing Group*
NTC/Contemporary Publishing Company

Originally published as *NTC's Dictionary of Trade Name Origins*

Contents

The detailed business of the lunch engaged our attention for a while, and then I leant across my plate. 'And *now?*' said I.

'It's the secret of vigour. Didn't you read that label?'

'Yes, but . . .'

'It's selling like hot cakes.'

'And what is it?' I pressed.

'Well,' said my uncle, and then leant forward and spoke softly under cover of his hand, 'It's nothing more or less than . . .'

(But here an unfortunate scruple intervenes. After all, Tono-Bungay is still a marketable commodity and in the hands of purchasers, who bought it from – among other vendors – me. No! I am afraid I cannot give it away.)

H. G. Wells, *Tono-Bungay*

Introduction

Our main medium of communication is language, and language we traditionally tend to regard as a battery of words and names that we arrange in a conventional manner, obeying certain rules of grammar, spelling and the like, in order to say what we want to say, in speech or writing.

If asked to define more closely what we understand by 'words' and 'names', we would probably say that 'words' are the speech units contained in standard dictionaries and that 'names' are the special words used to designate a particular object or concept.

Indeed, if we are to distinguish between the two categories, we would add that 'words' are used to convey meaning, whereas 'names' are used more to indicate – to name, in fact. 'Linctus', for example, means 'a soothing syrupy cough-mixture' (in the definition of the *Concise Oxford Dictionary*), but 'London' has no meaning in itself – it is the name used to designate 'the capital city of the United Kingdom'.

There is another difference, too, between 'words' and 'names'. Words, the everyday dictionary sort, usually have a well-defined origin or etymology. Names, on the other hand, frequently have an origin that is a good deal more obscure or complex. Thus 'linctus' derives from the Latin verb *lingere*, 'to lick', but the exact origin of the name 'London' is still much disputed. It may even itself derive from some other name.

In considering names we are aware, of course, that there are several categories of names. There are personal names, place names, house names, boat names, pet names (the ones we give our domestic animals) – and trade names, among others.

It is this latter category that this book is about. In particular, it is the *origin* of trade names that the book is about.

My objective in writing such a book is twofold. In the first place, it is to fill a gap. There have been a number of books dealing with the origins of personal names (surnames and first names) and with place names, but very few with trade names. Second, many trade names have extremely interesting origins, whether regarded from a linguistic angle or a socio-historical one. For a start, most trade names, unlike personal names and place names, are comparatively recent, and have appeared within the last hundred years. Then, again unlike personal and place names, the vast majority of trade names have been consciously and artificially devised, have been 'manufactured' much as the commercial products they designate have been manufactured.

There is another special feature about trade names that distinguishes them from other types of name. They not only designate – the particular product of a particular manufacturer, or that particular manufacturer himself – but they advertise. That, after all, is one of their primary functions, to persuade us, the consumers, to buy and use product A as distinct from product B.

The way in which this is done is a reasonably complex process. After a while, as with some of the older and most familiar trade names, a name comes to acquire its own kind of aura of positiveness, its own overtones of meaning. Just as 'London' not only designates 'the capital of the United Kingdom', it actually comes to *mean* 'the capital of the United Kingdom', with all that the concept implies (a large city, the seat of parliament, the focal point of the country, the location of headquarters of many of the country's institutions, and so on). In a similar manner, a trade name such as 'Lux' comes not only to indicate a particular brand of soap, it comes to acquire the meaning of 'soap', even to the extent that it can lose much of its association with a particular product. To say, 'I washed it in soap' and 'I washed it in Lux' is thus almost the same thing, since Lux *is* soap. (Legally, of course, such a suggestion of genericism can be damaging.)

And while 'Lux' comes to mean what 'soap' means (a medium for the effective washing of clothes, the skin, and other objects), it simultaneously fulfils another function. For the name 'Lux' in itself suggests other words, such as 'luxury' and 'luck'. These 'free associations', as they are known in the advertising business, can be very valuable in the promotion and marketing process of a particular product. True, many personal names and place names also have such associations (who is the prettier, Fiona or Florence? which is the more attractive, Bootle or Bournemouth?), but trade names have them much more readily and obviously. After all, they are intended to!

Trade names, thus, form a special and interesting category of name. At the same time they are, next to personal and place names, the most prominent and important in our day-to-day communications and in fact in our daily lives. How, indeed, can we actually go about our daily affairs and our lives without the use of commercial products, each of which has its name? The bread we eat and the butter we spread on it, the tea we drink and the sweeteners we put in it, the shoes we wear, the cars we drive, the TV sets we buy or rent, the soap we wash with (not necessarily Lux), the polish we clean with, the pens we write with, the mowers we mow with, the drinks we ply our guests with – all these, and many more, have a distinguishing trade name.

As with most categories of name, we tend to take trade names for granted, and accept that product A is called 'Splodge' and product B 'Bracknel'. Since our business in this book, however, is to examine the origins of trade names we must look more closely at the names themselves. What sort of words are they?

In general, it can be immediately seen that trade names seem to be based either on existing names, mainly personal names, or existing standard words, or a combination of both. On the other hand there seem to be several trade names that have no recognisable origin – there is no known existing name or word that we can relate them to.

There are thus 'name names', 'word names', and 'arbitrary names'. (Such colloquial terms may horrify linguists, but this is not a solemn linguistic work, but a popular, although considered, treatment of the way in which trade names originate.)

Among the 'name names' we find such familiar names as those of the major chain stores (Woolworth, W.H. Smith, Marks & Spencer, Debenham, and so on), those of patent medicines and household remedies (J. Collis Browne's Compound, Gee's Linctus, Pears Soap, Wilkinson Sword razor blades), as well as a whole range of household names, from Dunlop tyres to Ford cars, Clark's shoes to Ingersoll watches, Black & Decker drills to Lipton's tea, Robinson's orange squash to Wall's ice cream, and Parker pens to Lloyds bank. Most such names are those of the manufacturers or the founders of the company concerned, or else those of the inventor or patentee of the product. Among place names commonly found for commercial products are London (carpets, records, washbasins, pins, among other things), Cambridge (carpets, watches, shoes, scientific instruments, and so on), Oxford (doors, watches, carpets, urinals, hats, stationery, etc.) and many more. These particular three, of course, have good or favourable 'free associations'. Further, the names do not imply that the products originate from these cities, any more than Everest double glazing comes from the Himalayas.

Among well-known 'word' names we find some of the more modern food-chain stores (Pricerite, Safeway, Fine Fare), many actual food products (Mothers Pride, Sunblest, Crunchie), and a similar range of goods, products and services (Double Two shirts, Krooklok car locks, Silvo silver polish, Tuf shoes).

'Arbitrary' names, with no apparent meaning or reference, are much less common, but among the best known are such names as *Araldite, Bradosol, Drene, Kodak, Lenor, Omo,* and *Saxa*. These all occur in this Dictionary, and I have attempted to give a more or less satisfactory interpretation – in some cases, alas, less than satisfactory – of all of them.

There is little doubt that 'word names' are both more prolific and on the whole more satisfactory, because meaningful, than 'name names' or 'arbitrary names'. They offer much greater scope for inventiveness, wittiness, originality, humour, and 'pointedness' than do names derived from the name of a person or place. The fact that word names frequently have erratic or eccentric spelling (as Krooklok and Tuf above) is no drawback to their interpretation, indeed it makes them more memorable and, often, more 'homely'.

One of the most important factors in the creation of word names is, naturally, the choice of word or words, and in very many instances, a name-creator will deliberately choose a standard word or element with a clear 'prestige' association – something that suggests quality, class, power, modernity, exclusivity, versatility, popularity, wholesomeness, or whatever the desirable attribute of the product is. Among such words and elements are the following:

Ace, Acme, Aero-, Air, All, Auto, Bulldog, Castle, Champion, City, Conquest, Countess, Crown, Crystal, Diamond, Double, Dream, Duo-, Dura-, Eagle, Easi-, Electro-, Embassy, Ever-, Executive, Express, Fair-, Fairy, Fast-, Flexi-, Gay, Globe, Gold(en), Grand, Green, Guard, Handi-, Hi-, Ideal, Imperial, Inter-, Iso-, Jet, Kent, Kleen-, Lady, Life, Light, Lion, Long, Lotus, Magi-, Major, Master, May, Meta-, Mini-, Mod-, Monarch, Multi-, Nat-, New, Nova-, Old, Oxi-, Para-, Perma-, Pilot, Plasto-, Poly-, Premier, Presto, Princess, Pure, Queen, Quick, Radi-, Rapid, Ray, Red, Reliance, Robo-, Roll, Rota-(Roto-), Royal, Safari, San-, Select, Servo-, Silver, Simplex, Sky, Sol-, Sovereign, Speed, Standard, Star, Stay, Ster-, Sun, Super-, Sure, Swan, Swift, Tan-, Tech-, Tel-, The, Thermo-, Top, Trans-, Trident, Triumph, Tru-, Tuf-, Twin, Ultra, Uni-, Val-, Vari-, Victor, Viking, Vita-, Wel-, West, White, Wizard, Wonder, Young, Zodiac.

Some of the elements seem to be popular simply for their scientific or technological associations, as Iso- (suggesting 'isobar', 'isomer', 'isometric', 'isotherm', 'isotope' and the like – perhaps even the more ordinary 'isolation') and Meta-('metabolic', 'metamorphosis', 'metaphysical', 'metathesis', but also, of course, 'metal'). Others have more than one association. Nat-, for example, suggests both 'national' and 'natural', Radi- suggests 'radical', 'radiate', 'radio' and 'radium', and Tel- points to 'television', 'telephone', 'telex', 'telegraph' and any number of 'tele-' instruments. Val-, similarly, conjures up both 'value' and 'valour', while Uni- has a number of connections – 'universal', 'uniform', 'union', 'unique' and 'unity' among them. Ster- will do for both 'sterling' and 'sterile'. Tan- is rather more obscure. Its principal association would seem to be 'tandem' (i.e. referring to the 'duality' of a product), although 'tangent' and even 'tan' itself are also possible links.

It will be noticed that the particular 'prestige' association evoked will vary from one word or element to another. The 'royal' ones, for example, (Crown, King, Princess, Queen, Royal, Sovereign) evoke high class and quality, whereas the 'speed' ones (Express, Fast-, Quick, Rapid, Speed) are used to imply a rapid and efficient process or operation. A special 'prestige' word is The, used to suggest uniqueness. Among such products are The Club (sleeping bags), The Dale (men's boots), The Eyelet (brass eyelets), The Gripwell (shoes), The Little Nipper (mousetraps), The News (hats), and The Stronghold (padlocks).

Foreign words, too, are sometimes chosen for a stylish trade name, especially Latin words (both classical and 'classy') such as Lux ('light') and Rex ('king'), and French words (sophisticated) such as Beau or Bel ('beautiful'). The Latin Lux will thus give our Lux soap yet another favourable association.

Name-creators do not restrict themselves to standard words, though, as we have seen. Among popular 'prestige' names are not only the already quoted Oxford and Cambridge but 'royal' names such as Windsor and York and names from classical mythology, such as Ajax, Atlas, Hercules, Jupiter, Mercury and Vulcan. Saints' names are fairly popular, too, and are usually prefixed by 'St'. Among them are St Andrew, St Christopher, St George (the most popular in Britain), St Crispin and the Marks & Spencer *St Michael*. When it comes to selecting a personal name that is unconnected with the manufacturer, Peter is curiously popular – no doubt by association with Peter Pan, itself a widely used trade name for children's wear, toys and other youthful products.

Many of these words and elements are in effect prefixes, added to the beginning of another word or existing name. Certain suffixes, forming the final element of a name, are also popular and are their corollary. They are dealt with separately, in Appendix I (p.193).

A consideration of the trade names so far cited has given us an insight into the actual process of creating and forming a satisfactory trade name. We have seen that 'name names' derive ready-made from existing personal or place names, but that 'word names' are deliberately devised by the name-creators – who may also choose to exploit the favourable associations of an existing name such as Oxford or Cambridge.

Who are the name-creators?

Trade names can be devised by a single individual or by literally thousands of people, they can spring from the processes of human thought or from the bowels of a computer.

Many names created by a single person owe their origin to the inventor or initial marketer of a product, or to the founder of a company. A glance through the entries of this Dictionary will show several names that originated thus, such as *Durex* and *57 Varieties*.

Other names are evolved by a firm's marketing department or by a consumer research organisation, usually in conjunction with a consumer survey of some kind to test the reactions that certain proposed or short-listed names may have on members of the public or on potential buyers of the product. The results of such surveys may sometimes bring surprises. The American company *Socony-Vacuum* asked a marketing research organisation to test their proposed new and shortened name of 'Sovac'. This was related by members of the public to Communism and the Soviet Union so was hastily abandoned, with the company opting for *Socony Mobil* Oil instead. Another American company, the B.F. Goodrich Co., tested some proposed names for a new synthetic fibre among housewives. Four out of ten women felt that one name, 'Merex', suggested a soap, while the name 'Dicuna' brought no response at all, favourable or unfavourable. Eventually the name selected was 'Darlan', which the ladies regarded as suggesting a rich synthetic fabric. (Perhaps one of their 'free associations' was 'darling'?)

To choose a name is not the same as to devise it in the first place, however, and many such selected names are initially concocted by computer, especially where the product is the result of some sophisticated scientific or technical process, such as the synthetic fibre mentioned, or a new drug. Many such names are virtually meaningless, and so are 'arbitrary names'. They can, however, have free associations, as perhaps 'Darlan' did. (Appendix II, p.203, lists some examples of computer-devised names.)

There seems little doubt, however, that the most successful names are those devised by one or more human beings, and the final choice may very often be that of a single individual. If such a person is not himself closely connected with the product or the manufacturing company, he can be a member of the public, and have devised the name by entering a naming contest.

Such contests are popular with many members of the public, who hope that a felicitous choice of name for a new product may win them handsome prizes in the form of cash or goods. A few such contests have produced some famous trade names, as for example *Hovis*. In more recent times, one wonders whether the name 'Adam Goodmint' chosen by a Leamington housewife in 1959 for a new brand of confectionery was really worth the £1,500 first prize that she won. (Other prizewinners in the same contest – the aim was to choose a name for a mythical guardsman who symbolised the new confectionery – devised the equally terrible puns 'Lemmie Finish' and 'Ivan I. Dealmint'. For these each winner received a sports car!)

Similar naming contests are sometimes organised among the workforce of a company. In 1978 the marketing staffs of Austin Morris assembled a gigantic list of 8,500 possible names, derived from several sources, for the company's new *Mini* to be launched in the autumn of 1980. The names were eventually whittled down to a shortlist of three, and these were submitted to almost the total workforce at Austin Morris, over 19,000 employees, for a final choice. The winning name was the *Metro* (see *Mini* for the voting figures and the other two names). The prizes for the first two correct *Metro* votes drawn were a *Mini* 1000 each – these to be replaced by the new Metro itself when the car was eventually launched.

In the course of their search for a possible new name for the car, Austin Morris were wary of listing a name that could have an undesirable meaning in some foreign language. This is a hazard that besets all name-creators, even – perhaps especially – computers. Doubtless Austin Morris had learned from the classic case of Rolls-Royce, who seeking a suitable car name to follow their successful run of 'ethereal' names (Silver Ghost, Silver Wraith, Silver Phantom) came up with 'Silver Mist'. When it was pointed out, however, that 'Mist' is the German for 'manure' they were obliged to do a rapid rethink – and devised instead the 'Silver Shadow'. Ford, too, were nearly led astray in this way: one of the shortlisted (and computer-devised) names for the car that eventually became the Corsair was 'Copreta'. This was also dropped when it was discovered that Greek *kopros* has the same meaning as the German 'Mist'. . . Such undesirable meanings can range from the purely ludicrous – *Nescafé* in Portuguese has a name that suggests it is not coffee – to the scabrous. (For instances of these, also involving Portuguese, see *Cona* and *Foden*.) Other foreign blunderous names marketed in Britain have been the French soft drink Pschitt and a Finnish lock de-icing compound called Super Piss.

Virtually all trade names, of course, are also registered trade marks, and there thus exist well-defined constraints for names that may and may not be registered, apart from the obvious ones arising from an undesirable foreign meaning.

The current act that lays down the requirements for an acceptable trade name is the Trade Marks Act of 1938. In order to qualify for registration a proposed name must be at least one of the following:
1 The name of the company, individual or firm represented in a special or particular name.

2 The signature of the applicant for registration or of some predecessor in the business.
3 An invented word or words.
4 A word or words having no direct reference to the character or quality of the goods and not being, according to its ordinary signification, a geographical name or a surname.
5 Any other distinctive mark; but a name, signature or word other than such as fall within the above descriptions will only be registrable upon evidence of its distinctiveness being shown.

An 'invented word' is not necessarily simply a misspelt one, such as 'Uneeda' or 'Orlwoola' (both of which were in fact refused registration on the grounds that they were not distinctive.) It has come to be defined as a word that 'should be clearly and substantially different from any word in ordinary and common use'. Thus, examples of well-known invented names are *Bovril*, *Enkalon*, *Formica*, *Sanatogen*, *Copydex*, *Kodak*, *Ferodo*, *Dulux*, *Britvic* and *Ercol*. The fact that *Kodak* is a genuinely arbitrary word, unlike any existing word or name, while *Copydex* incorporates the recognisable everyday word 'copy' with the suffix '-dex' does not invalidate the legal acceptability of the names as 'invented'. *Dulux*, however, is closer to a foreign word – to French *du luxe*, 'luxury' – and although technically still an 'invented' word is a reminder that there exist today legally registered trade names that are, in fact, ordinary and common words in a foreign language. Some of these, such as *Persil* (French for 'parsley'), slipped through the net in the early years of tradename registration. (*Persil* might, however, have qualified on the grounds that it is a word that has 'no direct reference to the character or quality of the goods'.)

This fourth point – the 'character or quality' stipulation – explains the wide prevalence of trade names that *are* ordinary words. In the case of names such as *Carnation* (evaporated milk), *Harp* (lager), *Jaguar* (cars), *Lotus* (shoes) and *Gumption* (cleansing preparations) there is clearly no direct reference to the actual character or quality of the products. Moreover, the words make distinctive trade marks.

The whole point, of course, in registering a trade name is to secure exclusive rights to it. A company wishes to emphasise that it alone manufactures 'Splodge', and that although there may be other products in the same category (detergents or whatever) it, the Yahoo Company Limited, has sole rights to the use of the name 'Splodge' for its particular product. It follows that any other company that puts a similar product called 'Splodge' (or even 'Spludge') on the market is guilty of 'passing off' and can be taken to court for infringement of trade mark.

In order to avoid coming up with a trade name that is 'deceptive'

8

from the point of view of possible registration, a company may have to spend much time and effort combing through the pages of the Trade Marks Register to ensure that no similar name already exists. The search procedure involves the rather convoluted mental approach needed by a crossword-puzzle solver. Suppose, for example, that you wish to check the registrability of the name *Harpic* (which is already registered, of course). You must not only look under this spelling of the name, but allow for a Cockney version with dropped aitches and for regional variations in pronunciation. Your search pattern might then go something like this:

```
HARPIC HAPPIC ARPIC   APPIC  ORPIC  OPPIC  URPIC  UPPIC
HARPIK HAPPIK ARPIK   APPIK  ORPIK  OPPIK  URPIK  UPPIK
HARPIT HAPPIT ARPIT   APPIT  ORPIT  OPPIT  URPIT  UPPIT
```

and so on.

The actual degree of similarity between a registered name and one filed for registration, and the likelihood of confusion that may consequently result from it, may have to be legally determined. The name 'Galaxy', for example, was not permitted to be registered for a category of foodstuffs since it was confusingly similar to *Glaxo*. For the same reason 'Rysta' was not acceptable for stockings because of its similarity to *Aristoc*, and 'Alka-Vescent' could not be registered for a brand of tablets for making seltzer water since it closely resembled *Alka-Seltzer* tablets. On the other hand both Suncrush and Sunfresh are makes of fruit squash, and in spite of their similarity are held to be not liable to confusion in the mind of the purchaser.

Cases have been recorded where existing trade marks have not been carefully respected. Since the war many of these have originated with Far-Eastern firms, in such countries as Taiwan and Hong Kong. Goods of cheaper quality but of similar outward appearance may be marketed either under identical names, as has happened with so called 'Dunlop' tennis rackets,* or under slightly altered spellings of the name, as with the version of the Raleigh *Chopper* bicycle (which see) named 'Choper', 'Cropper' and 'Clopper', among others. In the late 1940s and early 1950s the Parker Pen Co. were more annoyed than amused to find versions of their '51' pens being mass produced in Italy (mainly Turin) under the name 'P.Arker'. Imitation Parker pens have also been produced in Japan – moreover in a town already named Usa so that the pens could be honestly said to be 'MADE IN USA'! This enterprise was undertaken apparently with the knowledge and even possible

---

* Reported in the *Dunlop News*, July 1979, under the agreeable headline 'TENNIS RACKET SMASHED'. The bogus rackets were exported from Hong Kong and supplied to European retailers by Leprechaun Fashions Ltd.

backing of the Ministry of International Trade and Industry in Japan. Usa continues to flourish as a city of over 50,000 inhabitants on the southern island of Kyushu.

One of the permanent fears hanging over a company is that it will for some reason lose the exclusive right to its registered trade name. When this happens, the name legally becomes a generic word – and any other company has the right to use it for its own products. This happened notably in the early days of trade-name legislation, with such household names as *Gramophone*, *Linoleum*, *Aspirin*, *Escalator* and Launderette being lost to the manufacturing companies who had previously owned them exclusively and used them for their products (these particular ones in the United Kingdom).

When a registered trade mark, either by design or default, becomes generic, it immediately assumes the status of a standard word, and is written with a small letter, not a capital. This now applies to all the names just quoted. (The *Gramophone* Company, however, still exists as a registered name.)

It does not follow that when a name loses its registered status in one country it will automatically lose it in others. The trade name *Thermos*, for example, is still registered – and rigorously protected – in Britain, but has become generic ('thermos') in the United States. Similarly, 'shredded wheat' can be used as a generic term for this type of cereal by any manufacturer (see this entry for the history of the name).

It equally does not follow that every new coined word is necessarily a valid trade mark right from the start simply because it is a new word that no one has used before. *Nylon*, for example, has never been a registered trade mark, although it is a protected word.

What happens – or should happen – in law, of course, and what happens in practice are often two different matters. Most manufacturers will try to insist on the accurate use of their registered names. By 'accurate' they mean the legally correct written form of the name, which must have a capital letter, be used as an adjective not a noun or verb, and even additionally appear within quotation marks. You are correct, therefore, to write that you propose to clean the sitting-room carpet with a 'Hoover' vacuum-cleaner. Some people, however, will not only use the name incorrectly (with a small letter and not as an adjective) but will sometimes apply it to a product that is not even manufactured by the registering company. 'I had to hoover that carpet three times last week,' a chatty aunt might write. And we are certainly almost all of us guilty of such indiscretions when we use the names in our everyday speech.

The owners of a registered trade name, however, have no right to prevent us, the members of the public, from using their names, or mis-using them, in any way we choose. The fact is simply that

10

from their point of view they are in danger of losing their rights to the names if the names are used descriptively, since as we have seen descriptive words cannot be registered. Put another way, companies wish to discourage members of the public from using the names to describe the product itself: legally the *Hoover* is a *Hoover* vacuum-cleaner – not just a *Hoover*. But who, in the long run, can say how the words of a language are actually to be used? Only the users and speakers of the language themselves.

This aura of legal sensitivity surrounding trade names has made most standard dictionaries very cautious in their handling of them. Some trade names are so wellknown that they simply cannot be omitted from a dictionary, especially if the named product is virtually part and parcel of a country's way of life. A typical example might be the name *Coca-Cola*. The actual handling of a trade name is a matter for each dictionary to decide individually. Some, such as the *Concise Oxford*, use a letter or symbol to denote a trade name - the *Oxford* uses 'P' for 'proprietary'. Others, such as *Collins English Dictionary*, follow the word with a label such as 'trademark'. Most dictionaries will print a separate statement disclaiming the implication of any special legal status for a name merely on the grounds of its inclusion in the dictionary or by its being labelled as a proprietary name. For similar reasons of caution, a number of dictionaries are reluctant to give the etymology of a trade name, even when it is fairly obvious or guessable. One undesirable consequence of the inclusion of a trade name in a dictionary, of course, is that the name is thus popularised and its generic use encouraged. This puts a dictionary into a quandary, since a good dictionary aims to reflect actual current usage. But when in the 1960s a new *Penguin* English dictionary included the name *Biro* to mean 'ball-point pen' – which after all is the way the word is actually used by many people – the company (*Biro Bic*) had to move extremely rapidly to get the name removed since such a generic definition of their product could have caused considerable legal damage.

The ramifications and implications of trade names and their legal usage are thus complex.

As with standard dictionaries, the actual status of a trade name is not usually relevant in this present Dictionary. Where a name's status deviates from the norm, however, as in the case with *aspirin* (now generic in Britain), *Thermos* (restricted) and *Shredded Wheat* (special), this will be indicated.

The main purpose of the book, however, is contained in its title: it is a Dictionary of Trade Name Origins. In each case I have tried to establish how a name came about, who devised it, and what the thinking was that lay behind the choice of a particular name.

Many trade names have obvious origins, and these for the most part have not been included. Most obvious names are the personal names, such as Marks & Spencer or Wrigley's chewing gum. Many are 'transparent' word-based names, such as Ansafone, Suncrush, Anglepoise or Mothercare. Most pet foods (with the notable exception of *Felix*) are 'transparent' and their meaning is obvious: Kit-E-Kat, Top Dog, Chum, Bonio, Trill and the like.

A fairly high proportion of personal names have been included, however, if only because it is not always immediately appreciated that they are indeed the names of people. This particularly applies to non-English names such as *Bally, Bata, Famel, Gestetner, Jaeger, Lancia, Max Factor* and *Schweppes*. These are all 'neat' personal names. It applies even more to trade names based on a non-English name, such as *Alfa-Laval, Bakelite, Chevette, Ercol, Nescafé, Toblerone* and (apparently) *Vono*. But even English (or American) names are not always spotted as the base of a trade name. It is not too easy to detect the source of *Ardente, Ban-Lon, Berlei, Birds Eye, Bovis* and *Tupperware* – as Dent, Bancroft, Burley, Birdseye, Bovis and Tupper.

The converse is also true, so that a number of trade names are included which may appear to be personal names but are not, in fact. Among them are *Alvis, Bush, Etam, Findus, Parkray, Thames & Hudson* and *Toni*. Furthermore, some names that are clearly personal names, such as *Anne French* and *Mr Kipling*, are purely imaginary – there was no real Anne French and no Mr Kipling.

Examples of other trade names that derive in some way from personal names are *Addis, Bejam, Be-Ro, Biba, Cessna, Cona, Cow Gum, Datsun, Ekco, Elsan, Evo-Stik, Ferodo, Foden, Gannex, Harpic, Honda, Idris, Kent, Kenwood, Lemon Hart, Meggezones, Nestlé, Oldsmobile, Post Toasties, Racal, Rawlplug, Rennies, Rowenta, Sanforized, Scotties, Tarmac, Tesco, Umbro, Vick, Vosene* and *Wolsey*.

Just as it is frequently difficult to recognise a 'name name' when you see it, so it is often hard to spot a 'word name'. *Askit*, for example, really is 'ask it', *Commer* derives from 'commercial', and *Spontex* is 'sponge texture'. Abbreviations, in fact, are among the hardest of all trade names to 'crack', especially when presented in the form of mere initials or stylised letters of the alphabet. *Esso* is 'Standard Oil', of course, but it is less wellknown that *Britax* is 'British Accessories' or that *Dettol* is ultimately based on the word 'disinfectant'. Names that are based on an abbreviation of both words and names are even harder to interpret. Among them are *Aspro, Dan-Air, Scotcade*, and the already mentioned *Elsan, Gannex* and *Umbro*.

'Name names', of course, are not restricted to personal names. Some derive from place names – with a place name here meaning any name of a place, from a whole country to a single house. Trade names of this type are *Abbey National* (named after a street), *Andrex* (a church), *Aston Martin* (a hill), *Avon* (a river), *Basildon Bond* (a village), *Bostik* (a city), *Bush* (a district), *Carlsberg* (a brewery), *Columbia* (a state), *Dolomite* (a mountain group), *Maxwell House* (a hotel), *Merrydown* (a house) and *Viyella* (a road).

Similarly, 'word names' are by no means limited to English words, as we know. We have *Atora* (from Spanish), *Badedas* (German), *El Al* (Hebrew), *Etam* (French), *Indesit* (Italian), *Kia-Ora* (Maori), *Lada* (Russian), *Lego* (Danish), *Mitsubishi* (Japanese), *Sobranie* (Bulgarian), and *Spar* (Dutch).

Of all languages, however, the most popular, because the most 'classy', has long been regarded as Latin. To a lesser extent, but for the same reason, Greek has also been frequently used for the base of a trade name. Latin words lie behind such names as *Aquascutum, Audi, Bovril, Calor, Corona, Creda, Cuticura, Denovo, Felix, Flora, Hovis, Innoxa, Linguaphone, Nivea, Novocain, Perspex, Primus, Pro-Plus, Ribena, Sanatogen, Solignum, Unitas, Valderma, Velox, Volvo* and *Wincarnis*. Greek words are the basis for names like *Bio-Strath, Cellophane, Cerebos, Cyclostyle, Dexion, Euthymol, gramophone, mimeograph, Silvikrin* and *Thermos*. Many names of drugs, too, come from one or both of these classical languages: *Benzedrine, Dexedrine, Dramamine, Nembutal* and the like.

The classical connection also provides, as mentioned earlier, a number of names from mythological sources, such as *Ambrosia, Apollinaris* (via a place name), *Cerebos, Dyane, Flora, Hermesetas, Milo, Pan* and *Zephyr*.

Thus the majority of trade names originate in either the names of people, places or ordinary words, in any language. The few trade names that fall outside these categories will be either purely 'arbitrary' words ('invented' in a real sense), as indicated before, or names derived from sources other than people or places, such as literature and the Bible (*Bovril, Brownie, Giulietta, Ivory, Marmion, Pickwick, Three Castles, Waverley*), ships (*Cutty Sark*), animals (*Master McGrath*) and existing trade names (*Bluebell, Chevette, Coke, Disprin, Electrolux, Kodachrome, Lil-lets, Minolta, Polyfilla, Range Rover, St Michael, Slimcea* and *Victrola*). There is little doubt that in this respect one particularly popular or successful trade name will inspire others, based on it. *Kodak*, for example, certainly influenced *Muzak*, and some of the original names ending in -ex produced many similar names (see Appendix I, p.197).

It cannot be over-emphasised that an important function of a trade name, however it is formed, is to suggest as well as to indicate. We have already examined the favourable 'prestige' associations that a trade name can have. After a while, a consumer will virtually expect a trade name to have such built-in connotations, and will subconsciously look for them. This process can even be extended to personal names, in their original form, that obviously were not expressly devised or even chosen with this function in mind. It is an odd fact that very many such personal names, even many not included in this book, do have acceptable or appropriate associations. It is not entirely frivolous, therefore, to say that Wrigley is a most suitable name for the manufacturer of a stretchable, twistable consumer product, or that Woolworth suggests value for money ('well worth' what you spend). Such names included in the Dictionary – but not just for this reason – are *Bass* ('deep', 'strong'), *Biro* ('giro'), *Boeing* ('ba-doing!'), *Braun* ('brawn'), *Cadillac* ('car de luxe'), *Ferodo* ('ferrous'), *Firestone* ('tough', 'hot'), *Gestetner* ('stenciller'), *Goodyear* ('success', 'durability'), *Hillman* ('hill-climber'), *Horlicks* ('licks'), *Jaeger* ('jaguar'), and so on. Is not *Liberty* just the right name for a trend-setting fashion store, or *Schick* for cosmetic products that are both 'slick' and 'chic'? Does not *Tootal* suggest 'total' variety and quality, and *Wolsey* clothing made mainly of wool? This last name may, possibly, have been at least subconsciously chosen for its suitability (it is not that of the founder of the firm), but the other names, and many more like them, give good value as favourable trade names.

Some marketing specialists hold that trade names have little effect on the positive 'sellability' of a product. In his *New Products and Diversification*, for example, Peter M. Krauschar states that the actual brand name seems 'relatively unimportant and certainly deserves less attention than is commonly given to it'. So long as a name does not arouse any strong negative reaction among its potential customers, 'a name which is distinctive and easy to pronounce will be adequate for most products' (Krauschar, pp.121–2).

True, the main purpose of the name is to distinguish a particular product, and it has been shown conclusively that the name is the most important factor in product recognition. A survey carried out in June 1975 among a sample of 1000 housewives in Britain found that nearly half the purchases bought had been recognised by their name, with less than a quarter identified by the colour of the packaging and only 6 per cent by the design or shape.* But the 'free associations' of a name must not be overlooked, even the unfavourable ones. One can only conjecture, of course, but it is possible that *Omo*, with its 'threat-face' appearance (see the entry) and suggestion of 'homosexual', may have had some adverse effect on its marketability and popularity. If, too, a potential customer is unsure how to pronounce a name, especially a foreign one, he may well opt for an alternative product. I have known more than one person who

* *Trade Marks: Report on a Survey among Housewives.* pp.12–13.

had decided against buying a tube of *Uhu* on the grounds that 'it's such a silly name to say'.

The pronounceability of a name can also have an undesirable effect on the attraction of a product, if only because many foreign names take a considerable time to settle to a single accepted spoken form. Does one make *Hitachi* rhyme with 'hit' or with 'high', for example? Japanese names in particular are especially alien to the English-speaker, to the extent that names such as *Hitachi* and *Matsushita* have been used for their comic effect in radio and TV entertainment programmes. This gives the names publicity, of course, but it cannot help a name's good image to have it used as a mock expletive or a joke sneeze (as has happened to *Hitachi* in the Morecambe and Wise Show).

This brings us to the key question: what is the ideal for a trade name?

If the named product or service is an international one, then the chief criteria for a good, successful name are these:

1 It must be instantly comprehensive visually. Here a short name, or one with distinctive or 'rare' letters such as 'O' and 'X' (see Appendix I, p.193) may score over a long or hyphenated name. This factor is responsible for such names as *Omo*, Daz and Dreft.

2 It must be easily pronounceable in all major languages, especially those of the countries where the product is to be marketed. Names ending in '-ex', '-o' and '-a' are popular here (see Appendix I), as are Latin and Greek names. On the other hand, for a smaller, more discerning market, deliberately difficult names may be promoted, such as Byrrh and Noilly Prat. The theory is that purchasers of these products pride themselves on being able to pronounce the difficult French names correctly! (An interesting sidelight to this is that the manufacturers of the *Biro* pen originally attempted to get the public to pronounce the name in the Hungarian way, 'beero'. They failed, however, when the pen became popular and people said the name in the way that seemed natural to rhyme with words like *Biro* that they already knew, such as 'autogiro', and with similar names such as *Li-Lo* and 'lino'.)

3 It must not have ludicrous or undesirable meanings in a foreign language. We have already examined some of these. But what is the association of the *Cortina* car in Spain, where its name simply means 'curtain'? This consideration frequently results in the name of a product or company being modified or changed altogether in another country (see *Cona* and *Foden*, for example). Thus the East German Wartburg 353 car was called the Knight in Great Britain. It may well be, too, that the *Vauxhall Viva* had its name changed to the Epic in France as much for the fact that French *vivier* means 'fish-pond' as for the fact that *Viva* does not have quite the same

associations as it does for an English-speaker. For similar reasons
the Russians chose to rename their Zhiguli car the *Lada* in export
markets: the native name is too close to 'gigolo' for comfort!

4   The name must, as we have seen, have favourable associations.
Witty or punning names (*Findus, Frog, Gunk, Hush Puppies, Jeep,
Lucky Strike, Odo-Ro-No, Sleepeezee, Teasmade, Veeto*) are fine so long
as they are not over-involved or too obscure, as are incongruous
ones (*Anchor* butter, *Camel* cigarettes, *Carnation* evaporated milk,
Cherry Blossom shoe polish, *Kiwi* shoe polish, *Monkey Brand* soap, *Owl*
pen-nibs, *Penguin* books, *Scotch* tape, *Shell* petrol, *Stork* margarine).
Such names have an additional point in their favour – their incon-
gruity makes them memorable.

5   The memorability of name is a further criterion. With this is
coupled its durability. A topical name may be a success at the time
when a product is launched, but later could become a drawback.
Sometimes an initially suitable name may lose its appropriateness
due to company diversification. This happened with *Hotpoint*, a
name that is very suitable for an iron but hardly for a refrigerator.

6   Finally, a name must, obviously, meet the necessary legal requirements if it is to be registered. We considered such requirements
earlier. In this connection – and even if a name is not to be registered
– it is surely wise to select a name that is straightforward to spell.
It is true that most trade names occur in spoken form among
consumers and the public generally, but manufacturers would have
less cause to complain of incorrect versions of their name if they
considered more closely in some cases how it could be mis-spelled.
Vulnerable names in this respect are ones that are themselves erratic
spellings, such as *Brylcreem* and Ansafone. Indeed, one may even
wonder whether the intended spelling (here the correct one) is quite
what it should be, and instinctively want to 'improve' it to something like 'Brylcream' or 'Ansaphone'.

An overall factor that links all these criteria is a name's actual
appearance. Regarded more as a symbol than as a word or words,
is it aesthetically pleasing? An awkward name can appear unattractive, such as (perhaps, for these things lie in the eye of the
beholder) *Hai Karate* or *Pomagne*. A short, symmetrical name such
as *Oxo* or *El Al*, on the other hand, is satisfyingly balanced. In
general, a name with a double letter is more attractive than one
without, so that *Allegro, Bournville, Chopper* and *Gannex* are more
pleasing visually than the rather top-heavy *Cuprinol, Duralumin* and
57 Varieties. Whether the six E's of *Sleepeezee* are attractive or off-
putting is a matter of taste. Some may regard the name as over-
frivolous anyway, and prefer a more 'solid' name such as
Slumberland.

Such psycholinguistic considerations are dealt with, where appropriate, in the main entries of the Dictionary. The entries also give relevant historical, legal and linguistic facts about a name where these are interesting or important. The etymology of a name, its actual origin, is of course the main purpose of an entry. In some cases this involves a fairly substantial narrative, a 'name story'. In others it is brief and to the point. In others again the etymology is only conjectural, either because it is in dispute or because it has not been possible for one reason or another to establish it.

How were the etymologies obtained?

In a few instances, they were provided by a standard reference book such as a dictionary or encyclopedia, or by a specialised book such as a company history. These are in the minority, however, and most origins were obtained direct from the manufacturers concerned. There were two hazards in this latter process. The first was that an unusually high proportion of written enquiries, even repeated ones, failed to reach their addressee (whether such letters strayed externally, in Post Office territory, or internally, in a company's administrative network, is not clear), the second was that many companies either could not or would not supply the information I asked for. Replies on the lines of 'We regret we cannot give you this information' were both tantalising and infuriating. Did they know but wouldn't tell, or did they themselves not know? In more than a few cases written (and even telephoned) enquiries failed to produce any response at all. True, there is no law of the land which obliges a respondent to correspond, but the proportion of those who chose not to was perhaps unnecessarily large. (Some, no doubt, were wary of a venture of this nature, and it turned out that a few misunderstood it, thinking I was compiling a directory and not a dictionary.)

Similar frustrations and refusals were tolerated with great patience and grace by my assistant, Margaret Dickson, when concentrating on firms in the London area, whom she initially approached by telephone. There is no doubt that without Margaret's help I could not have obtained the amount of material that I did, and I would like to acknowledge her careful and cheerful help right here, before that of all others. I owe her much.

There were, of course, hundreds of firms who did respond, and to all who did I express my sincere and grateful thanks, for without them this book could never have been written. Separate acknowledgments appear (on p.212) to the various officers of these firms and also to other persons who were good enough to help.

Where information for a name is sparse or possibly inaccurate – though I naturally hope such instances will be few – I should be very glad to hear from readers who have well-documented facts available to enable me to amplify and correct this information in future editions of the book. In particular I should welcome background information on a shortlist of names about which I have been able to find out little or nothing, and which therefore mostly lack their own entries. These names appear separately, in Appendix III, p.206. I would very much like to be able to incorporate some or all of them in a future edition. (Details of the information needed are given at the head of the list.)

In conclusion I must make it clear that any shortcomings the book may have are due to me alone. In a pioneer project of this kind all is not necessarily plain sailing, and in some of the rougher passages I may not always have been aware, from my stand on the captain's bridge, that down below decks a leak or two may have been sprung. I would like to think that readers and users of this Dictionary will help me to repair these for the next voyage, when I will hope for smoother waters.

All communications should be addressed to me c/o the publishers, whose address can be found on the reverse of the title page.

Petersfield, Hampshire   Adrian Room

Arrangement of the entries

The entries run in alphabetical order. Each entry opens with the trade name in heavy print followed by its identity in brackets. The identity states the nature of the product, enterprise or service and gives the name of the manufacturer or owner of the named product. The linking word 'by' here means that the product is manufactured by or marketed by the company that follows. The word 'and', as *Formica* (plastic laminate and manufacturer), means that the company name is identical to the name of the product. It should be stressed that the identity of the product is in most cases not a comprehensive one. This means that the company concerned may well manufacture other products under the same trade name. The identity given is usually the one for which the name is famous or well known.

In virtually every case the name of the manufacturer or company given in brackets is that of the firm immediately responsible for the product, usually a British firm (which in the case of non-British-based firms will be a subsidiary of the parent company). The full title of most companies officially ends with 'Ltd' (denoting 'private limited company' since the Companies Act, 1980) or 'plc' ('public limited company'), but to save space this suffix is omitted in all identity statements and, often, in the main text of an entry. Furthermore, the word 'Company', as part of the full title, is almost always abbreviated to 'Co.'. For 'Mars', therefore, 'Mars Ltd' should be understood, and for 'The Boots Co.' the full implied title is 'The Boots Company plc'.

In this connection it should be noted that the name of a company is not given only when it is exactly the same as that of the product. If the company name is at all different it will be given in full. Thus *Berec* batteries are made by Berec Group, not Berec, and *Nestlé* products are manufactured by The Nestlé Co., not just Nestlé. Names like these are therefore repeated in their full form, with the other words that form part of the name added.

A name printed in *italics* in an entry has its own entry in the appropriate alphabetical place. Trade names, therefore, that do not occur in italics, do not have an entry, even if they are apparently well known.

There are a few cross-references. These mostly occur when the trade name of one product can best be dealt with in the entry for another. This applies, for example, to some of the early names for different types of *gramophone*.

Names not given with a capital letter (as *gramophone*) are now officially generic in Britain – but not necessarily in other countries.

References to books by author's name only are to books listed in the Bibliography (p.208).

Dictionary

A

Abbey National (building society) The society is the result of a merger in 1944 between the Abbey Road building society and the National building society. The Abbey Road society, established in 1849, originally had its offices on Abbey Road in north-west London.

Acrilan (acrylic fibre by Monsanto) The name originated in 1950 in the United States as the result of a contest conducted by the Chemstrand Corporation. Two conditions were that the name should consist of three syllables and should not end in '-on' (presumably because of the wealth of names of the '*nylon*' type). The name is easily associated with 'acrylic'.

Adamsez (sanitary appliances and manufacturer) The name originated in Newcastle-upon-Tyne, possibly as a surname. Tyneside lore, however, claims that the name is simply a phonetic rendering of 'Adams's'.

Addis (toothbrushes and plastic products and their manufacturer) The name derives from the founder of the company in 1780, William Addis, of Clerkenwell, London.

Adidas (sportswear and equipment and manufacturer) The firm was founded in the 1920s as a German company by Adolf ('Adi') Dassler (1900–78), with the name coming from his 'pet' first name and the first three letters of his surname. Adidas sports goods are distributed in the UK by *Umbro* International.

Aero (chocolate by Rowntree Mackintosh) The chocolate is 'aerated', i.e. contains hollow 'bubbles', and the name presumably refers to this property. Its association with 'aeroplane' is a favourable one for virtually any decade of the twentieth century, from cross-channel hops to the jet age.

23

Aeroflot (state airline of the USSR)   The name is Russian for 'air fleet'. The airline was founded in 1923 as 'Dobrolyot', an abbreviation of one word of its full title of Vserossiyskoye obshchestvo *dobro*vol'nogo vozdushnogo flota (The All-Russian Company of the Voluntary Air Fleet) plus the second half of *polyot*, Russian for 'flight'. This name was changed to *Aeroflot* in 1930.

Aertex (cellular cotton fabric and shirts and blouses made from it by William Hollins & Co.)   The official designation of *Aertex* is a 'leno-woven cotton cellular fabric', this fabric being distinctive for its *'airy' tex*ture – from which words the name derives. The fabric was invented in 1888. William Hollins & Co., who manufacture it, also produce *Clydella* and *Viyella*.

Aga (cooker by *Glynwed* Domestic and Heating Appliances)   The cooker was first produced by the Swedish company *Svenska Aktiebolaget Gasaccumulator* ('Swedish Gas Accumulator Company') with the name deriving from the initials of '*A*ktiebolaget', '*G*as' and '*A*ccumulator'. There is a fortuitous prestige association with the Persian title *aga*, meaning 'lord', 'sir', as in the name of the Aga Khan.

Agfa (photographic products and manufacturer)   The name is an acronym for *Aktiengesellschaft für Anilinfabrikation* ('limited company for dye manufacture'), the title of the German firm established in 1867 at Rummelsburger See, near Berlin, but only so abbreviated from 1873. In 1908 the *Agfa* works was set up in Wolfen (now in East Germany), where production continued until 1945. After the Second World War the factory was re-established in West Germany at Leverkusen and Munich. In 1964 *Agfa* amalgamated with *Gevaert* as *Agfa-Gevaert*.

Ajax (cleanser by *Colgate Palmolive*)   The name must be a classical allusion: Ajax was the Greek hero of the Trojan War who went mad when Achilles' armour was awarded to Ulysses instead of to him. But presumably the name of the cleanser was chosen not for this but for the Greek's strength: in his madness Ajax was said to have slaughtered a whole flock of sheep.

AJW (motorcycle by Chinwood)   The name is the initials of the firm's founder, Arthur John Wheaton, who established the company in 1926. It must not be confused with the AJS, now out of production, whose name derives from the founder of the motorcycle business in 1897, Albert John Stevens.

Alcan (aluminium foil and products and manufacturer) The name is an abbreviation of *Al*uminium of *Can*ada, now Alcan Aluminum (in Britain, Aluminium), founded in 1928. The association with 'cans' is perhaps rather misleading.

Aldis (film projector and audio-visual products by The Rank Organisation) The company acquired in 1951 by the Rank Organisation was formed in 1937 as *Aldis* Brothers, in turn acquiring a business of manufacturing opticians run by a Mr Aldis and a Mr Smith. This is not the same Aldis as the inventor of the Aldis lamp: he was Arthur Cyril Webb Aldis whose signalling lamp originally came into use in the Navy during the First World War.

Alfa-Laval (milking machine and manufacturer) The firm derives its name from that of Gustaf de Laval (1845–1913), Swedish engineer and inventor of a centrifugal cream separator. De Laval patented his machine in 1878 and started a firm to manufacture it, this company being incorporated in 1883 as AB Separator. Six years later, de Laval acquired the patent rights to the 'Alfa' disk, a conical insert, which improved the efficiency of the separator, its own name being a stock prestige one ('alpha'). The parent company – in Tumba, Sweden – adopted the name Alfa-Laval in 1963, the name already being used by companies marketing the separator abroad.

Alfa Romeo **Alfa Romeo** (car and manufacturer) The French engineer Alexandre Darracq, who was to produce the Darracq car (and who actually began his commercial business with a cheap bicycle, the Gladiator), began to make taxicabs in Italy, at Portello, Milan, in 1906. Within four years, however, he had sold out to the Società Anonima Lombarda Fabbrica Automobili ('Lombardy Automobile Works Company'), who started to make their native version of this under the name ALFA (from the initials of their full title). In 1914 Nicola Romeo became the firm's manager, and its name was changed to Società Anonima Ing. N. Romeo ('Engineer N. Romeo Limited Company'). After the First World War, the company's cars were renamed *Alfa-Romeo*. 'Alfa', as the Italian for 'alpha', is coincidentally a standard prestige name, as in *Alfa-Laval*.

Algipan (medicinal balm for the relief of muscular and joint pain by Wyeth Laboratories) The name seems to be derived from a combination of two Greek words: *algos*, 'pain' and *panakeia* (English 'panacea') 'all-healing remedy'.

Alka-Seltzer (analgesic soluble preparation by Miles Laboratories) The preparation is *alka*line, i.e. antacid, and when in solution

25

effervesces like *Seltzer* water (which properly is a medicinal mineral water from Nieder-*Selters* in Germany).

Alkit (tropical wear, menswear and manufacturer)   The name suggests versatility: does the firm aim to provide *all* types of *kit*?

Allegro (car by Austin Morris)   The name is typical for a car model. It is both foreign sounding and hence on the exotic side, and suggests an agreeable speediness or liveliness. As a musical term 'allegro' is used to mean 'briskly', and is actually the Italian word for 'lively', 'gay'.

Almay (skincare and cosmetic products by *Aspro*-Nicholas)   The products originated with the American firm *Almay* Inc., whose parent company was the Schieffelin Corporation. This was in 1920, when the young chemist, Schieffelin, had devised an eye shadow for his wife that would not irritate her very sensitive skin. His first name was Al, and hers was May – hence the brand name. A special feature of *Almay* products is that they are hypoallergenic, i.e. they guard against allergic reactions.

Altoids (peppermint lozenges by Smith Kendon)   The lozenges were first manufactured in the second half of the nineteenth century, when '-oid' was a fashionable suffix for patent medicines. When *Altoids* were introduced as a very strong peppermint, they were originally intended for the chemist trade and were promoted as the best or highest '-oid' there was on the market. Hence the name, with the first part of the word from the Latin for 'high', *altus* (as in English 'altitude').

Alvis (car and manufacturer)   The name is said to have no specific meaning, but to be simply a name easy to pronounce in several languages. This is not very satisfactory, however, and various stories have been circulated concerning the name. One, for example, says that the first two letters of 'aluminium' were used in combination with the Latin word *vis*, 'force', 'power'. Another suggests that the name is based on the name of a woman, Avis, with 'L' added to give the word symmetry when displayed on the car. Something of a seed of the first story can be found in the fact that the name was first used on a piston manufactured by Aluminium Alloy Pistons Ltd, which was established in 1914 by Geoffrey de Freville in Wandsworth, London. The *Alvis* company was founded by Thomas George John in 1919, and the first cars of the name were manufactured in the following year. (Alvis is in fact a surname, but no one of the name seems to have played a part in the development of the company or its cars.)

Ambi (lightening cosmetic for coloured skins by *Aspro-Nicholas*)   The product was invented by a British pharmacist, Harry Atkinson, who set up his business in Salisbury, Rhodesia, and was first marketed by his African Pharmaceutical Distributors and aimed at white skins, not coloured. From this came the product designed for native African skins manufactured by the *Am*algamated *Bio*chemical Division – a grand name (avoiding reference to politics or colour) which provided the name of the cosmetic. *Ambi* was launched after some delay in 1963, being first marketed in African countries other than Rhodesia (such as Zambia, Malawi and finally South Africa), and then eventually the United States. It is in fact a clever name, since apart from its actual origin it suggests 'ambi-', i.e. a two-way switch (as in 'ambidextrous'), and is also an easy name to say, spell, and remember.

Ambrosia (rice pudding by *Bovril*)   The name was appropriated by the joint founders of the company of the same name, an American and an Englishman (the latter being one Alfred Morris), when in 1917 they discovered ways of drying milk in order to produce rice pudding commercially. The name already existed as that of an American company and with its basic meaning of 'food of the gods' – and its literal meaning in sixteenth-century Latin, from Greek, 'immortality' – was felt to be suitable for a delectable foodstuff.

Amilcar (car and manufacturer)   The little French sports car had a name that was said to be an anagram of something although it is not certain of what. The financial backers of the car, first manufactured in 1921, were the Frenchmen Lamy and Émile Akar, and the name could derive from their surnames or from a variant of 'Émile Akar'. In French, Amilcar is an alternative spelling of Hamilcar, the name of the Carthaginian leader who was the father of Hannibal. This is a prestige bonus. Also, of course, there is an association with 'car' – although this would not have been as significant for Frenchmen as for English speakers.

Amm-i-Dent (toothpaste by Stafford-Miller)   The toothpaste contains ammonium phosphate as an agent in preventing dental caries. The origin of the name is therefore obvious. What is rather unusual is the hyphenated infix '-i-', where one might have expected '-o-', for example. This presumably represents 'in' here, as well as supplying a further letter from 'ammonium'. (The name also coincidentally suggests 'ammunition' – an apt association for a toothpaste that can 'shoot' germs.)

Ampex (magnetic tapes by *Ampex* Corporation)   One might expect a link with 'amplify' or 'amps', but these are simply fortuitous associations. The name in fact derives from the initials of the founder of the company, and one of the pioneers of the videotape, *A*lexander *M*athew *P*oniatoff, a Russian immigrant to America in 1927, when he was thirty-five. The suffix '-ex' here is specifically stated to denote 'excellence'. Poniatoff founded *Ampex* in 1942, and demonstrated his first video recording in 1956. The name perhaps unfortunately also suggests *Amplex*, with which of course it must not be confused.

Amplex (deodorant by Ashe Laboratories)   The name was first used in April 1951. When under development in the laboratory, the com*plex* of chlorophyll compounds forming the basis of the product was designated by the code name 'Plex'. To this, when the finished product was first marketed, were added the letters 'Am-' standing for 'a.m.', since early instructions accompanying the deodorant suggested it should be used first thing in the morning. The association with 'amplify' is perhaps unfortunate, since the suggestion could be made that the product actually increases body odour rather than reduces it.

Amytal (sedative and hypnotic drug by Eli Lilly)   The name is a part-conventional adaptation of the scientific title of the drug, isoamyl ethyl barbituric acid. It was registered by Eli Lilly & Co. in 1930.

Anadin (analgesic tablets by International Chemical Co.)   The product originated in the United States, where in 1918 it was invented by a Wisconsin dentist and sold as 'Anacin' – the name under which it is still marketed in the rest of the world apart from South Africa. A modification of 'Anacin' had to be used in the United Kingdom, where it was introduced in 1931, as the name 'Anacine' already existed in the Trade Mark Register. Presumably 'Anacin' owes its derivation at least partly to the Greek prefix *an-*, 'without', with the '-cin' element either from some Greek or Latin word (Latin *acinus*, 'berry', seems unlikely) or arbitrary.

Anchor (butter by *Anchor* Foods)   The brand name was first used in New Zealand in 1886 by an emigrant Cornishman, Henry Reynolds, who had taken up dairy farming on the Waikato plain, south of Auckland on North Island. The reason behind the choice of name

28

for the butter Reynolds first churned on 3 November 1886 is not recorded, but possibly the name is an appropriate one for use by a settler who was seeking a safe arrival in a new country. As applied to butter, it suggests reliability and stability, both desirable qualities. The first wrapped packs of *Anchor* butter were introduced in 1924 and the brand was first marketed in Britain in 1929 by Empire Dairies (renamed *Anchor* Foods in 1978).

Andrews (laxative or 'liver salt' by Sterling Health)   *Andrews* Liver Salt was registered as a trade mark in 1909, when Scott & Turner Ltd, originators of so-called 'health salts' (in fact laxatives) adopted the name for the product from the church of St Andrew near their offices in Newcastle-upon-Tyne. The 'cleanliness-next-to-godliness' association is an enjoyable bonus in the name. Mr Scott and Mr Turner had first sold their 'health salts' in 1893, and their expanding business was partly due to the popularity of their product among sailors visiting Newcastle port.

Andrex **Andrex** (toilet paper by Bowater-Scott)   St Andrew answers for this name as well, since the product was originally made in 1945 by a small firm in St Andrews Road, Walthamstow, London, and sold as 'Androll'. The name was changed to *Andrex* in 1954 and was taken over by Bowater-Scott in 1956 when this company was formed by a merger between the Bowater Organisation in Britain and the Scott Paper Company in America. The '-ex' suffix presumably has the standard connotations (see p.197). (St Andrews Road is itself named after the church on its north side, thus equating the origin of *Andrex* with *Andrews* Liver Salt.)

Anne French (toiletry products by International Chemical Co.)   The name was invented in 1937 on the basis that a 'French connection' was a desirable attribute in toiletries. It was promoted before the Second World War on Radio Normandy by a young lady who claimed to be 'Anne French'.

Apollinaris (table water distributed by *Britvic*)   The sparkling mineral water was discovered in the mid-nineteenth century when the German farmer Georg Kreuzberg was digging an irrigation system in his vineyard in Bad Neuenahr, south of Bonn. The spring from which the water came was named Apollinaris after a nearby chapel (presumably having some pagan association with Apollo) and the name was itself transferred to the water, which was first distributed in England in 1878 by one of Kreuzberg's cousins. An affectionate form of the name became current in the interwar years when a 'whisky and Polly' was a popular drink in some fashionable circles.

Aquascutum (raincoats and manufacturer)   The name is Latin for 'water shield' and was first used in 1853 for a chemically treated rain-repellent fabric that had been patented in 1851 by the Regent Street, London firm of Bax & Co. The name is an awkward one, and its pronunciation will vary from country to country – perhaps to a degree depending on the speaker's treatment of Latin words. This awkwardness, arguably giving the name a certain mystique, is offset by the name's classical origin, since in a number of trade names 'classical' has the desirable connotation of 'classy'. The name has itself promoted other fabrics and coats produced by the company, such as the Eiderscutum light overcoat and (1962) the multicoloured wool-yarn weave, Aquaspectrum.

Araldite (epoxy resin by *Ciba*-Geigy)   The adhesive was developed by Aero Research of Duxford, Cambridgeshire, in the 1930s. This firm was known as 'ARL', and the name seems to derive from this.

Arborite (laminated plastics and manufacturer)   The name suggests an association with trees (Latin *arbor*). Perhaps the idea is that some of the plastics resemble a wooden surface?

Ardath (tobacco manufacturers)   The *Ardath* Tobacco Co., makers of *State Express* cigarettes, was founded in the late nineteenth century by Albert Levy (later Sir Albert) as 'La Casa de Habana' (Spanish for 'The House of Havana'). In 1895 Albert Levy changed this title to *Ardath* from the novel of this name by Marie Corelli, who in turn had taken it from the Book of Esdras in the Apocrypha. In the ninth chapter of this source comes the passage, 'So I went my way into the field which is called Ardath . . . there I sat among the flowers and did eat of the herbs of the field and the meat of them satisfied me.' A prestigious biblical-cum-literary origin, therefore, for a cigarette company! The name still appears on the *Three Fives* pack.

Ardente (hearing-aid and manufacturer)   The company of this name was set up in 1919 by a family named Dent, as 'R.H. Dent for Deaf Ears', who in their premises in Wigmore Street, London, sold hearing-aids imported from the Continent. The firm subsequently came to manufacture its own aids, but continued trading under its original name until 1937 or 1938, when the name was streamlined to *Ardente*. The obvious association with 'ardent' is a favourable one, although not one that primarily belongs to hearing-aids, since these are delicate, refined instruments rather than 'burning' ones. The firm also manufactures alarm systems, however, for which the association is much more valid.

Ariel (washing powder by Procter & Gamble)   The name has suitable connotations for the product: light, airy, and classical (the spirit Ariel in Shakespeare's *Tempest*, for example). A possible association with 'aerial' and thus with the modern world of television is also favourable. The name formerly belonged to the European manufacturers of *4711* perfume and, in Britain, to Reckitt & Colman. Procter & Gamble, who now own it, also manufacture a similarly named product, Fairy (soap and detergent), which for *Ariel* as a name is a further fortuitous link.

Aristoc (stockings and manufacturer)   The name was suggested to the stocking manufacturer A.E. Allen in 1924 by a business acquaintance. The opportunity to blend the word for a product (in this case, stockings) with a favourable association ('aristocratic') does not arise all that frequently, and Allen applied to register the name on the afternoon of the day that it was offered to him.

Ascona (car by *Opel*)   As with a number of car names, the derivation lies in a fashionable place name. In this case it is Ascona, a holiday resort on Lago Maggiore, Switzerland. The association with *Ascot* may also be helpful.

Ascot (gas water-heater by TI Domestic Appliances)   Here is what seems to be another obvious origin in a fashionable place name – Ascot in Berkshire, with its famous race-meeting attended by royalty. The link with the place is more oblique than direct, however, since the firm that manufactured the water-heaters was founded in London by a German, Dr Bernard Friedman, as an agency for marketing the heaters made by Junkers in Germany. The original heaters thus carried the name 'Junkers'. Friedman changed the name of his firm to *Ascot* Gas Water Heaters in 1933, when no doubt he felt (this was the year that Hitler came to power) that a more specifically English name was desirable. He also needed a shortish name to fit into the inverted blue triangle that until then had contained the 'Junkers' name. The *Ascot* company subsequently became part of the Radiation Group, and this in turn became part of TI (Tube Investments) in 1967.

Askit (analgesic powder by *Aspro*-Nicholas)   The product was originally sold, without a name, in Laidlaw's Pharmacy, Glasgow. The story runs that one day in 1919, Mr and Mrs Laidlaw heard two girls whispering together in their shop: 'You ask it', said one, 'No, you ask it', said the other, this exchange continuing for some time. The Laidlaws decided to adopt *Askit* as a brand name for their powder and subsequently the *Askit* Company was formed (later *Askit* Laboratories). In 1959 the firm was acquired by *Aspro*-Nicholas, who still manufacture the product.

aspirin (tablet or other form of acetylsalicylic acid used as an analgesic) The famous trade name, now generic in Britain and many other countries, was derived from the Greek by the German scientist C. Witthauer in 1899, this being the short form of the full German title, *Acetylirte Spirsäure* ('acetylated spiraeic acid'), plus the chemical suffix '-in'. The product was first manufactured by the German firm of Bayer, who lost the exclusive right to the name when, as with *Cellophane*, it was decided by the courts that the article had no other general name and that, on the expiry of the patent, it could be manufactured by other firms (as W.J. Bush & Co. in Britain in 1914). *Aspirin* is sold in a number of still patented forms, as for example *Aspro*, *Disprin*, and *Alka-Seltzer*. (See next entry for more on the fate of the name *aspirin*.)

Aspro (form of *aspirin* by *Aspro*-Nicholas) The name has its origin in Australia. When this country's supply of *aspirin* from the German firm of Bayer was cut off in 1914 at the start of the First World War, the Australian Attorney-General suspended the German patent and trade-mark rights in the name and granted them to any native manufacturer who could meet the required standards. (As it happened, Bayer had not applied for a patent on *aspirin* in Australia, so no breach of patent law would have been involved.) Thus an Australian chemist, George Nicholas – whose name gave the second half of the firm *Aspro*-Nicholas – set out to make his own *aspirin*, assisted by another chemist, one Harry Shmith (*sic*). On 12 June, 1915 they had succeeded in manufacturing the product to the required standard, and hurried to take over the Bayer trade name of 'Aspirin'. Permission to do so was granted. However, sales were not good, mainly due to hostile associations with the product, which still bore its German name. Nicholas, therefore, decided to change the name and did so in 1917 by combining the last two letters of his own name with the first three letters of 'product', thus emphasising that it was a 'Nicho*las pro*duct' and not a German one. This name also, of course, still strongly suggested the nature of the article, *aspirin*. Sales subsequently picked up, and were helped by the ending of the war. *Aspro* was first sold in Britain (by import from Australia) in 1925, and the *Aspro* company formed in 1927, becoming *Aspro*-Nicholas in 1956. The name is virtually international, but the product sells as 'Naspro' in Indonesia.

Aston Martin (car by *Aston Martin Lagonda*) The car was first manufactured in 1921 by the founder of the company, Lionel *Martin*, who as a racing driver had won a number of races on *Aston* Clinton hill, near Aylesbury in Buckinghamshire. Early in 1981 the *Aston Martin Lagonda* company was taken over by two British firms, C.H. Industries and Pace Petroleum.

Atco (motor mowers and manufacturer) The mowers were originally manufactured by Charles H. Pugh Ltd in 1921. The directors were looking for a short, catchy name for their product, and took it from the full name of a firm within the group that manufactured cycle chains, the *At*las Chain *Co*mpany. 'Atlas' itself is a standard prestige name suggesting strength (from the mythical Greek giant who held the heavens on his shoulders).

Atcost (concrete buildings and manufacturer) The exact origin of the name is uncertain, although the implication seems to be that the firm's buildings will be erected 'at cost'. The name was in use from 1948.

Atora (shredded suet by RHM Foods) The name originated towards the end of the nineteenth century. At the time the beef fat which went to make up shredded suet came from South America, and the exporters there were said to have referred to the fat as *a toro*, Spanish for 'from a bull'. This, at any rate, is one of the more likely explanations of the name.

Atra (twin-blade razor by *Gillette* Industries) The razor so named superseded the *Trac II* in 1977. Its cartridge is a pivoting one, and names such as Hugger, Face Hugger and Contour were considered, to reflect the razor's ability to adjust to the contours of a shaver's face. The eventual name chosen was that of an earlier twin-blade razor, itself originally called Contra, that had been consumer-tested in Australia and was thus the *A*ustralian *t*est *ra*zor. (This had been shelved in 1971 in favour of the *Trac II*.) It was subsequently found that the name could also be the acronym of *a*utomatic *t*racking *ra*zor *a*ction.

Audi (car and manufacturer) The car was established in 1909 by Dr August Horch, founder of *Horch*-Werke, Zwickau (now East Germany). Horch originally manufactured the car under his own name, but lost control of the company and for legal reasons could not give his name to another car. He therefore ingeniously translated his surname into Latin, with *audi* meaning 'hear!', as does German *horch*. This, although certainly a classical name, is more punning than prestigious. Financial difficulties led to the acquisition of *Audi* by *DKW* in 1931. In 1971 the car passed to the *Volkswagen* company when *VW* took over the *Audi NSU* Auto-Union-Aktiengesellschaft.

Avia (watches by Louis Newmark)   The association would seem to be with 'aviation', and thus suitable for a modern precision instrument that needs to keep up with the times. In fact the origin of the name is recorded as a random one 'conjured out of the air' (*sic*) by senior executives of Louis Newmark, together with senior executives of an associate Swiss company that is now no longer in existence.

Avis (car-hire company)   If not an acronym ('*a*ll *v*ehicles *i*nstantly *s*upplied'?) the name might derive from Latin *avis*, 'bird', the reference being to the firm's provision of speed and distance.

Avon (cosmetics by *Avon* Cosmetics)   The firm, well known for its 'door-to-door' selling, was launched in the United States in 1886 by David H. McConnell, who at the age of sixteen had been selling books door-to-door. In his rounds, McConnell found that he was not always welcomed with his goods, so hit on the idea of giving each prospective customer an 'enticer' in the form of a small flask of perfume. He subsequently found that his lady customers preferred the perfume to his books, so founded The California Perfume Company, named in honour of a friend who came from California and who had been the first to invest in his company. The firm prospered, engaged female 'door-to-door' sellers of the perfume (one Mrs P.F.E. Albee was the first 'Avon lady') and expanded. McConnell chose the name *Avon* for its prestige connotations – he himself was a lover of Shakespeare – with the name of his native village, Suffern-on-the-Ramapo, New York, suggesting 'Stratford-on-Avon'. The non-English origin of the name is reflected in its usual pronunciation as two full syllables, 'A-von'. Compare the next entry.

Avon (tyres by *Avon* Rubber Co.)   The firm was founded in a former clothmill at Limpley Stoke, Wiltshire, in 1885, was acquired by Browne & Margetson Ltd soon after, and in 1889 was transferred to a larger premises, also once a clothmill, a few miles away at Melksham, Wiltshire. The company name was changed to *Avon* India Rubber Co. in 1891, and shortened to *Avon* Rubber Co. in 1963. Both clothmills were on the same river Avon, hence the name.

(Wiltshire has three Avons: the one involved here is the 'Bristol' Avon, rising just west of Sherston, Wiltshire.)

Avro (aircraft by A.V. Roe & Co.) The firm was founded in 1910 by the English aircraft designer (and first Englishman to fly his own aeroplane) Alliott Verdon Roe (1877–1958). The origin of the name is thus self-explanatory, although the absence of the final 'E' needs accounting for: Roe had hired a shed at Brooklands race-track, where early flying tests were carried out, and in painting his name on the top gable could not fit in the last letter of 'A.V. Roe'. In 1924 Roe severed all ties with his company and founded Saunders-Roe Ltd to manufacture flying boats. In 1962 A.V. Roe became an integral part of *Hawker Siddeley* Aviation.

Babycham (perry by Showerings) The Showering family business of brewing and cider making began in Shepton Mallet, Somerset, in the eighteenth century. The business was incorporated as a limited company in 1932, and the four Showering brothers, who were its directors, began to look for special lines to manufacture. In 1949, one of them, Francis Showering, produced a clear perry which was test-marketed for three months in the Bristol area. Results were highly encouraging, and a name was devised that was based on a 'baby chamois', a cute creature depicted to accompany the name *Babycham* and the slogan 'I'd love a Babycham', the general image being of a product that was attractive to women and girls. The name coincidentally suggests 'champagne', of course, which is a bonus.

Badedas (bath additive by Linguer & Fischer) The full name of the product is 'Badedas Vita Bath Gelee'. It originated in Germany in the 1950s near Baden-Baden, and the name of this city, plus *Bad*, German for 'bath', lies at the basis of the name. Possibly the suffix '-das' derives from the German for 'the', and in fact *das Bad* means 'the bath' (implying '*the* bath' when the product is added to it).

Bakelite (plastic moulding material by *Bakelite Xylonite*) In spite of the suggestion of 'baked light' or something similar, reinforced by the product's use for plastic wares and telephones, it actually derives from the material's inventor, the Belgian-American chemist, L.H. Baekeland, who first evolved it in 1909 (under the German name 'Bakelit'). The trade name is thus based on the first half of 'Baekeland' with the chemical suffix '-ite'. The product is sometimes spelled with a small letter, especially as applied to a number of varieties of early plastics. Properly, however, the name belongs to BXL. Baekeland also invented the photographic paper, *Velox*.

BALLY **Bally** (shoes by *Bally* Group)   The name for English speakers has somewhat unfortunate associations ('Where are my bally shoes?'). As is to be expected, therefore, the origin is a foreign one, and the name is that of the Swiss shoe manufacturer, Carl Franz Bally, who founded his company in 1851. The firm expanded and subsequent branches were set up in France and Great Britain. In 1977 the majority shareholding of C.F. Bally Ltd was acquired by Oerlikon-Bührle Holding. The correct pronunciation of the name approximates to 'Bah-yee'.

Banda (duplicating machine by *Ozalid*)   The name derives from the initials of an earlier company, *B*lock *and A*nderson, acquired by *Ozalid* in 1962. The suggestion of 'band' is a suitable one for a machine that handles 'bands' of paper. The name is still in use, in spite of a merger between the *Ozalid* Company and Nig *Banda* in 1972 (the latter firm having been formerly Nig Mason and before that Nig Securities), and the subsequent absorption of *Ozalid* itself into the Dutch company Océ-van der Grinten in 1977.

Ban-Lon (stretch elastic *nylon* by J.T. Bancroft & Sons)   Once the name of the manufacturer is known, the origin is obvious: *Ban*croft ny*lon*. The firm is an American one.

Bantam Books (paperback books by *Bantam Books*, Inc.)   The American paperback publishers were established in 1945 by Ian Ballantine, previously the manager of the American branch of *Penguin Books*, itself set up in 1939. (*Penguin* had been founded in Britain four years earlier.) The name of *Bantam Books* was chosen by Bernard Geis, at the time a young editor for the American publishing firm of Grosset & Dunlap. The bantam is a pugnacious bird, and was at least in part selected as a name and pictorial symbol for the new firm in order to 'do combat' with an already established American paperback publisher – Pocket Books, whose symbol was a kangaroo. Doubtless, too, the name lined up well with the *Penguin* that was a third paperback animal of standing. See also *Corgi Books*.

barathea (silk and wool or cotton and *rayon* fabric)   The name was originally a trade mark for a fine cloth made with a silk warp and worsted weft dyed black and commonly used for military ties, suits, and other wear. Its origin (around 1862) is uncertain: the word looks Greek, but can hardly derive from *barathron*, 'gulf', 'pit'.

Basildon Bond (notepaper by John Dickinson Stationery) The brand of this name was launched in 1911 by Millington & Sons – a firm acquired by John Dickinson in 1918. The Basildon in question is not Basildon New Town in Essex but the village of Basildon, near Pangbourne in Berkshire. The story runs that Millington's directors were looking for a name for their new bond notepaper ('bond' being a term for a superior type of strong white paper that was formerly used for bonds) and that some of them, on holiday near Basildon, saw the name on a signpost and realising its alliterative potential forthwith adopted it. (Millington's factory was in fact in Tottenham, London.)

Bass (beer by *Bass*-Charrington) The name is a personal one, that of William Bass, a master carter of Burton-on-Trent, who founded his brewery in 1777. The name came to be specifically applied to the '*India Pale Ale*' or 'Bitter' manufactured by *Bass* & Co., now part of *Bass*-Charrington. The association of 'deep' is probably a favourable one: drink deep, deep colour, deep glass. The name is not pronounced as 'base', however, but as 'gas'.

Bata (shoes by The British *Bata* Shoe Co.) The name is not an acronym but that of Tomas Bata, who founded the firm in Zlín, Czechoslovakia, in 1894. By 1932 *Bata* had spread its shoe manufacturing to twenty-eight countries, including Canada, where the *Bata* International Centre is located (at Don Mills, Ontario). Tomas Bata was killed that same year in an air disaster at the age of fifty-six and was succeeded as chairman by his son Thomas J. Bata, a Canadian citizen.

Bear Brand (hosiery and manufacturer) The name may perhaps have been originally used for a brand of clothing, with the animal name either arbitrary or chosen to suggest warmth and durability. (Or is there a connection with 'teddy bear' to suggest homeliness and cosiness?)

Beaucaire (dry-cleaning fluid by LRC Products) The name was chosen to imply 'good care'. It coincidentally is reminiscent of the aristocratic hero of Booth Tarkington's novel, *Monsieur Beaucaire*, published in 1900, and may also suggest to some 'bouquet', another favourable association.

Beetle (synthetic resin by BIP Chemicals) The name was registered in 1898 by the British Cyanides Co. (now British Industrial Plastics) for use on all its products, some of which were employed in the African goldfields. This prompts one theory for the origin of the name, which is that as a creature of ill-omen the beetle was intended to serve as a toxicity warning to native workers. On the other hand, the reference may have been to the insect's activity and industry. In 1925 the name was specifically adopted for the new synthetic resins and resultant products made by the company. Hence the rather incongruously homely name for an impersonal scientifically engineered product.

Bejam (food freezers and manufacturer)   The origin of the name lies with John Apthorp. Having bought a home freezer in the mid-1960s – a rare thing at a time when freezers were almost exclusively used by hotels and restaurants – the future chairman of *Bejam* realised that there was a considerable market in Britain for frozen foods and that such foods, especially meat, could be sold from special freezer centres. The first such centre was opened in 1968 and the name of the new company formed from the initials of members of John Apthorp's family: *B*rian his brother, *E*ric his father, *J*ohn *A*pthorp himself, and *M*illie his mother (as well as *M*arion his sister).

Bendix (washing machines and manufacturer)   The name is ultimately that of the American inventor and industrialist, Vincent Bendix (1882–1945), best known for his contribution to automobile and aircraft technology. He founded the *Bendix* Co. in 1907 to produce cars, and although the company failed two years later he established another firm, the *Bendix* Brake Co., in 1912. The *Bendix* Aviation Corporation was organised in 1929. Perhaps because of its final 'x' the name is often taken to be a concocted word rather than a genuine surname.

Benzedrine (amphetamine drug)   The drug is a carbonate of *benz*yl-methyl-carbinamine, and to this full name was added the suffix '-edrine', as in 'ephedrine' (an alkaloid drug providing relief from hay fever, asthma, etc.). The name *Benzedrine* was first used in 1933, and, especially among addicts, acquired the popular form 'Benny'. The name is now sometimes spelled with a small letter, although the *Concise Oxford Dictionary*, seventh edition (1982), gives it a capital, as do most dictionaries and reference works.

Berec (dry batteries and manufacturer)   The name is the changed version of the *B*ritish *Ev*er *R*eady *El*ectrical *C*ompany, better known as *Ever Ready*, and was first introduced to Great Britain, as the *Berec*

Group, in 1978. To the British it was a new name, but *Berec* had long existed as the company name in many countries of the world, with 'Berec' apparently even meaning 'battery' in some African countries. *Ever Ready*, on the other hand, was used only in Britain, Eire, and South Africa. (In Germany the company's name is Daimon, and in Italy it is Superpila, *pila* being the Italian for 'battery'.) The British Ever Ready Electrical Company was itself formed in 1906, and was in turn the changed name of the American Electrical Novelty & Manufacturing Company, a small firm set up by three American businessmen in London in 1901. This firm produced electrical novelties powered by batteries trade-named 'Ever Ready'. When the company announced early in 1978 that it was about to change its name to *Berec*, the *Sunday Telegraph* accused it of seeking anonymity by 'coyly concealing the familiar Ever Ready battery company'. The change itself was mainly motivated by competitors using similar names. In 1982, however, the company reverted from *Berec* to the old, familiar *Ever Ready*.

Berlei (foundation garments and manufacturer)   The name is an adaptation of the founder of the company, Fred Burley, who in 1910 acquired an interest in a small corset business in Sydney, Australia. He and his brother Arthur formed a limited company two years later, at first named directly after them but in 1919 becoming *Berlei* Ltd, presumably for distinctiveness. In 1929 Fred Burley established *Berlei* (UK) in Slough, Buckinghamshire.

Bermaline (brown bread and manufacturer)   The name seems to be of somewhat uncertain origin. According to a previous managing director's secretary, who had been with the firm from 1926, the story is that the founder of the company, John Montgomery, had sailed as a young man on commercial ships as a baker (he himself was from the Hebrides), and had been impressed with a group of islands in the South Seas called the Bermalino Islands. On his return to Glasgow he needed a name for the malt loaf in which he specialised and gave it that of the islands, setting up his firm in 1868. The islands, however, do not seem to exist with this or any similar name on present-day maps. Since 1972 the company has specialised in malting, rather than producing *Bermaline* bread.

Be-Ro (flour by RHM Foods)   The name is a contraction of 'Bell-Royal', which was the name of the flour manufactured by Thomas Bell & Son of Newcastle and Nottingham, a firm acquired by RHM in the 1950s. The 'Royal' element of the name is presumably a stock prestige word. Thomas Bell founded his company around 1880 in a yard near the Groat Market in Newcastle.

Berol (pencils and manufacturers)   The manufacturing company was founded by the Berol family as the Eagle Pencil Company in 1856, at Yonkers, New York. A British subsidiary of the firm was set up at Tottenham, London, in 1906. In 1969, the Eagle Pencil Corporation in the United States was renamed the *Berol* Corporation, while at the same time in Britain the Eagle Pencil Co. became *Berol* Ltd. The change from a standard prestige name (Eagle) to a family one at such a late stage is rather unusual: normally such a progression is the other way round.

Biba (fashion store)   The 'swinging London' fashion store was founded by Barbara Hulanicki in the 1960s and named after her youngest sister, Biruta, affectionately called Biba. In the 1970s the store closed through insolvency – only to reopen in 1976 in Brazil. In 1978, however, Biruta opened a *Biba* boutique in Conduit Street, London and two years later Barbara herself opened a new boutique, 'Barbara Hulanicki's', also in London. The original *'Biba'* store had been in the fashionable Kensington High Street.

Bic (ballpoint pen and manufacturer)   Once again the name of the company's founder lies behind the trade name. In this case it was the Frenchman, Marcel Bich, who with his brother pioneered the disposable or 'throw-away' ballpoint pen in the 1950s. The first successful pen of this type was the *Bic* Crystal, introduced to Britain from France in 1958. *Bic* pens are now manufactured by *Biro Bic* Ltd. In France the word 'bic' has been sometimes used to mean 'ball pen', much as 'biro' has in Britain. In one of its correct forms as a registered trade mark, *Bic* is not only spelled with a capital letter but in the style *BiC*.

Bile Beans (laxative pill and general tonic by Fisons)   The product was originated, and the name devised, by Charles Fulton in Australia in 1898. It claimed to stimulate the flow of bile and the pill was originally oval, or bean-shaped. *Bile Beans* were still being produced in the 1980s.

Bio-Strath (health food by Vessen)   The first element of the name is Greek *bios*, 'life', the second derives from the German who formulated the product, Dr Strathmeyer. The suggestion of some rarefied scientific term, as 'stratosphere', is no doubt of value.

Bird's (food products by General Foods)   see **Birds Eye**.

Birds Eye (food products by *Birds Eye* Foods)   The ultimate origin of the name lies with Clarence Birdseye (1886–1956), the American

40

businessman and inventor, who devised a process for freezing foods in packages small enough for retailing. Birdseye (who was always actually called Bob, not Clarence) hit on his idea while fur trading and trapping in Labrador: he discovered that fish and caribou meat frozen in the dry Arctic air were still tender and fresh when thawed and cooked months later. This was in 1915. Eight years later he launched Birdseye Seafoods Inc. in New York, and in 1926 founded General Seafoods in Gloucester, Massachusetts. In 1929, however, he sold this company to the newly named General Foods. Birdseye claimed that his unusual surname – which was originally written in two words, as the trade name today – came from an English ancestor, a page in the royal court, who had been nicknamed 'Bird's Eye' by the queen after he had shot a diving hawk through the eye with an arrow. The name must not be confused with *Bird's* (food products by General Foods): this derives from the original firm of Alfred Bird (1813–79), a Birmingham chemist. The confusion is compounded by the fact that there is an identity of name and products, although *Birds Eye* is a *Unilever* name (in Britain) and *Bird's* a General Foods one (as part of the USA Corporation).

Biro (ballpoint pen by *Biro-Bic*)   The name is that of the inventor of this particular type of ballpoint pen, the Hungarian László Biró. Biró left Hungary before the Second World War on the rise of Nazism and settled in Argentina. There he patented his invention of a pen with quick-drying ink that would not blot in 1943, and the first commercially produced *Biro* was produced in 1945: in Britain by the Miles-Martin Pen Co. and in the USA by Eterpen Co. of Buenos Aires. The great popularity and relative cheapness of the pen caused the name to be sometimes used generically to apply to any ballpoint. The Hungarian surname is a curiously attractive name for the product, with the final '-o' and the association with 'giro' reinforcing the visual concept of a pen whose 'nib' is a ball-bearing.

Bismag (indigestion remedy by International Chemical Co.)   The name is simply a contraction of two main ingredients, *bis*muth and *mag*nesia. Compare the next name.

BiSoDol (indigestion remedy by International Chemical Co.)   The name is presumably from '*bi*carbonate of *so*da', a basic ingredient, with '-Dol', absorbed from Latin *dolor*, 'pain'. The three elements of the name are graphically distinguished by capital letters in the correct form of the trade mark.

 Bisto (gravy powder by RHM Foods)   The famous name, popu-

larised by the urchin children savouring the gravy's aroma (the
Bisto Kids and their 'Ah! Bisto!'), seems to be of unrecorded origin.
The association with 'bistro', although apt, would not seem to be
a pointer to the true derivation. The product was introduced in
1910, and one possible explanation of the name is that it could be
an anagram of an advertising slogan used then and ever since:
'*B*rowns, *S*easons, *T*hickens *I*n *O*ne'. It is in fact a first-class international trade name for a product that is peculiarly English.

BL (motor-vehicle manufacturers)   The name became the official
abbreviation (from 1978) of the British Leyland Motor Corporation,
in turn founded in 1968 as a result of the merger of British Motor
Holdings (itself the result of several previous mergers) and the
Leyland Motor Corporation. The latter firm was founded in 1919
at Leyland, then a village but now a town, south of Preston, Lancashire. *BL* still has a factory at Leyland, as well as at Longbridge,
Coventry, Cowley and Solihull (England) and Bathgate and Glasgow (Scotland). In 1980 BL's famous Marina was relaunched as
the Morris Ital, and in the same year the company produced the
popular *Mini* Metro (see *Mini*).

Bluebell (metal polish by Reckitt & Colman)   The association
between the flower and the polish is an unusual one, and the true
origin of the name does not seem clear. Doubtless, it applied in a
general way to all products of the firm who first manufactured it,
the Bluebell Polish Co., who registered the name in 1907. (The firm
could have acquired its name for a variety of reasons; for example,
simply as an attractive name or for an actual geographical location
near some bluebells. The latter would seem unlikely, however, since
the firm's address was Wandsworth Bridge Wharf, Carnwath Road,
Fulham, London.)

Blue Circle (group name of parent company of cement manufacturers)   The story behind the name, which may be apocryphal, is
as follows: shortly after the First World War a unifying name was
needed for Associated Portland Cement Manufacturers and British
Portland Cement Manufacturers, who manufactured cement, and
the Cement Marketing Co., who sold it. This was considered at a
high-level meeting at which, after a lengthy discussion, one of the
directors drew a blue circle round all three names with a large blue
pencil that he affected. Thus the symbol, and the name, was born.

BMW (car and manufacturers)   The name is an abbreviation of
the full title of the German firm: *Bayerische Motoren Werke* ('Bavarian
Motor Works'). The company was founded in Munich in 1916 and
42

originally, as BFW (*Bayerische Flugzeug-werke*, 'Bavarian Aircraft Works'), made aero engines. In 1923 it branched out into motorcycles, and in 1928 produced its first car on taking over the Fahrzeugfabrik Eisenach. This latter firm had the previous year started to make the British Austin Seven under licence, calling it the Dixi. The car was renamed the *BMW* on the takeover.

Bodley Head (publisher)   The firm was founded in 1887 by Elkin Mathews and John Lane (the latter being the uncle of Allen Lane who founded *Penguin* Books). Its name comes from the sign that hung outside the shop: this showed the head of Sir Thomas Bodley, founder of the Bodleian Library at Oxford. Sir Thomas was a Devonian, like the two booksellers, Mathews and Lane.

Boeing (aircraft and manufacturer)   The firm was set up in 1916 by William Edward Boeing (1881–1956), an American aircraft manufacturer, as the Pacific Aero Products Co. The following year it was renamed as the *Boeing* Airplane Co. The *Boeing 747* was the first of the so-called 'jumbo jets', and was introduced into service in 1970. That this aircraft should have a name that suggests a rapidly propelled missile ('boing!') is a comic book coincidence.

Bonjela (oral pain-relieving gel by Reckitt & Colman)   The name was registered by a Yorkshire firm, Walfox Ltd, in 1938. It derives from a combination of French *bon*, 'good', plus an element suggesting 'jelly' or 'gel'.

Bostik

Bostik (adhesive and manufacturer)   The name has its origin in the Boston Blacking Co., a Leicester firm founded in 1898. This obtained its adhesives from the firm of the same name in America (hence 'Boston'). On expanding, and subsequent to the development of a rubber latex adhesive for the shoe industry in 1931, the firm changed its name to *Bostik* (*Bos*ton plus a form of 'stick') in 1962. There is in fact an English surname Bostick, but for once the name of the firm does not derive from one of its founders.

Bournville (chocolate by Cadbury *Schweppes*)   The chocolate is made at *Bournville*, Birmingham, in a factory that was set up on a specially planned housing estate laid out here in 1879, in what was then a rural setting, by George Cadbury. The name was originally to have been 'Bournbrook', after the river here, but *Bournville* was chosen for its French associations, since French chocolate was regarded as the best. See also the next entry.

43

Bournvita (chocolate drink by Cadbury *Schweppes*)   The name is a blend of *Bournville* and Latin *vita*, 'life', a fashionable early-twentieth-century trade name element (compare *Ryvita*).

Bovis

Bovis (building contractors)   A name that must surely be an acronym or at least an anagram! Yet it is actually the surname of C.W. Bovis, who in 1885 acquired a small builder's business set up thirty years previously by a Mr Sanders. On acquiring the business, Mr Bovis changed the name of the firm to C.W. Bovis & Co. In 1909, when the firm was sold to Sidney Glyn and Samuel Joseph, this was streamlined to its present form of *Bovis* Ltd. (The surname is akin to Beevers and Bevis; of French origin it means 'fine son'.)

Bovril (concentrated essence of beef and manufacturer)   The name is not only one of the most firmly established of household names but has an unusual derivation from an artificial word. It is a combination of two elements: Latin *bos*, *bovis*, 'ox', and *vril*. The latter word occurs in Lord Lytton's novel, *The Coming Race*, published in 1871. This tells how the members of a community, living at some time in the future, had discovered an 'electric fluid called Vril, which was capable of being raised and disciplined into the mightiest agency of all forms of matter, animate and inanimate'. (In his *A Concise Etymological Dictionary of Modern English* (John Murray, 1924) Ernest Weekley suggests that 'vril' may in turn derive from Latin *vis*, *vires*, 'force', or *virilis*, 'manly'.) The name was first used by the inventor of the essence in 1887, John Lawson Johnston. Its classical-cum-literary origin are typical of late-Victorian pomposity. Yet the 'deep-sounding' name with its two labials (*b* and *v*) is just right for a lip-smacking product. Its resemblance to the word 'brothel', on the other hand, caused it to be used as a slang term for this establishment in the 1930s.

Bradosol (antibiotic throat tablets by *Ciba*-Geigy)   The name may be either arbitrary or have some meaning that is now lost. One possibility might be the combination of a surname such as *Brad*man and the element 'sol' to denote a *sol*ution.

Brasso (metal polish by Reckitt & Colman)   The origin is obvious. The ending '-o' is typical of the period when the name was registered, 1905.

Braun (electric shaver by *Gillette* Industries)   The name has its origin in a German company, Braun AG, set up to manufacture kitchen blenders and home-food preparation equipment by a Prussian, Max Braun, in 1921. The company merged with *Gillette* in

44

1967. The German pronunciation of the name resembles English 'Brown'. The English way of saying the trade name, however, is 'brawn', thus providing a masculine association that, for the product, is highly suitable.

Brillo (cleaning soap pad by *Brillo* Manufacturing Co.)   The name is obvious ('brilliant'). The '-o' suffix is roughly of the same vintage as *Brasso* – *Brillo* was introduced in 1913. (That *brillo* is Italian slang for 'tight' or 'sozzled' is not too damaging a coincidence, perhaps.)

Bri-Nylon (form of *nylon* by ICI Fibres)   The fabric was manufactured by *Bri*tish *Nylon* Spinners, a company owned jointly by ICI and Courtaulds. Courtaulds subsequently sold its interest in British Nylon Spinners to ICI and the company was then renamed as ICI Fibres Ltd.

Britax (car seat-belt and manufacturer)   The name is an abbreviation of *Bri*tish *Acc*essorie*s*, a firm set up by a Mr Percy Steer early in the twentieth century and purchased by Mr O.A. Proctor, the present managing director of Securon Manufacturing, in 1937. It later became part of the *Britax*-Excelsior Co.

British Leyland see **BL**

Britvic (soft drink and manufacturer)   The name would seem to suggest 'British Victory', but in fact derives from *Bri*tish *Vi*tamin Produc*ts*, a firm that as James MacPherson & Co. had been acquired by Ralph Chapman in 1938. Chapman changed the name to reflect his introduction of fruit juices to a business that formerly manufactured only flavoured mineral waters. In 1954 he sold *Britvic* Ltd, as the firm had then become, to Vine Products, which in turn merged with Showerings in 1962. Eventually Showerings (with its full title of Showerings, Vine Products and Whiteways, or SVPW) made its final merger when in 1968 it joined with Allied Breweries. The name is rather cumbersome one – perhaps 'Brivit' or something similar with less consonants would have been better. See also *RSVP*.

Brobat (bleach and detergent by Jeyes Group)   The name is alleged to be formed from letters (or syllables?) taken from the names of the original two proprietors of the firm that manufactured the product. Their identity has not been revealed, but any names such as *Bro*wn and *Bat*ten would produce the trade name.

Brolac (paint by Berger, Jenson & Nicholson)   The first half of

45

the name represents *Bro*admead, Bristol, where in 1897 the firm of John Hall & Sons was set up to manufacture paints and putties. The second half of the name comes from the '*lac*quer paints', previously known as 'hard-gloss paints', produced by the firm in the 1920s as '*Bro*admead *Lac*quer Paint'.

Bronco (toilet paper by British Tissues) In the 1930s the newsprint firm of Peter Dixon & Son added the manufacture of toilet paper to their standard product. For this purpose one of their mills at Oughtibridge, Yorkshire, was modified to manufacture hard toilet tissue and one of its first customers was the maker of *Bronco*, the British Patent Perforated Paper Co. (In 1955 this latter firm was acquired by Peter Dixon.) The name seems to derive from a combination of *Br*itish and some other word, either the 'co-' of 'company' or possibly even 'bronco' itself, the reference being to the toughness of the Scandinavian tissue used ('strong as a horse', i.e. as a bronco). Another theory put forward by the managing director of Peter Dixon & Son, Anthony Dixon, is that the British Patent Perforated Paper Co. aimed to choose a name similar to a toilet paper called Bromo, which was supposed to have some chemical association (bromide?) and which was manufactured in Britain for export to India and Africa. Yet another theory maintains that the name is onomatopoeic: 'Bronco' represents the sound made when a sheet of (hard) toilet paper is detached sharply from its roll! The first explanation, however, seems the most likely, since the *Bronco* firm originally made two main types of toilet paper called British No.1 and British No.2.

Brooke Bond (tea by *Brooke Bond Oxo*) The name originated (as 'Brooke, Bond & Co.') in a shop in Market Street, Manchester. Here in 1869 a twenty-four-year-old tea merchant, Arthur Brooke, set up his business. Hence the derivation of 'Brooke'. But who was Bond? He did not exist. Arthur Brooke invented the name because to him it 'seemed to sound well'. (Subconsciously he was no doubt attracted by the monetary significance of 'bond' as well as the alliteration.)

Brownie (camera by *Kodak*) George Eastman, the American photographic inventor and founder of *Kodak*, wanted a cheap, simple camera that anyone could operate with ease, especially children. The first model was introduced to the public in 1900, with its name chosen by Eastman from the 'Brownies' – not the traditional fairy folk, but the miniature humanoids that populated the books and poems of the Canadian writer and illustrator, Palmer Cox. Like their fairy-tale counterparts, however, Cox's creatures were helpful, cheerful, and efficient, and this was the image that Eastman wanted for his new popular camera, with a name to match. The similarity of the name to that of its designer, Brownell, seems to have been a genuine coincidence: his family have confirmed that it was Palmer Cox's characters that were the real inspiration for the name. The *Brownie* camera was manufactured in the United States until 1962 and in Britain until 1967, the latter model being the *Brownie* 127. In 1980, however, a new *Brownie* model appeared on sale in Britain. This was the inexpensive 'starter' camera that had previously been marketed as the *Kodak* Pocket A-1.

Brylcreem (hair dressing by Beecham Group) The name is a combination of '*brill*iantine' and '*cream*', with stylised spelling. *Brylcreem* was first marketed in 1928 by the County Chemical Co., Birmingham, whose manager, Wilfrid Hill, had asked his chief chemist to formulate a new-style hair cream which would be different from the brilliantines, oils and gums then in use. The new product contained no gum or starch, and was originally sold only to hairdressers. The County Chemical Co. (as the County Perfumery Co.) passed to Beecham in 1939. During the early years of the Second World War, a nickname for young RAF officers was 'the Brylcreem Boys', mainly as the result of an advertisement picturing such an officer who had dressed his hair with *Brylcreem*. An early but short-lived name for the product was 'Elite'.

Bukta (sports clothing and manufacturer) The name comes from the surname of the founder of the business in the 1870s, Edward Robinson Buck. Perhaps T. and A. are the initials of his partners or sons?

Burco (washing machines and manufacturer) The name is a contraction of *Bur*nley *Co*mponents, a firm originally manufacturing machine parts but specialising in washing machines from 1926. The name was shortened to *Burco* in 1936, and the firm still has its headquarters at Burnley, Lancashire.

Burmah Oil (petroleum products by Burmah-*Castrol*) The Burmah Oil Co. produced oil in Burma when it was still a province of India. The company has retained the nineteenth-century spelling of the name with the final 'h', if only as a reminder of the days of the 'pukka sahib' who had made his colonial home in 'Poonah' and 'Simlah'.

Bush (radio and television sets by Interstate Electronics) *Bush* Radio Ltd was founded in Woodger Road, Shepherds *Bush*, London, in 1932. It became part of the Rank group in 1942, but was sold by them in 1981 to the London-based electronics company Interstate Electronics.

Cadillac (car and manufacturer) The Cadillac Motor Car Co. of Detroit produced its first car in 1903, taking its name from the founder of Detroit in 1701, the Frenchman Antoine de La Mothe, sieur de Cadillac. His own name – strictly a title – comes from the small town so called in south-west France, near Bordeaux.

Calor (gas by *Calor* Gas) The name is Latin for 'heat'. The gas is supplied under pressure in containers in the form of liquefied gas that is mainly butane. Such gas was first marketed by ICI in 1936.

Camel (cigarettes by R.J. Reynolds Tobacco Co.) Richard Joshua Reynolds founded his tobacco company in Winston (now Winston-Salem), North Carolina, in 1875, producing such brands as Old Rip, Fat Back, Red Meat, Wine Sap, and Minnie Ogburn. In 1907 he introduced a pipe tobacco called Prince Albert. Shortly after, Reynolds decided that the time was ripe to introduce a brand of cigarettes, and with an eye on the then current fashion for exotic names, chose *Camel* for his new product, the name evoking the mysterious Orient and suiting the Turkish tobaccos that the cigarettes would contain. He began his advertising campaign in 1913, taking advantage of a coincidental visit to Winston of Barnum and Bailey's Circus. The public was 'teased' by a series of strange slogans reading 'Camels', and 'The Camels are coming!', and accompanied by a drawing (made from a photograph) of Old Joe, Barnum and Bailey's circus dromedary. The *Camel* cigarette pack, with its haughty-looking 'camel' and stylised pyramids and palm trees, was to become a classic.

Camp (instant liquid coffee by R. Paterson & Sons) *Camp* Coffee was introduced by a Scotsman, Campbell Paterson, in the late nineteenth century. From the earliest days the brand has been associated with a colonial military image: the coffee is shown on the bottle label being savoured by a Scots army officer outside his tent with a native Indian manservant in attendance. The design originated in colonial days and thus pertains to that era. Sales of the coffee, however, have been made chiefly to British, not overseas

48

users. The name would appear to have two references: to 'camp' itself and to its inventor, *Camp*bell Paterson.

C & A Modes (clothing chain-store group)   The firm was founded in Holland in 1841 by two Dutch brothers, *C*lemens *and A*ugust Brenninkmeyer. Popularly (and facetiously) the name has often been held to stand for '*c*oats *and* '*a*ts'. Originally, it seems, the brothers' trade name was 'Canda'. This was later changed to 'Cyamodes' and finally to 'C & A's'. The subsequent change to *C & A Modes* was designed to repeat the earlier name, with the brothers' initials, while at the same time standing for 'Cheap & Artistic Modes'. The original name 'Canda', however, is still in active use, and of course has good overtones of 'candour'.

Caran d'Ache (coloured crayons and pencils and manufacturer)   The Swiss firm, founded in 1924, took its name from the French caricaturist and illustrator who worked under the name of Caran d'Ache, a pseudonym based on the Russian word for 'pencil', *karandash*. The artist's real name was Emmanuel Poiré, and he was born in Moscow in 1859 and died in Paris in 1909. When the Swiss pencil factory adopted his name in his honour, they overlooked the fact that he had left a widow in Paris, and she brought a case against the company which she eventually won. The firm was obliged to pay her a life annuity of 20,000 francs. Madame Poiré, however, died soon after and the company escaped with the payment of only one annuity. The legal predecessor of *Caran d'Ache* was a Genevan pencil factory founded in 1915. To improve its poor reputation, this firm took the name 'Ecridor' in 1920 (from French *écrit d'or*, 'written in gold'), but went into liquidation two years later. Its assets, personnel and premises were acquired in 1924 to form the present-day company. It is fortuitous that the name *Caran d'Ache* bears something of a resemblance to 'crayon'. In the United Kingdom and Ireland the company's products are distributed by Jakar International.

carborundum (abrasive substance)   The name was first registered by the American company, the Carborundum Co., in 1892, with the substance itself patented by E. G. Acheson. The material is a misnomer, since although the name combines '*carb*on' and '*corundum*' the actual composition contains carbon and silicon as silicon carbide (SiC).

Carlsberg (lager by *Carlsberg* Brewery)   In 1847 J.C. Jacobsen, a Danish brewer, established a new brewery on a hill outside Copen-

---

hagen. Jacobsen's wife had just given birth to a son, whom the parents named Carl: the son's name, plus Danish *berg*, 'hill', was chosen by the brewer for the name of his brewery. The name made a natural transfer to the lager.

Carlton (car by *Vauxhall* Motors) The names *Carlton* and *Royale* were both selected, members of the public assisting, for the new models introduced by *Vauxhall* in October 1978. The association is a 'luxury' one: the Carlton is the London Tory club *par excellence* and the Junior Carlton is another noted London club, with Carlton House (which gave its name to Carlton House Terrace) being the name of the London home of the Prince Regent, later George IV. As a name, too, *Carlton* is easily pronounced and has the initial 'C' that marks many successful trade names.

Carnation (evaporated milk by *Carnation* Foods) The *Carnation* Co. was founded in the American town of Kent, Washington, by Elbridge Amos Stuart in 1899. The story runs that Stuart was looking for a good name to match an as yet undesigned brightly coloured label that he intended to put on his cases of evaporated milk. On business one afternoon in nearby Seattle, he noticed in a shop window a pile of cigar boxes with the incongruous name, 'Carnation cigars'. He bought a box – and decided that he had found the name he was looking for. To this day the can labels portray three red carnations to match the name. As for the cigars, 'Carnation', with its simultaneous suggestion of opulence and 'Corona', was perhaps not such an absurd name as it may have appeared to Stuart!

Castrol (motor oil by *Burmah*-Castrol) The association with 'castor oil' is a correct one. Originally named Wakefield Motor Oil in 1906 by the founder of the lubricating oil firm, Charles Wakefield, the product, which has *castor oil* as its base, was renamed *Castrol* 'R' for the first British aero meeting (Doncaster 1909) and Castrol Motor Oil, for car engines, in 1912. (The 'R' was presumably for the rotary engines of the aircraft, for which *Castrol* 'R' was one of the few suitable oils available. Today most *Castrol* automotive oils are based on mineral oil, not vegetable oil.)

Caterpillar (tracked vehicles by *Caterpillar* Tractors) The name seems to have been first used by Benjamin Holt, of Stockton, California. He registered the name as a trade mark in 1910 but reported in his application that he had been using it since 1904. He did not record the reason for his choice of name but presumably the inspiration lay in the 'caterpillar-like' progression of the tracks as they

50

moved over the ground, the many shoes of the track suggesting the legs of a caterpillar. (The first such track shoes for Holt's steam tractor were made of wood.) At the same time the *Supplement* to the *Oxford English Dictionary* (1972) enters a quote from *Scientific American* of 16 May 1908, to the effect that the British military authorities had been testing a tracked tractor at Aldershot, and that the soldiers there had 'promptly christened it the "caterpillar" '. But possibly the soldiers had heard of Holt's invention, even though the name was not yet registered. The Caterpillar Tractor Co. was set up in 1925 in California.

Celanese (artificial silk fabric by British *Celanese*)   The name some-what exotically, but erroneously, suggests 'Ceylonese'. It in fact almost certainly derives from 'cellulose' (the fabric was patented in 1894 as cellulose acetate *rayon*) with either an arbitrary suffix or one deliberately chosen to suggest 'ease', with reference to the fabric's comfort of wearing. Its chief use for ladies' underwear when spun commercially after the First World War would seem to support this theory. The firm who first introduced the fabric in 1921 on a commercial scale were British *Celanese* (formerly the British Cellulose and Chemical Manufacturing Co.) The actual name was devised in 1923 by an employee of the company, Dr Henri Dreyfus, as the result of a competition.

Cellophane (transparent wrapping material by British *Cellophane*)   *Cellophane* was first manufactured under this name in Paris in 1913, with its name composed of '*cell*ulose', the infix '-*o*-', and the element '-*phane*' meaning 'showing through' (as in 'dia-phanous'). The substance was first produced in France in 1869 by its Swiss inventor, Jacques Edwin Brandenberger. He, however, or rather his American assignee, Du Pont, lost his exclusive right to the name in the USA when the courts decided that, on the expira-tion of the patent, the article had no other general name, and that 'cellophane' was thus descriptive. (Much the same thing happened with *aspirin* and *linoleum*.) In America, thus, the name is generic, but in the UK is a registered trade mark and the property of British *Cellophane* Ltd (BCL).

celluloid (thermoplastic material)   Originally an American trade mark, 'celluloid' was the name used for a plastic material made from camphor and *cellul*ose nitrate in the late 1860s by John Wesley Hyatt of Albany, New York, to whom a patent was granted in 1870. (The '-oid' suffix denotes the relationship of the material to its basic constituent, cellulose nitrate.) The name is now often used generi-cally, and spelled with a small letter, especially for the many cel-

51

lulose derivatives used for coating film (hence the jargon use of the word to mean 'cinema film').

Cerebos (table salt by *Cerebos* Foods) The name is a classical concoction, and although possibly suggesting a bull in wax (Greek *keros*, 'wax' and *bous*, 'ox') actually seems to stem from Ceres, the Greek goddess of agriculture (as in 'cereal'), with the second element indeed being 'ox', although Latin (*bos*, *bovis*) rather than Greek. (Compare *Bovril*.) At the same time the first half of the name could also relate to Latin *cerebrum*, 'brain', and the last two letters, if one is really intent on a search for classical roots, also happen to be Latin for 'bone'! But this is no doubt to read too much into the name. However these connotations were mentioned in a piece of doggerel that appeared by way of advertising the product in the 1900s, two of whose verses ran:

'Ceres' is Greek for the goddess of grain,
'Cerebrum' stands for the best of the brain,
'Bos' is an ox, and 'Os' is the bone –
A rare combination, as critics will own.

Now 'Cerebos Salt' is the strength of the grain,
That is needed to nourish the bones and the brain,
Thrown out with the bran, but restored to the good,
Is a salt for the table, rich, dainty and good.

Cerebos salt itself first appeared in 1894 as the invention of a chemist, George Weddell, who wanted something to strengthen his young daughter's teeth and bones.

Cessna (light aircraft and manufacturer) The company was founded in Wichita, Kansas, in 1911 by Clyde V. Cessna, an American aviation pioneer.

Chad Valley (toys and games by General Mills UK) The company's headquarters are in Birmingham, where the *Chad Valley* is an actual location two miles south-west of the city centre. The Chad does not seem to be anything to do with the saint Chad to whom Birmingham's Roman Catholic cathedral is dedicated.

Chase Manhattan (bank) The American bank was created in 1955 as a result of a merger between the Bank of Manhattan (founded 1799) and the Chase National Bank of the City of New York (founded 1877). The latter took its name from Salmon Portland Chase (1807–73), the American lawyer and statesman, who originated the United States national banking system in 1863.

Cherry Blossom (shoe polish by Reckitt & Colman) The name was originally used by the Chiswick Soap Co., London, for a perfumed toilet soap packed in a tin. After a period of non-use the name was revived for similarly packed boot polishes manufactured by the same firm, with the name being registered in 1903, and the company's name changed to the Chiswick Polish Co. The firm in due course was acquired by the company that today is Reckitt & Colman. Hence the unlikely link between an attractive spring flower and a basic shoe-cleaning substance. (Compare *Carnation* and evaporated milk.)

Chesterfield (cigarettes by Liggett & Myers) When the American Tobacco Co. trust was broken up in 1911 Liggett & Myers acquired some top-selling brands of cigarettes. One of these was *Chesterfield*, a name which they reintroduced in 1912. It had formerly been used by the Drummond Tobacco Co. and in 1898 had been the subject of litigation when Lichenstein Bros of New York sued Drummond, claiming that *they* had originally used the name on a cigar. The New York Supreme Court ruled against Lichenstein on the grounds that 'Chesterfield' was a geographical name as well as that of an actual person. As a brand name, of course, the reference is a 'prestige' one to Lord Chesterfield, the fourth Earl of Stanhope, who had achieved world renown as a symbol of gracious living (and whose name had passed to such upper-class household objects as the Chesterfield coat and the elegant type of sofa called a chesterfield).

Chevette (car by *Vauxhall* Motors) The car is based on the American *Chevrolet*, hence a 'Chev-ette', or smaller *Chevrolet*. At the same time the name is attractively and elegantly (although meaninglessly) French.

Chevrolet (car and manufacturer) The name is that of Louis Chevrolet, a Swiss engineer engaged in the bicycle business in France, who at the turn of the century went to America to race *Fiats*. By 1909 he was experimenting with a six-cylinder design car on behalf of William Crapo Durant, for whom he had been working as a racing driver. Two years later Chevrolet launched the *Chevrolet* Motor Co., whose name, thought Durant, 'had a musical sound and the romance of foreign origin'. He might have added that for a car to bear the name of a famous racing driver was an added sign of prestige, since racing drivers were the heroes of the day.

Chinon (camera by Dixon Photographic UK) The name, rather like *Chevrolet*, has 'the romance of foreign origin' – in this case conjuring up the royal châteaux of France. In actual fact the name

53

derives from the president of *Chinon* Industries Inc. of Japan, Hiroshi Chino. It was first used in 1963.

Chopper ('high-rise' bicycle for boys by Raleigh)   The actual design of the bicycle, the so-called 'arrow wedge', came from the United States as a result of a visit there by Raleigh's subsequent director of design, Alan Oakley, in 1967. The name can therefore be said to be American in inspiration, and was primarily designed to suggest a powerful machine that could 'chop' its way along. Only when the model was first marketed in the United States in 1969 (it was on sale in Britain the following year) did the connection with 'chopper' as a slang term for a helicopter become significant. (The association was not over-emphasised, since this was the time of the Vietnam war.) Raleigh have had trouble over the name. Not only have the press tended to refer to any 'high-rise' bike as a 'Chopper', but in some countries similarly designed models have been produced, and notably in Taiwan, where versions of the bicycle named 'Choper', 'Cropper', 'Clopper' and 'Rally Chopper' have appeared on the market. A name that was originally considered for the machine but subsequently rejected was 'Marauder'.

Chrysler (car and manufacturer)   In spite of associations with 'crystal' and 'chrysalis' (and thus with Greek *khrusos*, 'gold') the name is actually that of the American engineer, Walter Percy Chrysler (1875–1940), who not only headed the *Chrysler* Corporation but was president and manager of the Buick Motor Co. for four years from 1916. He launched the car that bore his name in 1923.

Ciba (chemical manufacturers)   The initials stand for *C*hemische *I*ndustrie *B*asel *A*ktiengesellschaft ('Chemical Industries of Basel Company'), a firm founded in Basle, Switzerland, in 1859. The abbreviated form of the name was registered in 1904. In 1970 *Ciba* merged with J.R. Geigy, founded in 1758, to form *Ciba*-Geigy.

CinemaScope (cinema film projection system using a wide screen)   The name arose in 1953 from '*cinema*' and '*-scope*', rather obviously, and was copyrighted the same year by Twentieth-Century Fox. The actual system had however been invented some years before by Henri Chrétien. Other companies produced their own version of it, such as WarnerScope and SuperScope, but rather surprisingly Fox dropped the process in the mid-1960s and switched to Panavision. (Compare *Cinerama*.)

Cinerama (cinema film projection system using a wide screen)   The name, from '*cinema*' and 'pano*rama*', predates Cin-

54

emaScope by two years. It was invented by Fred Waller, an American film research technician, and the process made a striking visual impact in the first film using it, 'This is Cinerama', shown in New York in 1952 (and stunning the audience with its impression of a roller-coaster ride). The difference between *Cinerama* and *CinemaScope* was that *Cinerama* projected the film by three projectors but *CinemaScope* used only one projector, this having an anamorphic ('distorting') lens.

CINZANO   **Cinzano** (aperitif and manufacturer)   The name is that of two Italian brothers, Carlo Stefano Cinzano and Giovanni Giacomo Cinzano, who in 1757 started their family business as distillers in the village of Pecetto, near Turin. The vermouth was first exported in 1860 and the business incorporated as a limited company in 1921, with *Cinzano* (UK) established in 1966. English-speakers at first tended to pronounce the name 'Sin-zah-no', but later acquired the more Italian pronunciation of 'Chin-zah-no', perhaps with half an ear for the associated toast 'chin-chin' or the like.

Citroën (car and manufacturer)   The name is that of the French engineer and industrialist, André-Gustave Citroën (1878–1835), who did for the European car industry what Henry Ford did for it in America. He began production of the small car bearing his name in 1919, with the *Citroën* 10CV being Europe's first mass-produced car. The diaeresis in his name gives it an added touch of class, but is necessary in French to show that the second of the two vowels is sounded separately from the first.

Clairol (hair conditioner by Bristol-Myers)   The name is almost certainly a French spelling of 'clear' (for elegance) with the '-ol' suffix meaning 'oil', as it often does.

Clydella (cloth fabric by William Hollins & Co.)   The name is based on *Viyella*, with which it, and the fabric it represents, is sometimes confused. *Clydella* owes the first part of its name to its source or origin: a mill in Glasgow on the banks of the river Clyde. As a fabric, *Clydella* is made from 81 per cent cotton and 19 per cent wool and is somewhat lighter in weight than *Viyella*. It was originally developed as a lightweight shirting for military wear in the First World War.

Coalite (smokeless fuel by *Coalite* and Chemical Products Co.)   With the suffix '-ite' simply indicating a commercial product, *Coalite* was first produced in 1906 as a smokeless fuel by heating, and so refining, bituminous coal. The suggestion of 'coal light' is a fortuitous one.

Coca-Cola (aerated drink and manufacturer)   As one of the best known and most 'international' of trade names, *Coca-Cola* was created in May 1886 by Frank M. Robinson, bookkeeper to the creator of the drink itself, Dr John S. Pemberton, a druggist from Atlanta, Georgia, and was registered as a trade mark on 31 January 1893. The name was based on two of the drink's constituents: extracts from *coca* leaves and from the *cola* nut. That coca leaves also yield cocaine is a connection that the manufacturers do not now prefer to emphasise, and it is certainly true that although the drink once contained a form of the drug, especially in the early days when it was advertised as an 'Esteemed Brain Tonic and Intellectual Beverage', it contains none now. The name itself is a remarkably successful one as a memorable and easily pronounceable trade name, having alliteration and three desirable 'k' sounds (compare *Kodak*). *Coca-Cola* gained popularity rapidly – it was first bottled in 1894 – to such an extent that the manufacturers were obliged to register a second name for it used by the public as a 'pet' form: *Coke*. The second element of the name is not a registered trade mark, so that 'cola' drinks exist on the market in a number of varieties. Among names of rival brands (impostors) were Coca, Cola, Fig Cola, Candy Cola, Cold Cola, Cay-Ola and Koca-Nola. All these were outlawed by the courts in 1916.

Codis (analgesic tablets by Reckitt & Colman)   The name was registered in 1949 and was devised to describe the nature of the product as a form of *co*deine that *dis*solves. (Compare *Disprin*.)

Coke (alternative name of *Coca-Cola*)   The name originated as a popular alternative for *Coca-Cola* before the First World War, with the popular abbreviation boosted by a rival firm, the Koke Company of America, who produced a similar drink. Fearing loss of identity and the substitution of other drinks under the name, the company adopted it in 1920 when the Supreme Court of the United States ruled that '*Coke*' was the exclusive property of the *Coca-Cola* Company. 'The name now characterizes a beverage to be had at almost any soda fountain', declared Mr Justice Oliver Wendell Holmes. 'It means a single thing coming from a single source and well known to the community.' In fact the Court had had doubts about the name, since 'coke' was – as it still is – a slang term for cocaine, which originally was present in the drink in microscopic quantities. Later, when cocaine was eliminated from the formula, the company found the name a successful one, free from undesirable

or misleading associations. The name *Coke* first appeared on bottles
in 1941 and was registered in 1945.

Colgate (soap and cosmetic preparations by *Colgate-Palmolive*)   The firm was founded in 1806 as a tallow chandlery
and soap-manufacturing business by William Colgate (1783–1857),
an English-born soap manufacturer brought to America as a child.
His son, Samuel Colgate (1822–97), expanded the business, and *his*
son Sidney Morse Colgate (1862–1930) became chairman of the
board of the consolidated *Colgate-Palmolive*-Peet Co. shortened to
Colgate-Palmolive in 1953 (see also *Palmolive*). The name is an easily
pronounced one, and free from any particular association, desirable
or not.

Colibri (cigarette lighters and manufacturer)   The firm bearing
the name was founded in 1927 by Julius Lowenthal, who the previous year had invented a lighter in which the user could light the
flame without touching the flint wheel directly with his thumb. On
the face of it an unlikely name, *Colibri* was chosen to impart to the
new type of lighter the elegance, lightness and swiftness of the
humming bird so called. The name's 'foreign-ness' (the word 'colibri' is actually of Caribbean origin) gives it an added exotic flavour.

Colt (ventilation appliances by *Colt* International)   The firm was
founded in 1925 not by a Mr Colt but by his business partner, later
the company's chairman, I.J. O'Hea. Mr O'Hea chose the name of
his partner, W.H. Colt, rather than his own as he regarded it as a
less awkward one. Ironically – and somewhat amusingly in the
circumstances – Mr Colt's real name was actually Gleischner, and
he had adopted his wife's maiden name on coming to England for
virtually the same reasons that prompted Mr O'Hea not to use his
name for the company! In 1932 the two partners agreed to part
company on an amicable basis, with Mr Colt taking on the timber
side of the business as W.H. Colt Ltd and Mr O'Hea continuing
with the newly named *Colt* Ventilation, from which was formed *Colt*
International. The name thus has no connection with any other
Colt: the gun, the beer (Colt 45), the car, or the lawn mower.

Columbia (gramophone records by EMI)   The records were originally produced by the *Columbia Phonograph* Co. in the 1890s. This
company had its headquarters in Washington, DC (i.e. in the District of Columbia). It was the sole sales agent for the American
Graphophone Co. (see *gramophone*). The original English subsidiary,
later autonomous, was the *Columbia Graphophone* Co. This was subsequently acquired by EMI.

Commer (commercial vehicles by *Chrysler* United Kingdom) The name is short for 'commercial', and originated with the firm Commercial Cars Ltd which was founded in London in 1905, becoming *Commer* Cars Ltd in Luton some years later. The company subsequently became part of *Chrysler* United Kingdom, who, however, do not use the name *Commer* on any of their vehicles.

Cona (coffee machine by The *Cona* Coffee Machine Co.) In spite of its foreign-seeming spelling, the name is of English origin, and is that of the company's founder, Alfred Cohn, who started his coffee-machine production in 1910. (The name is his surname, minus the 'h', with his initial added.) An English-devised but foreign-sounding name can however have its disadvantages. In Portugal, for example, and other Portuguese-speaking countries to which the coffee machine is exported, the name has had to be changed to 'Acolon', since the English name is the Portuguese slang word for the pudenda (as it almost is in a number of other languages, including English itself). The name is coincidentally suitable for the cone shape of the seat of the upper vessel of the machine.

Condor (tobacco by Gallaher) A rather unusual name for a tobacco, or indeed any consumer product. Thanks to television documentaries, however, at least most people will know what a condor is. The bird eats carrion, but presumably this is not part of the intended image. It is also the largest bird of prey in the world, which must be nearer the mark: size, power, and rarity. Perhaps the name sounds slightly exotic, with a hint of French *d'or*, 'golden'.

Consul (cars by Ford Motor Co.) A typical prestige name for a car. Consul, of course, is a diplomatic title. Through the Romans, it is also a historical one.

Contac (decongestant capsules by Menley & James Laboratories) The name of the 'unblocking' capsules suggests 'contact', which is perfectly suitable for a drug that aims to attack a cold and its symptoms. It in fact derives, however, from '*conti*nuous *ac*tion', since the product's 'time capsules' are effective over a number of hours.

Cookeen (cooking fat by Van den Berghs & Jurgens) The unusual part of the name is its suffix. But presumably '-een' is an eye-catching variant of the traditional '-ine'. This particular spelling also ensures a correct pronunciation (rhyming with 'keen' and not 'fine').

Copydex (adhesive and manufacturer)   How can an adhesive be used to copy? The answer lies in the evolution of the firm of this name, founded in 1946 in London for the purpose of selling office supplies, including carbon paper (used of course for *copy*ing), typewriter ribbons and, as with most office-supply firms, adhesives. The firm specialised in adhesives after a salesman, by chance, found that the firm's particular brand was effective in repairing holes in potato sacks at his home. The ending '-dex' is unexplained. Possibly it is simply the 'trade suffix' '-ex' with '-d-' used as a convenient infix. Or perhaps a more obvious name, such as 'Copitex', already existed as a registered trade mark.

Corgi (metal scale models by *Mettoy* Playcraft)   *Corgi* die-cast models were first on the market in 1956. Their name seems to have two main associations: the corgi dog is a miniature breed noted for its sturdiness; *Corgi* toys are manufactured in South Wales (at Swansea) and the corgi dog is a Welsh breed. The fact that the corgi is a 'royal' dog is a fortuitous bonus! (Compare the next entry.)

Corgi Books (paperback books by *Transworld* Publishers)   *Transworld* Publishers are a British subsidiary of *Bantam Books* (which see). In 1951 the company first published *Corgi Books*, having been organised the previous year by Ian Ballantine who established *Bantam Books* in the United States in 1945. At the time of this organisation of *Transworld*, the *Bantam* name and trade mark were unavailable in Britain, so *Transworld* was chosen as the company name ('across the world' from Bantam in America) and the corgi dog was selected for the symbol from a list of more than a hundred animals, birds and pocket-sized articles. It was hoped that *Corgi Books* would become favourite reading of the subjects of Queen Elizabeth II, whose own favourite pets were corgi dogs. (Compare the previous entry.)

Corniche (car by Bentley Motors)   Many car names are foreign-sounding, but this one may have some people baffled. What exactly is a corniche? Is it a form of cornice (whatever that is)? Is it even an English word at all? Recourse to the *Concise Oxford Dictionary* reveals that a corniche is a 'coastal road with wide views' (which is in fact related in origin to 'cornice', the architectural term for a length of wood or stone that runs along the top of a building). So the image is of a stately car-ride along a cliff-top. All well and good, but isn't the name rather too rarefied, even for majestic Bentley owners? Not everyone, either, will have heard of the *corniches* (or *routes en corniche*), the coastal roads of the French Riviera that run along rocky ledges.

Corona (soft drinks by Beecham Group)   The word is Latin for 'crown', and this seems to be the origin, i.e. a prestige name. It was devised by a Welsh grocer, William Evans, who first marketed his soft drinks – previously called Welsh Hills drinks – in England in 1927.

Cortina (car by Ford Motor Co.)   The *Cortina* has for many years been Britain's top-selling car. Its name, too, has an image that manages to be both exotic and popular – that of the north Italian resort of Cortina d' Ampezzo, site of the 1956 Winter Olympic Games, and one of the most popular summer and winter resorts in the Dolomites. (To an Italian, however, the name may seem more humdrum: not only is it a 'home' town but *Cortina* is simply the Italian for 'curtain'.) Since 1972 the Ford *Cortina* has had a rival in the *Triumph Dolomite*.

Coty (perfumery by Helena Rubinstein)   The name, familiar in its flourished handsigned form, is the surname of the Corsican-born industrialist François Coty, who after a period at Grasse in the south of France, a region noted for its flowers and perfumes, opened a perfume plant near Paris in 1905. Coty's short and simple name is a successful trade name – much more so than his real name of Francesco Giuseppe Spoturno would have been. The firm of *Coty* was registered in Great Britain in 1923.

Courtelle (synthetic fabric by Courtaulds)   The name derives from *Court*aulds with a suffix '-elle' that suggests either femininity (as 'mademoiselle') or a homely diminutiveness (as 'bagatelle').

Cow Gum (adhesive and manufacturer)   In spite of a link between gum and glue and knackers' yards, *Cow Gum* adhesive does not come from cows, or parts of cows, but from a firm that manufactured rubber goods in Cheapside, London, owned by Peter Brusey Cow. A modern offshoot of the business that began in the nineteenth century is Cow Industrial Polymers, rubber manufacturers of Streatham Common, London.

 Creda (domestic appliances and manufacturer)   The name is an abbreviation of *Cred*enda, a company that in 1919 joined with Simplex, Accles and Pollock and Tubes Ltd to form Tube Investments.

60

Credenda is Latin for 'things to be trusted' (just as 'agenda' literally means 'things to be done'), and so is an effective classical-sounding name for the reliability of a firm and its products.

Crimplene (synthetic fibre by ICI) The fibre is a modified *Terylene* filament yarn, noted for its crease-resistant properties. The name seems to point to the yarn's 'crimped' quality. At the same time it is curious that near Harrogate in Yorkshire, where ICI Fibres has its headquarters, there is a stream called Crimple Beck.

Cubs (breakfast cereal by *Nabisco*) The name was first registered in 1938, although the actual product, a small-sized *Shredded Wheat* cereal, was not marketed until 1957. As a trade name, *Cubs* was intended to indicate a 'junior' version of the 'adult' *Shredded Wheat*. It is a short, snappy name, and an effective one for a breakfast cereal that is aimed at a much wider consumership than Cub Scouts, with many of whom, nevertheless, it must be popular.

CUPRINOL **Cuprinol** (wood preservative and manufacturer) There would seem to be some link with copper here (as in 'cupric', 'cupro-nickel' and the like) – or is there an association with 'recuperative'? Perhaps the base of the name relates to some chemical used to preserve wood. The suffix '-ol' almost certainly indicates 'oil', since oils and oil-soluble chemicals are widely used in wood preservation.

Cutex (nail varnish by Chesebrough-Pond's) The name, and the product, originated with Northam Warren, an American who began marketing a liquid cuticle remover in 1911. Five years later he introduced America's first liquid nail polish, calling it *Cutex* after the *cut*icle remover, with the suffix '-ex' meaning 'out'. Warren had opposition from a foreign manufacturer, who duplicated the name and packaging of *Cutex* for his own product and defended himself in court on the grounds that 'cutex' was a generic term for nail polish. The challenger lost.

Cuticura (skincare products by *Cuticura* Laboratories) The origin of the name, which dates back to the nineteenth century, is not 'cuticle curer', as has been suggested, but Latin *cutis*, 'skin', and *cura*, 'care'. (Could there also be a hint at the rarer Latin word *curatura*, 'attention to the body'?) The original *Cuticura* product was an ointment designed for Newfoundland fishermen, whose hands became very sore in the course of their work.

Cutty Sark (whisky by Berry Bros & Rudd) How did a Scotch whisky come to have the name of a famous tea clipper? The story

61

goes that one day in 1923 in the offices of Berry Bros in London a guest was entertained to lunch. This was the Scottish artist James McBey. After lunch Francis Berry asked his guest for his suggestions for a name for. the whisky that he planned to put on the export market. McBey came up with the name of the sailing ship, that he had recently been reading about. To his surprise, Berry agreed to the proposal. Thus the name of the tea clipper (which literally means 'short shirt', and originates from the garment worn by the witch Nannie in Burns's poem 'Tam o'Shanter'), was transferred to the whisky that became the largest selling brand of scotch in the United States.

Cyanamid (pharmaceutical and chemical products and manufacturer) The company was founded in 1907 by an American civil engineer, Frank Washburn, whose speciality was building dams. Washburn had heard of a German process for extracting nitrogen from the air and combining it with lime and carbide to form *cyanamide* (or *cyanamid*, as it can also be spelled), a basic element in fertiliser. Such a process, Washburn was pleased to notice, demanded a large supply of electricity. He went to Germany, bought the American rights for the process, then set up American *Cyanamid* to use the electricity generated by his dams for the production of fertilisers. *Cyanamid* of Great Britain Ltd was established in London in 1923, and the American parent company acquired *Formica* in 1956. The name is reflected in several of its products, such as the agricultural Cyfac and Cycocel, the industrial Cymel and Cyanamer, and the perfume Cie (presumably intended to evoke 'sigh').

Cyclostyle see **Gestetner**

Cydrax (non-alcoholic cider by Whiteways of Whimple) The firm, founded by Henry Whiteway in the 1890s, has always spelled its product 'cyder', so that when it became a public company in 1934 it took the name of Whiteways Cyder Co. 'Cyder' is presumably thought of as a more rural, 'wholesome' (because old-fashioned) spelling of the word, with the 'y' conjuring up names on the lines of 'Ye Olde Tea-Shoppe'. The '-ax' suffix is doubtless an alternative for '-ex', and was passed on to another of the company's drinks, Peardrax, a non-alcoholic perry. In 1972 the word 'Cyder' was nevertheless dropped from the company owing to the wide diversification of its products, one of which is *Sanatogen*.

D

Dacron (polyester fibre by du Pont de Nemours & Co.)   The name is almost certainly, like *Orlon*, a concocted one, with, however, the final two letters suggesting *nylon*. True, the initial 'D' could have been chosen for *d*u Pont, or *D*elaware, where the company has its headquarters (at Wilmington), but this may be simply coincidental. *Dacron* is the American equivalent of *Terylene*.

Daddies (sauce by Smedley-*HP* Foods)   The name was registered around 1903, but seems to have no traceable story behind it. Perhaps the name was chosen simply as a homely one: if Daddy liked the sauce, maybe the rest of the family would. Or perhaps this was the only type of 'sauce' children could legitimately give their fathers? A contemporary sauce named Burma Sauce was advertised with the words, 'The only sauce I dare give father.'

DAF (car and manufacturer)   The abbreviation is a Dutch one – for Van *D*oorne's *A*utomobiel*f*abrieken ('Van Doorne's Motor Works'). The brothers Hub and Wim van Doorne started up their car-repair business in 1928. In 1930 they branched out into the manufacture of trailers, and proceeded from these to trucks, military vehicles and buses, with their first cars produced in 1959.

Daimler (car by *BL*)   The *Daimler* has always been regarded as a typically British car. It would probably be more accurate to say that the *British* Daimler has always been truly British, and that the car dates in this respect from 1896, when the English *Daimler* Motor Co. was founded to exploit the German Daimler patents bought the previous year by financier H.J. Lawson's British Motor Syndicate. These patents were specifically for the engine designed by the German mechanical engineer and inventor Gottfried Daimler (1834–1900), whose company *Daimler-Motoren-Gesellschaft* ('Daimler Motor Company') built the first *Mercedes* in 1899.

DAKS (menswear by *DAKS*-Simpson)   The firm's history began in 1894, when Simeon Simpson set up a bespoke tailoring business in London. His 'House of Simpson' fulfilled a demand for ready-made suits and jackets, however, caused by the First World War, and a development was the patenting of a self-supporting waistband for trousers in 1934 by Simpson's second son, Alexander. He it was who devised the name DAKS for such trousers, the origin apparently being a blend of 'dad' and 'slacks', and a pleasant-sounding compromise in itself. The name is thus neither an abbreviation nor an acronym of the initials of the first Mr Simpson.

Dan-Air (commercial airline)   The airline does not have specific Danish links, commercially or routewise. Its name comes from *Da*vies & *N*ewman Ltd, a London shipbroking company that entered the aircraft broking market in the early 1950s and established its own air service, with its main base at Southend Airport, in 1953. (Two years later the company moved to Blackbushe and when this airport closed in 1960 made a further move to Gatwick.) The name is a trifle awkward: might not a sleeker name for an airline have been something like 'Danline', or a weightier one such as 'D & N Lines' been more suitable?

Dannimac (raincoats and manufacturer)   The manufacturer must presumably be named something like Daniel or Daniels. Or is the name meant to suggest a 'dandy mac'?

Datsun (car and manufacturer)   The original car, manufactured in 1913, was called the DAT, the initials being those of the three financial backers of the Japanese Kwaishinsha Motor Car Works, K. *D*en, R. *A*oyama, and A. *T*akeuchi. In the early years, the name was changed to 'Datson', intended to mean 'son of DAT'. However, when 'son' was pronounced by the Japanese it sounded too much like the Japanese word for 'loss' so the name was modified to *Datsun* (in 1932). In 1933 the Jidosha Seizo Co., the forerunner of the present company, was established, and the following year it produced the Austin Seven under licence (as the *Datsun*) and changed its own name to the Nissan Motor Co.

Day-Glo (fluorescent paint by Dane and Co.)   The name is of American origin, and was devised by the Switzer Bros Inc. of Cleveland, Ohio, in the early 1950s to describe their daylight fluorescent colours. These are four or five times brighter than conventional colours, so thus seem to *glow* in *day*light. The name is sometimes used generically of any fluorescent colours, and spelled indifferently, as 'day-glow', 'daglo' and the like. Such a practice, although utterly unacceptable to the owners of the trade mark, is characteristic of the English language, which will designate a popular new commonplace object by its best-known name. In Britain the name is dangerously close to that of Dayglow Signs, a company in Worcestershire manufacturing highly coloured signs and display plates.

DECCA   **Decca** (*gramophone* records and manufacturer)   The exact origin of the name appears to be unrecorded. It was, however, first used for a portable *gramophone*, the *Decca* Portable, manufactured by Barnett Samuel & Co. in London in 1913. One theory behind the name, offered by a descendant of the Samuel family, is that *Decca* was chosen to match the names of other products of the company beginning with 'D', and in particular the main Barnett Samuel name of Dulcet. The advantage of Decca, it was thought, was that it would be pronounced reasonably accurately in all European languages, whereas 'Dulcet' was said differently, for example, by the Italians. But this explanation has not been authenticated. Nor has the one that claims the name to represent the musical notes D, E, C, C, A, attractive and apt as the idea might seem.

Deeko (household paperware and manufacturer)   The name derives from a partnership formed between a Mr Dailley and a Mr Wilkinson in 1899 to manufacture paper doyleys and ornamental paper for mantel shelves in Islington, London. Mr Wilkinson left the partnership in 1907 and the company of *D*ailley & *Co* was then set up. And there is the name, with the '-ko' ending a variation on the usual '-co' for 'company'.

Denovo (tyre by Dunlop)   The name is Latin for 'from new' (*de novo*) and resulted from a company contest that produced 9500 suggested names, most of which (such as 'Jack the Gripper' and 'Safeway') were eliminated for language reasons or because they were already in use. The final selection was made by a Paris company called Novamark – whose own name was licensed in the UK to form Novamark International, the London trade name creators.

Dequadin (throat lozenges by Farley Health Products)   The name is based on Dequalinium chloride BP (i.e. listed in the *British Pharmacopoeia*), a compound possessing antibacterial and antifungal properties. The lozenges were first marketed in 1955.

Dettol

Dettol (antiseptic and disinfectant by Reckitt & Colman)   One might ingeniously derive the name from '*d*isinfectant' and 'Co*l*man', or '*d*isinfectant' and 'Reckitt & Colman'. The true origin is simpler. When the product was about to be marketed in the 1930s (it first went on sale in 1933) there was a debate as to whether it should be promoted as a disinfectant, perhaps called 'Disinfectol', or as an antiseptic. The decision finally was that it should be introduced as a disinfectant through doctors for medical uses at first, and that the name should not be 'Disinfectol' but something that had a medical flavour without giving a preconceived idea of the nature of the product. This name, thus based on the suggested 'Disinfectol', was *Dettol*. (At first the name of the manufacturer appeared on the bottle as the 'Suffolk Chemical Co.', since it was thought that Reckitt's name, which would be associated with blue and black lead, would be a handicap to sales. Later it was realised that it was better to have the name of a familiar firm, even if it was associated with non-medical products.)

Dexedrine (stimulant drug by Smith, Kline & French Laboratories) The name was introduced in 1942 for a drug that was a preparation of *dex*amphetamine sulphate, with '-edrine' based on *Benzedrine*.

Dexion (steel storage equipment by *Dexion*-Comino International) The name is based on the Greek word for 'right'. This had a twofold intention: to denote the slotted or right-angle design of the product and to suggest its correctness or 'rightness' for the job. The latter concept is reflected in the tick symbol of the company's logo. *Dexion* was registered as a name about 1939 by the founder of the company, Demetrius Comino, an Australian of Greek extraction.

Dimplex (domestic electric heaters by *Dimplex* Heating) The name seems to have originated from the 'dimpled' design of the first oil-filled electric radiators produced by the company, with the suffix '-ex' (or '-lex') perhaps suggesting the powering agent, *el*ectricity.

Dinky Toys (die-cast model vehicles by General Mills UK) The colloquial word, more British than American, means not only 'small' but also 'pretty', 'dainty', 'neat'. The models are no longer made.

DISPRIN **Disprin** (analgesic tablets by Reckitt & Colman) The name is reasonably transparent, indicating a *dis*solvable as*pirin*. It was registered in 1944 by Roy Vickers of Liverpool.

DKW (car and motorcycle and manufacturer) The initials have been given various interpretations, including *D*eutsche *K*raftfahrzeug *W*erke ('German Motor Vehicle Works'), *D*ampf *K*raft *W*agen ('steam power vehicle'), *D*as *k*leine *W*under ('The Little Wonder'), and *D*es *K*naben *W*unsch ('the boy's wish')! The truth of the tale seems to be somewhere between all four. In 1916 a firm in southeast Germany started by a Dane, Jorgen Rasmussen, was producing steam-powered engines. Three years later a German engineer from Berlin offered Rasmussen the production of a small 30cc toy two-stroke engine (every boy's wish). In 1921 an enlarged version of this engine was assembled to power a normal bicycle (a little wonder). In 1927 Rasmussen's firm produced its first motor car. The changing interpretation of the initials thus marked the gradual expansion and progress of the firm – which in 1932 joined with *Audi, Horch* and Wanderer to form the Auto-Union consortium.

Do-Do (decongestant by International Laboratories)   A name that could suggest the product is 'dead as a dodo', which is hardly conducive to ready sales! The name was in fact registered in 1934 by the owner of the company, Harry Pickup (see *Harpic*), who devised it from the first syllables of the names of two previously unsuccessful tonic products, 'Dovim' and 'Dovite', commercialese Latin for 'I give strength' and 'I give life.'

Dolcis (shoes and manufacturer)   The name is presumably from the Latin word *dulcis*, 'pleasant', 'delightful'. Perhaps the spelling was changed slightly since the 'u' version was already in use as a trade mark?

Dolomite (cars by *Jaguar Rover Triumph*)   The name, although used for the car launched in 1972, was in existence as a car name well before the Second World War. It is that of the Dolomites, the Alpine mountains in northern Italy popular among tourists. Compare the 'rival' name of the *Cortina.*

Domestos (liquid bleach by *Unilever*)   *Domestos* was first introduced in 1930 and was being nationally distributed by 1952. The name seems to be a blend of '*domest*ic' and the brand name of a bleaching chemical, Chlor*os*.

Dormobile (motor vehicle with elevating roof and manufacturer)   Another fairly obvious name: a blend of '*dorm*itory' (the vehicle was designed as a camper for people to sleep in) and 'autom*obile*' (or perhaps just 'mobile').

Dorothy Perkins (womenswear chain stores)   The original shop from which the chain came was built in the style of a red-tiled gable-roofed cottage. The wife of one of the partners of the founder, Samuel Farmer, suggested the name since she felt that the popular climbing rose so called fitted in well with the cottage style. The name of the rambling rose itself dates back to the turn of the century.

Double Century (sherry by Pedro Domecq)   The firm of Pedro Domecq was founded in 1730. In 1930 they blended a special golden oloroso sherry to mark their two-hundredth anniversary – their 'Double Century'.

Double Diamond (beer by *Ind Coope*) In a pre-Christmas advertising campaign in 1979, *Ind Coope* promoted *Double Diamond* as their 'best' *India Pale Ale* for which in 1876 they had 'adopted the double diamond symbol'. The name would thus seem to originate from a conventional graphic device, this being a triple 'X' (XXX) to denote a strong beer. (The 'double diamond' can be discerned in the enclosed parts of this symbol, between the 'Xs'.)

Dralon (acrylic fibre by Farbenfabriken Bayer) The name is of German origin, and thus may be derived from *Draht*, 'wire', 'thread', 'strand' (referring to the manufacturing process) and the last three letters of *nylon*. To English-speakers it will probably suggest 'drape', which is a reasonable association since the material is used not only for upholstery but also for curtains (which are draped). It is unfortunate that a number of English words beginning 'dra-' have undesirable connotations, as 'drain', 'draggle', and 'drab'.

Dramamine (travel-sickness tablets by Searle Laboratories) The name is a contraction of '*d*iphenhyd*ramine* theoclate', with the middle syllable repeated.

Drambuie (liqueur by The *Drambuie* Liqueur Co.) The name has a proper history. After the Jacobite rebellion of 1745 ('The Forty-Five'), the Young Pretender ('Bonnie Prince Charlie') fled for his life to the Isle of Skye. On leaving for France the following year he gave to John Mackinnon of Strathaird who had rowed him to a safe hiding-place the secret formula of his personal liqueur. For nearly 150 years the Mackinnons kept the secret to themselves. Then in 1906, and after the name had been registered in 1892, Malcolm Mackinnon decided to produce the liqueur commercially as *Drambuie*, a name deriving from the Gaelic *dram*, 'drink', and either *buidheach*, 'satisfying', 'pleasing', or *buidh*, 'yellow', 'golden'.

Drene (shampoo by Procter & Gamble) A rather unpleasant name, in fact, suggesting a number of off-putting words starting 'dr-' ('dreary', 'drain', 'dregs', 'drone', 'drench' and the like). There is of course 'dream' and the rarish girls' name Drene, but these are not ready associations, although favourable. *Drene* was the first soapless shampoo to be marketed in the United States, in 1933.

Drinamyl (stimulant drug by Menley & James Laboratories) The drug is named from its active ingredients, *d*examphetamine and *amyl*barbitone, with the first four letters also based on Dexa*drine*.

Dubonnet (aperitif by Cadbury *Schweppes*)   The name is that of a Parisian chemist, Joseph Dubonnet, who in 1846 prepared a wine containing quinquina (cinchona), a drug from a South American tree or shrub famed as a tonic and febrifuge. *Dubonnet* today still contains quinquina. The company of the name was formed in 1908. The famous slogan 'Dubo, Dubon, Dubonnet' first appeared in the 1920s. (To a Frenchman this suggests 'beautiful, good, Dubonnet'.)

Du Maurier (cigarettes by BAT Industries)   The cigarette was launched in 1903 by Peter Jackson Ltd after the actor Gerald du Maurier had made requests for 'a cigarette less irritating to his throat'. Peter Jackson were a subsidiary of the International Tobacco Co., which company was taken over by Gallaher in 1934. In 1979 the brand passed to BAT, who had owned the trade mark overseas since they acquired Peter Jackson (Overseas) Ltd in 1955.

Duraglit (metal polish by Reckitt & Colman)   The name was first registered by the *Duraglit* Polish Co. in 1927, passing to Reckitt & Colman in the late 1950s. It is thought to derive from Latin *durus*, 'hard', and '*glit*ter'. It also, of course, suggests a *durable glitter*.

Duralumin (aluminium alloy)   The name, which is now generic ('duralumin'), was created in 1910, presumably from Latin *durus*, 'hard' and '*alumin*ium'. There may however be a link with the West German city of Düren, since heat-treatable light aluminium alloys were first produced by the *Dürener Metallwerke Aktiengesellschaft* ('Düren Metal Works Company').

Durex (contraceptives by LRC International)   The name was devised by the former chairman of LRC, Mr A.R. Reid, to whom it came 'out of the air' when he was travelling one evening in 1929 on his usual train home from London to Southend-on-Sea. Some subconscious process must have been at work, however, since there is a strong hint of 'endurable' in the name. The name also is (or was) that of a brand of adhesive tape in Australia, and a consequent embarrassment to at least one lady visitor to England who should have asked for *Sellotape* or *Scotch* tape.

Dyane (car by *Citroën*)   The name is classically based – on Diana (French *Diane*), the goddess of the moon and of the hunt. A 'classy' name, therefore.

Dymo (addressing systems by *Dymo* Business Systems)   Presumably the suggestion intended is '*dyn*amic' or '*dynamo*'? The name would not seem to be an acronym.

E

Earex (ear drops and manufacturer)   The 'ex-' suffix here must certainly mean 'out'. The product was originally named 'Aurex', but this more classical version was objected to by a company who were using the name 'Orex' for a brand of aspirin. A change was therefore necessary. There is also, of course, a suggestion of 'ear-aches' (*'Earex* for earaches').

Echo (margarine by Van den Berghs & Jurgens)   Is the margarine meant to be an 'echo' of real butter? The name is also a classical one in Greek mythology, which gives it added prestige.

Eden Vale (dairy products by Express Dairy Foods)   The name would seem to be an 'idyllic' one, conjuring up the countryside and all that is good in its natural state (the Garden of *Eden*). On the other hand there may well be a geographical connection with the valley of the river Eden, in Cumbria, or, more likely, with the place named Eden Vale near Castle Eden, east of Durham.

Ekco (radios and manufacturer)   The name is that of the original firm, E.K. Cole Ltd, who merged with Pye in 1960 to form British Electronics Industries Ltd, which in turn became Pye of Cambridge Ltd in 1963. *Ekco*, of course, is an ideal name for a radio.

Ektachrome (photographic film by *Kodak*)   The first half of the name seems to have no reliable record: could it perhaps be based on George *E*as*t*man, who founded *K*odak? But this is not very satisfactory, since an original element such as 'Ekta-' must surely have a specific derivation. (Perhaps 'echt', from the German, meaning 'genuine', 'authentic'?) The '-chrome' element is Greek for 'colour'.

El Al (Israeli airline)   The name was devised by David Remez, Israeli first minister of transport, in 1948 for a DC-4 Skymaster setting up a civilian 'airline' from Israel to Geneva, Switzerland. He took the name from the Hebrew version of a phrase in the Old Testament, where in Hosea 11, 7 come the words 'though they called them to the most High'. The Hebrew version of this runs literally 'though they call him to "Al"', the latter word or title perhaps meaning 'him on high'. (Peake's *Commentary on the Bible*, ed. Matthew Black. Nelson, 1972, p.611.) The more prosaic suggestion of 'Air Israel', made by some of the top men in Israel's Southern

Bomber Command, was thus rejected in favour of a more meaningful name for the newly born state's embryo airline.

Elan (car by *Lotus*)   The name was chosen fairly arbitrarily – mainly to match the existing names of Elite, Eclat, and Esprit. All four names are both French and 'fast', however, and of course all begin with 'E'. Among names considered for the new model, but rejected, were 'Epee' and 'Excalibur'.

Elastoplast (adhesive plasters by Smith & Nephew)   The name is obvious, but originally existed in the longer form Elastic Adhesive Bandages when the dressings were first put on the market in about 1928.

Electrolux (refrigerators and vacuum cleaners and manufacturer)   The company grew out of a small Swedish company, AB Lux, founded in 1901 for the manufacture of paraffin lamp mantles. ('Lux' in this case was intended to mean 'light' rather than 'luxury'.) In 1919 the same Swedish firm changed its name to AB *Electrolux* to reflect its new line of manufacture – electric domestic appliances. The British company was founded in 1921.

Elf (petrol by *Elf* Petroleum (UK))   The parent company is the French Société Nationale Elf Aquitaine (SNEA). When this was formed by the purchase of a few small oil companies, it was decided to choose a name by computer, preferably one of only three or four letters. When the computer selection was considered, and all the unpronounceable and undesirable letter combinations were eliminated, a short list was further whittled down to just two names: *Elf* and 'Elan'. *Elf* was chosen and became an international name except in Austria, where 'Elan' was used since *elf* in German means 'eleven' and such a connotation for an oil product is misleading. In Germany itself, however, *Elf* was retained since the name was already well known before the company began operations there. The name is pleasant sounding – gentle rather than harsh – but whether the meaning suggested in English ('fairy') is a fitting one for a powerful fuelling agent is perhaps debatable.

Elida (pharmaceutical products by *Elida* Gibbs)   The name is that of a company originating in Vienna, Austria, and was part of *Unilever* before 1939. The derivation does not seem to be recorded: the name could be an anagram or an obscure Christian name, for example, or a composite name with letters from different words.

Elsan (chemical closet by LRC International)   The inventor of

71

chemical sanitation and founder of the *Elsan* Co. in 1920 was Ephraim Louis Jackson. His first two initials, plus the 'san-' of 'sanitation', gave the name of the product. In the Second World War 'Elsan gen' was service slang for news that was unreliable. (*Elsan*s were fitted on bombers.)

Energen (dietetic foods by RHM)   The name was first used for a type of biscuit produced by a baker in the Cotswolds in 1908. It was marketed by the founder of *Energen* Foods, Richard Maurice. The name appears to be a blend of '*energy*' and the then popular 'health' suffix, '-gen' (as in *Sanatogen*). This was vaguely scientific and at the same time suggested 'generate'. A biscuit that generated energy, therefore. The word was originally printed with thick bars over the first and last letters, 'E' and 'N', the capital being lowered to accommodate its bar. During the First World War, however, this device was abandoned in case it was thought to indicate a name of German origin.

England's Glory (matches by Bryant & May)   The origin of the name was not revealed until 1959, when a Gloucester man unearthed an old advertising poster. This named the ship that is portrayed on the *England's Glory* matchbox label: she was HMS *Devastation*, a twin-screw iron-turret battleship. The ship had been first used in the 1870s on the label of a Gloucester match manufacturer, Thomas Gee. Gee's business soon closed, and the trade mark was taken over by Moreland, another Gloucester manufacturer, in 1891. In 1972 Moreland's company was in turn taken over by Bryant & May. The name is not thus that of a ship, but the patriotic epithet of a ship – and an almost ridiculously lofty name for a humble box of matches.

Enkalon (form of *nylon* by British *Enkalon*)   The '-lon' undoubtedly derives from *nylon*, while the first part of the name is the abbreviation of the original manufacturers, the Dutch firm *N*ederlands *K*unstzijde Fabriek ('Netherlands Artificial Fibre Factory'), founded in 1911. And if 'NK' does not seem to produce 'Enka-', it is because the name is based on the Dutch pronunciation of these two letters.

Eno ('fruit salt' by Beecham Group)   The product – actually a laxative – was originally produced by J.C. Eno, a Newcastle pharmacist, in the nineteenth century. As with *Andrews* 'liver salt', the product was in demand among seamen visiting the port, and this boosted business so that by 1880 *Eno* had moved to London and set up a subsidiary trade in North and South America.

72

En-Tout-Cas (hard tennis court and manufacturer) A French name for a typically English product (for a typically English game). The patent on the court was taken out in 1910, with its name meaning literally 'in any case' (i.e. usable in any weather). The phrase existed before this to apply to a type of combined umbrella and parasol – also suitable for variable weather. (Legend has it that a lady from Paris with such a waterproofed parasol was present at the opening ceremony of the first *En-Tout-Cas* court – and that her requisite inspired the choice of name!)

Erasmic (shaving cream by *Elida* Gibbs) One must presumably seek elsewhere than in the name of the Renaissance Dutch humanist Erasmus for the origin of this brand name. The *Erasmic* Co. was purchased by *Unilever* some time before the Second World War. Perhaps the name is a blend of two other words, such as '*erase*' and '*cosmic*'? Coincidentally it is an anagram of 'is cream'!

Ercol (furniture by *Ercol* Furniture) The name is an abbreviation of the family name *Ercol*ani. The company was established in 1920 by Lucian Ercolani, an Italian born in 1880, who came to Britain with his parents when he was seven.

ERF (commercial motor vehicles and manufacturer) The trucks and the company derive their name from the initials of Edwin Richard Foden, who having resigned from his own firm of *Foden* Ltd in 1932, formed a team the following year with his son Dennis and another resigned Foden manager, George Faulkner, to build their own oil-engined truck chassis.

escalator (moving staircase) The word was originally a United States trade name, from '*escal*ading elev*ator*', patented in 1900 by the Otis Elevator Co. for the use of passengers of the Manhattan Elevated Railway. In 1949 the name was legally adjudged to have become public property through popular use, and so became generic. Based in turn on *escalator* is the Travolator, a moving inclined walkway more like a conveyor belt than a staircase.

Esso (petrol by *Esso* Petroleum Co.) The name is a version of the initials SO, the abbreviation of the *S*tandard *O*il Co. of New Jersey. This was the chief company of the Oil Trust set up by Rockefeller in 1888 in the United States. When the Trust was broken up in 1911 the company retained the name. In Britain the *Esso* Petroleum Co. is wholly owned by *Exxon*, the name assumed in 1973 by Standard Oil. The name is also Italian for 'it' and suggests French *essence*, 'petrol', as well as 'essence' itself.

Etam (womenswear and chain stores) Not an anagram ('team', 'mate'?) or the initials of the founder, but the abbreviation of the name of the original French hosiery company, *Établissement Meilleur* ('best company'). This company opened retail outlets in Europe in 1916 and came to Britain in 1923.

Eucryl (toothpaste by LRC Products) In 1899 a series of toilet preparations was manufactured by a chemist in the North of England who based his products on a mixture of three chemical substances, each of which was individually an antiseptic. The name *Eucryl* apparently derives from the words for the two most important of these. What they were has not been revealed, but they could well have been *euc*alyptus and some chemical containing or ending in 'cryl' or 'ryl'.

Euthymol (toothpaste by Warner-Lambert) The product was launched in about 1898. Its name would seem to be a blend of the Greek element *eu-*, 'good' and '*eu*calyptus', plus the 'thymol' (also Greek) that is the word for an antiseptic phenol.

Ever Ready see **Berec**

Evo-stik (adhesive by Evode Holdings) The name of the adhesive is based on that of the company. The forerunner of Evode was Spic and Span Shoe Polishes, established in 1932. The firm changed its name first in 1938 to Spic and Span Chemical Products, then later that year to Dove Chemical Products, then finally two years after that to Evode Chemical Works. The reason for the final change was that there was a possibility of confusion between the chemical products being marketed by Dove Chemical Products, and similar products produced by another company, Wailes Dove Bitumastic. Evode was thus evolved by reversing 'Dove' and adding an 'E'.

Exide (batteries by Chloride Group) The name seems to have been first used by an American firm, ESB Inc., in 1900. The rights to use the name in Britain were acquired in 1903 by The Chloride Electric Storage Co., now Chloride Group. The origin of the name seems to lie in 'oxide', with 'E' for 'electric' substituted for the first letter of this word. (The initials of ESB Inc. stand for 'electric storage batteries'.)

Ex-Lax (laxative and manufacturer) The original name for the laxative, as devised with a chocolate flavour by a Hungarian-born scientist in New York in 1905, was 'Bo-Bo' (from 'bon-bon'). When, however, a Hungarian newspaper one day reported that there had been an 'ex-lex in Hungary' (this being a Latin term, literally 'outside the law', applied to the disagreement between senate and congress and consequent suspension of government functions), Bo-Bo was immediately renamed *Ex-Lax*. Or so the story goes. At any rate, the name is an eminently suitable one for a *lax*ative, with the prefix '*Ex-*' (more usually a suffix) meaning either 'excellent' or 'out'!

Exxon (name from 1973 of Standard Oil of New Jersey)   The name resulted from the split-up in 1911 of the Oil Trust united by *Esso* in America. Part of the court decision leading to the break-up involved an injunction that the name *Esso* should not be used in certain states where the newly formed Standard Oil companies resulting from the split were established. The consequence was that Standard Oil had to look for another name in these states. With the help of a computer 10,000 possible new names were produced – and reduced to six, including two existing company trade marks, Enco and Enjoy. After extensive tests and surveys, *Exxon*, with its two 'Xs', was found to be the most easily recognised, readily remembered, and easily written name. In 1981 the Corporation lost a legal case against a firm named Exxon Insurance Consultants International in which they claimed that their own American *Exxon* name was an 'original literary work' and thus entitled to copyright protection. The judge ruled that a single invented word could not be the subject of copyright although *Exxon* was, of course, entitled to judgment for an injunction for 'passing off' by the insurance consultants.

Faber and Faber (publisher)   In 1924 Geoffrey Faber (1889–1961) was invited to become chairman of The Scientific Press. The following year he established his publishing firm of Faber and Gwyer, the latter name representing the original owners of The Scientific Press. In 1929 the firm was reconstituted as *Faber and Faber*, with the Gwyer interest entirely withdrawn. The second Faber was fictional, and rumour has it that the repetition of the name was suggested by Walter de la Mare (father of one of the original directors of the firm, Richard de la Mare) 'because you can't have too much of a good thing!'

Fablon (self-adhesive plastic covering by Commercial Plastics)   The product was launched in 1957. Its name would seem to derive from a fairly conventional prestige element 'fab-' ('fabulous') with the common suffix for artificial fabrics '-lon' based on *nylon*.

Famel (cough linctus and pastilles by *Optrex*)   The product was probably first marketed around 1916 and was formulated by a Monsieur Famel, of Paris. The name was registered in Britain in 1931.

Fanta (sparkling orange drink by *Coca-Cola*)   The name was first used in Germany during the Second World War. It was derived from *Fantasie*, 'fantasia' (with implied 'fantasy'), since considerable imagination was needed to create a palatable drink from the limited means available in years of austerity.

Farola (wheat-based pudding by James Marshall (Glasgow))   The trade name was registered in 1885. The base of the word is Latin *far*, 'corn', with the fashionably Victorian ending '-ola' (as in *pianola*).

Felix (cat food by *Quaker Oats*)   In 1970 *Quaker Oats* acquired *Felix* Cat Food Ltd, a firm that had been manufacturing dry cat foods since before the Second World War. 'Felix' by then had already become an almost generic name for a cat, deriving partly from the cartoon character (in Pat Sullivan's film cartoons of the 1920s, in which Felix the Cat 'kept on walking'), and partly from the Latin scientific name for the cat genus, Felis (itself suggesting the Latin *felix*, 'happy').

FERODO **Ferodo** (brake linings and manufacturer)   The founder of the company in 1897 was a Mr Herbert Frood. Shortly after setting up the firm he invented a name for its products based on his own surname – *Ferodo* is an anagram of 'Frood' with an extra 'e'. The name is a good international one – easily pronounced in several languages – with the 'Fero-' suggesting the powdered iron ('ferro-') present in brake linings.

Ferrograph (tape-recorder by *Ferrograph* Professional Recorder Co.)   The technical-looking name is based on Latin *ferrum*, 'iron', and the Greek element 'graph' meaning 'writing', 'recording'. The tapes for tape-recorders are coated with iron oxide.

FIAT **Fiat** (car and manufacturer)   The name is the abbreviation of the

Italian firm founded in Turin in 1899: *F*abbrica *I*taliana *A*utomobili *T*orino ('Turin Italian Automobile Works'). By chance the acronym makes the favourable word 'fiat' (authorisation, decree), thus giving the name the suggestion of high legal or commercial status.

Fiesta (car by Ford Motor Co.) The car was given the code name 'Bobcat' in 1972, three and a half years before it came into production. This particular name was chosen since it began with 'B' (it was a 'Class B' car, i.e. was a small car like the *Fiat* 127, Renault S and *Volkswagen* Polo) and was the name of an animal that was sturdy and fast-moving, as the car itself was intended to be. The original idea was to retain the name, but it was already in use for a model of the Ford Mercury, so had to be changed anyway. A name was sought that was: short, easy to pronounce, preferably continental in flavour, easy to combine with 'Ford', understood in most countries, of identical meaning in most languages, original and pleasant, simple, credible and apt (i.e. conjuring up a small, economical but lively and sound car), and not in use by anyone else. Of the suggestions offered, a short list of fifty was made, then a final list of thirteen. These were: Amigo, Bambi, Bebe, Bolero, Bravo, Cherie, Chico, *Fiesta*, Forito, Metro, Pony, Sierra and Tempo. Although after a survey it was found that 10 per cent of those questioned confused Sierra with 'siesta', while continental interviewees felt that Pony was British (but the British themselves did not like it), Amigo, *Fiesta*, and Sierra seemed too Spanish, and the Germans for some reason were not keen on Bambi, this nevertheless reduced the names to these five: *Fiesta*, Amigo, Bambi, Pony, and Sierra. A further factor was considered at this point: apart from the Escort, all Ford cars are named after a town or region (as the Taunus, *Cortina*, *Granada*, Capri). Thus the name Nice was proposed, but rejected since in German the name should be Nizza – an unattractive and, to most people, meaningless name. Here Henry Ford II himself put in his word. He felt that Bravo was not a good name for a car: it was meaningful in Spanish or Italian, but virtually meaningless in English. He liked the alliteration of 'Ford Fiesta'. This, therefore, was the final choice. (It had once been used by *Oldsmobile* and permission had to be obtained by Ford from General Motors for its use.) The official 'name-choosing' took place on 22 September 1974. Other names proposed early for the car, as Adonis, Sonata, Gato, Piccolo, and Ischia, were thus non-starters.

57 Varieties (food products by H.J. Heinz) The number 57 is an arbitrary one. It was devised by the firm's founder, Henry Heinz, when riding one day in 1896 in an elevated train in New York. He saw an advertisement card in the train for a brand of shoes offering

'21 Styles'. Heinz appreciated that his new firm did not have styles of products – it did, however, have varieties. He therefore counted them up, and counted more than 57. This, though, was the number that 'stuck' (not 58 or 59, say), so *57 Varieties* it was. Perhaps the 'luckiness' of the numbers five and seven influenced his choice (five for the heavenly pentad or quincunx, seven with its many mystical associations), but might not 73 have been an even better choice, with greater significance and suggesting a higher number of varieties?

 Findus (frozen food products and manufacturer)   The name is not a surname in origin, but an abbreviation of '*Fruit Indus*tries', a business formed in Sweden in the Second World War by two chocolate companies, Marabou and Freia. In Britain *Findus* is owned by *Nestlé*.

 Firestone (tyres by *Firestone* Tyre & Rubber Co.)   In spite of its appropriateness for motor tyres (toughness, reliability, good for a 'burn' or car race), the name is actually that of the company's founder, the American industrialist Harvey Samuel Firestone (1868–1938), who set up the Firestone Tire & Rubber Co. in Akron, Ohio, in 1900. The company, in fact, received its charter as a corporation under the laws of West Virginia, since Ohio's corporation laws at that time imposed double liability on stockholders. This provision no longer applied when the company expanded and was reorganised under an Ohio charter in 1910.

Flora (soft margarine by Van den Berghs & Jurgens)   One can only assume that the name is simply an agreeable one, with a slight classical touch. Flora was the Roman goddess of flowers.

Flymo (air cushion mower and manufacturer)   The name seems to be a blend formed from '*fly*ing *mo*wer'. The *Flymo* works on a Hovercraft principle, moving on a cushion of air ejected downwards.

Foden (commercial vehicles and manufacturer)   The name is that of the company's founder, Edwin Foden (1841–1911), who in 1876 took exclusive control of a business, Hancock and Foden, in which he had been a partner and in which also, when it was Plant and Hancock, he had started his career as a sixteen-year-old apprentice twenty years earlier. The first *Foden* vehicle was a steam traction engine, built in 1880. Foden's son, Edwin Richard, founded his own firm *ERF* Ltd in 1933. In Portugal the company name has an undesirable connotation (the same that the German Fokker aircraft has in English), so is in that country modified to 'Poden'. In 1980 the company went into liquidation, and the American trucks firm of Paccar (*Pa*cific *Car* and Foundry) acquired it.

Formica (plastic laminate and manufacturer)   The *Formica* Corporation have always vigorously protected their trade mark in the several legal battles in which they have been involved for fear that the name should become generic, as happened with *aspirin*. The company has always won its contests, although the outcome is still awaited of a petition filed in 1978 by the Federal Trade Commission, an American government agency, to cancel the mark on the grounds that the name is descriptive of the product itself. *Formica* have also consistently endeavoured to ensure that their name is used as an adjective, not as a noun, so that it is legally correct to speak of a '*Formica* plastic laminate', say, but not to talk of a 'tabletop made of *Formica*'. The name seems to suggest some connection with ants or formic acid. The word was in fact devised in 1913 by two young American scientists, Herb Faber and Dan O'Connor, who were instrumental in discovering a natural resin substitute *for mica* as an insulation material for electrical wiring. The two men founded the *Formica* Corporation in this same year, and the company subsequently become part of the American *Cyanamid* Co.

4711 (eau-de-Cologne by Ferdinand Muhlens)   The unusual name owes its direct origin to the gift of a scrap of paper made to Ferdinand Muhlens, a Cologne banker, by a monk to whom Muhlens had given refuge. The paper simply contained the figure 4711, an allegedly secret formula for making 'Aqua mirabilis', the 'miracle water' that was genuine eau-de-Cologne. Six years later, when Napoleon occupied Cologne, French soldiers had difficulty reading names in the German script and chalked this number on the wall of the original factory building on the Glockengasse ('Bell Lane') by way of an address. The number was adopted by Muhlens as a brand name, but could not be registered in Germany until 1915 because of a regulation in the German Trademark Act which excluded the registration of marks consisting of numbers or letters. Only when the firm pointed to its lengthy use of the name, establishing it as a characteristic symbol of the company, was registration allowed. Internationally the name was registered in 1923.

Fray Bentos (meat products by *Brooke Bond Oxo*)   The name, virtually synonymous with corned beef, derives from the once small town of Fray Bentos in Uruguay, South America, where the country's first industrialised meat-packing plant was established in 1861.

Frigidaire (refrigerators by White Consolidated Industries)   The

79

name is said to have been devised from 'frigid air' by the founder of General Motors, William C. Durant, in 1918, when he purchased with his own money a small American company called the Guardian Frigerator Co. The following year he sold his acquisition to General Motors, when it was renamed *Frigidaire* Corporation. The *Frigidaire* was the first refrigerator to be marketed in Britain, in 1924. In France *le frigidaire* was sometimes used as an alternative word for a refrigerator. A number of French dictionaries, as *Larousse* and *Robert*, give the origin of the word as Latin *frigidarium*, 'cold chamber', rather than the English name. The *Frigidaire* Corporation remained a division of General Motors until 1979, when the name and assets (except the original plant at Dayton, Ohio) were sold to White Consolidated Industries.

Frisbee (plastic disc thrown in the air as a game)   The name of the disc is said to be derived from that of the Frisbie Bakery, in Bridgeport, Connecticut, whose pie-tins could be thrown as a game thus. The first *Frisbee* was brought out in 1957 by the Wham-O Manufacturing Co. of San Gabriel, California, who had purchased the rights from a Los Angeles building inspector, one Fred Morriso. Morriso had based his discs on the bakery's pie-tins but had changed the spelling to avoid legal problems. (The bakery itself went out of business in 1958 – presumably not just because it ran out of pie-tins.)

Frog (model aircraft kits by Hornby Hobbies)   What connection can there be between an earthbound creature, even if a leaping one, and an airborne model aircraft? The answer is none, as such; the name is an acronym for '*f*lies *r*ight *o*ff the *g*round'. This was the base of the name coined in 1931 by International Model Aircraft Ltd to describe a model plane they had designed. Subsequently the firm produced non-flying models, for which *Frog*, as a word in its own right, is perhaps a more appropriate name.

Fujica (camera and manufacturer)   The name comes from that of the manufacturers, the *Fuji* Film Co., plus the 'ca-' of *ca*mera. The company's headquarters are located near Japan's highest mountain, Fuji (also known as Fujiyama). Camera names ending in 'ca-' are quite common: compare *Leica* and *Konica*.

Gannex (clothing by Kagan Textiles)   The name is a combination of the name of the company's founder, Joseph Kagan, later Lord Ka*gan*, and the second and third letters of '*te*xtiles'. Lord Kagan, who founded the firm in 1951, had originally planned to use the name 'Gantex' but on the advice of linguists decided to amend this to *Gannex*, thus ensuring a more uniform pronunciation in different languages. The association with 'gannets' is not an unfavourable one: bird names are in fact used by a number of clothing manufacturers (see, for example, *Tern*, and compare Robin wools and Emu knitting yarns).

Gauloise (cigarettes and manufacturer)   The name of the French cigarettes means 'Gallic', 'of Gaul'. Gaul, of course, was the name of France in early times when the Romans inhabited it, the Gauls being the Celtic people who populated the country. The name is thus both a historical one and a patriotic one – rather like having an English brand of cigarettes called 'Celts' (except this would be associated, for different reasons, with Scotland).

Gaumont (cinemas by The Rank Organisation)   The name is that of the French motion picture inventor, Léon Ernest Gaumont (1864–1946), who developed in 1901 a method of synchronising a film projector with a *gramophone*. He went into business in France in the 1890s and was soon also active in Britain. In 1909 the Gaumont Co. was formed in Britain to manage the United Kingdom side of the business, and this company was acquired in 1927 by the *Gaumont*-British Picture Corporation which was specifically formed to bring about the acquisition. In 1942 *Gaumont*-British became part of Rank. The Frenchman's surname sounds as if it derives from a French place name, but there is no place in France so called. The use of the initials 'GB' by *Gaumont*-British, especially in their newsreels, fortuitously suggested 'Great Britain', a patriotic association welcomed by the British cinema-going public in the Second World War.

Germolene (antiseptic ointment by Beecham Group)   The first part of the name is obvious; presumably the latter half, the suffix, either denotes 'clean' or is simply a fairly arbitrary trade-name ending.

Gestetner (duplicating stencils and machines by *Gestetner* Dupli-

81

cators)   The name is that of David *Gestetner*, a Hungarian immigrant to Britain, who invented and manufactured the *Cyclostyle* pen,
using a wax pencil for the first time, in London in 1881. Seven years
later he introduced the first typewriter stencil, and in the same year,
1888, patented both in Britain and the USA an improved type of
Cyclostyle pen called the Neo-Cyclostyle in Britain and the Neostyle
in America. Further developments in both the product and its name
involved the introduction of a rotary duplicator called the *Roneo*.

Gevaert (photographic products by *Agfa-Gevaert*)   Lieven Gevaert
was a Belgian who started the manufacture of calcium paper in
Antwerp in 1890. In 1920, the year that saw the introduction of
celluloid to the motion-picture film industry, *Gevaert's* company became *Gevaert* Photo-Producten NV. The merger between *Gevaert* and
Agfa to form *Agfa-Gevaert* took place in 1964.

Gillette (safety razors, blades, and toiletries by *Gillette*
Industries)   The name comes from the company's first president,
King Camp Gillette, who traced his name back to the Gillet family
of Somerset, England. Gillette patented the first disposable razor-
blades in 1902, having the previous year founded his company for
the manufacture of razors and blades, initially as the American
Safety Razor Co. In 1908 Wilkinson Sword tried unsuccessfully to
trade mark the name 'Gilledge' as a stropper to resharpen used
blades. *Gillette* as a name has a favourable French appearance
(although a bogus one) for products in the sophisticated toiletries
market. Gillette's original blade had been perfected by William E.
Nickerson, who designed equipment for the company. It was for-
tunate that he had not been the actual inventor, since 'Nickerson'
would hardly make a suitable name for a company selling razors
and blades.

Gitane (cigarettes and manufacturer)   *Gitane* is French for 'Spanish gipsy' or 'gipsy' in general. Perhaps Spanish gipsies, as a brand
name, were thought to be more exotic or romantic than the Bohe-
mians who gave the other standard French word for 'gipsy',
bohémien.

Giulietta (car by *Alfa-Romeo*)   The association between Romeo
and Juliet is obvious, and the Italian form of the name makes it
even more apt. The first *Giulietta* appeared in the 1950s. A new
model with a 'flying wedge' shape came on the market in 1979.

Glaxo (industrial holding company)   The *Glaxo* Group was
founded in Wellington, New Zealand, in 1873 as Joseph Nathan

and Co., a small import-export company. In about 1900 Nathan, who had emigrated from London in 1853, bought a milk-drying process and began to export dried milk from Australia. Originally, it seems, he tried to register the name 'Lacto', but this proved unacceptable to the Registrar of Companies. Nathan offered other names, and *Glaxo*, which was among them, was accepted.

Gloy (adhesive and manufacturer) The name was originally owned by the British firm of A. Wilme Collier Ltd. Its obvious connection would appear to be the word 'glue'. Perhaps the spelling *Gloy* was influenced by the Greek word for 'glue', *gloia*, which would give it a classical (and thus favourable) association. The trade name dates back to before 1930. The fact that there is a Scottish river and glen named Gloy, near Lochaber, is a mere coincidence – the glen and the glue have no connection.

Glynwed (engineering and building products by *Glynwed* Group Services) The name sounds something like a British regional electricity or gas board (as MANWEB, the Merseyside and North Wales Electricity Board), but it is in fact a contraction of the two original companies, *Glyn*n Bros and the *Wed*nesbury Tube Co. The former was founded in 1890, the latter in 1921, and *Glynwed* became a public company in 1941.

Golden Syrup (treacle by Tate & Lyle) The name does not belong exclusively to Tate & Lyle, although the brand is most familiar – if only because of its dead-lion and swarm-of-bees trade mark – as the product of this company. 'Golden' obviously is a prestige name for any product, as well as, in this case, describing the colour of the syrup. The name was first used on the tins of treacle produced by Abram Lyle's company in 1885. Tate & Lyle itself resulted as a merger of this company and the sugar firm, Tate's, in 1921. Within the company – and perhaps outside it? – the treacle is affectionately known as 'Goldie'.

Golden Wonder (potato crisps and manufacturer) An apparently obvious name. It was devised – seemingly on the spur of the moment – by the son of an Edinburgh baker, William Alexander, who wanted a name for the potato crisps he was baking around 1947. Doubtless it was prompted by the variety of potato so called, although these are in fact unsuitable for making crisps. William Alexander died in Jersey in 1963. The story behind the name, in abbreviated form, was printed on crisp packets for the munching public to read in the latter half of the 1970s.

GOODYEAR **Goodyear** (tyres by the Goodyear Tyre & Rubber Co.) Like *Firestone, Goodyear* is an apt name for motor tyres, suggesting successful and long running. Like *Firestone*, it is actually the name of the man who was indirectly responsible for the business, Charles Goodyear (1800–60). He invented the vulcanisation process that made possible the commercial use of rubber. The company's name must not be confused with that of the B.F. Goodrich Co. of Akron, Ohio, who were the first company to test-market puncture-proof tyres (in 1947). The *Goodyear* Tyre and Rubber Co. was founded in Akron in 1898 by two brothers, Frank and Charles Seiberling.

Gor-Ray (skirts and manufacturer) The company was set up in the late 1930s by two brothers, C. Joseph Stillitz and Louis Stillitz, who traded as C. Stillitz Ltd. They sold pleated skirts in the so-called *gore*d and sun*ray* styles – the former shaped with tapering or triangular pieces of material, the latter having pleats that are narrower at the top than the bottom. The company was renamed after the two styles. It is an awkward name, and perhaps the brothers might have done better to choose something more mellifluous for their fashions.

 Goya (perfumes and cosmetics and manufacturer) The name was first registered in 1936. An initial suggestion for the name of the perfumes was 'Loya', but there already existed a firm making toilet preparations called Loy Products. By working through the alphabet, *Goya* was selected. Only afterwards was it discovered that the name was that of the Spanish painter, Francisco de Goya (1746–1828), who may have painted a naked and a clothed 'Maja' (favourable for a perfume, presumably), but who also depicted executions, garrottings, and gory bullfighting scenes (most unfavourable).

 G-Plan (furniture by E. Gomme) The name was devised in 1953 by the firm's advertising agents, J. Walter Thompson. It is based, apparently, not so much on the name of the founder of the firm, Ebenezer Gomme, who started making furniture on his own account in 1898, but was selected simply as a suitable letter of the alphabet. (But does the association with 'g-string' help or hinder?) The company has unsuccessfully tried to prevent other, smaller, furniture manufacturers from using the word 'Plan' in their names, prefixed by a letter of the alphabet, but did win an action against a firm called G-Pine.

gramophone (instrument for reproducing sound recordings) The first *Gramophone* (as a trade name, with a capital letter) was patented by Emile Berliner in Washington, DC, on 8 November 1887. Berliner, a German immigrant, chose the name to differentiate his instrument from its predecessors – his used discs, the earlier machines used cylinders. He devised the name by reversing the two parts of the word '*phonogram*', an instrument which in turn based its name on the *phonograph*. The latter word was apparently invented (again, as a trade name, *Phonograph*) by a Frenchman, the Abbé Lenoir, when popularising the invention of Charles Cros, a minor French poet and amateur scientist. Cros's invention was meanwhile being paralleled by Edison's machine in America, and subsequently the word *phonograph* came to be used generically in the United States for what in Britain was the *gramophone* (now usually referred to as a 'record player'). Another instrument that played a significant part in the early evolution of the instrument was the *Graphophone*. This was an improvement on Edison's *Phonograph* invented by an American engineer, Chichester A. Bell, cousin of Alexander Graham Bell, the better-known Scottish-born inventor, together with Charles Sumner Tainter, a scientist and instrument maker. This machine used a wax coating on the cylinder instead of tin foil. Bell and Tainter applied for a patent on their instrument on 27 June 1885, Edison's original *Phonograph* having been invented eight years earlier in 1877. In America one company that was formed to manufacture *phonographs* was the American *Graphophone* Co., while in Britain The *Gramophone* Co. was set up for the same purpose, although using the English name of the instrument. As mentioned, the name *Gramophone* was initially used in America, both specifically and generically, as a result of Berliner's improved version. The word disappeared from American English as the result of an injunction sought against the Consolidated Talking Machine Co. in 1901 by Frank Seaman (who was to manufacture yet another type of instrument, the *Zonophone*). Seaman wanted to prevent the company from using the word, to which, he claimed, it did not have exclusive rights. The decision went against him, but the company was, however, enjoined not to use the word. Even though this injunction was itself reversed in the Court of Appeal two months later, the owner of Consolidated Talking Machines, Eldridge R. Johnson, decided to drop the word *gramophone* from his advertising and to refer to his product as the *Victor* Talking Machine, which would play *Victor* records. The name, he felt, was 'euphonious and evocative of success'. (It subsequently developed into *Victrola*, which see.) Meanwhile in Britain The *Gramophone* Company was refused the right to the trade mark in 1910, when the name became legally generic. The *Gramophone* Co. itself merged with the *Columbia Graphophone* Co. in 1931 to form Electrical and Musical Industries (EMI), a merger joined by virtually every important European record company except the Deutsche Grammophon Gesellschaft (DGG). The *Gramophone* Co., famous for its record label *His Master's Voice*, continued as a private company within EMI, the latter's name being changed in 1973 to EMI Records Ltd. In this same year a new company was formed, The *Gramophone* Company (1973) Ltd, merely to keep the name alive. The whole picture is thus a somewhat complex one, with more than a few legal entanglements. At least we can be reasonably sure of the order of appearance of the early basic names: *phonograph* (1877), *phonogram* (1884), *graphophone* (1885), *gramophone* (1887).

Granada (film, television, theatre, TV rental and publishing group) How did the name of a Spanish province come to be associated with a leading British enterprise? The answer is in a holiday taken in the 1920s by the group's chairman, Sidney Bernstein (born 1899). One Easter he took a ship to Gibraltar, travelled overland to Barcelona, and continued by ship to Majorca. On his way from Gibraltar he arrived late at night in Granada, and was greatly impressed with the city, especially the Alhambra Palace, on viewing it the next day. At the time he was looking for a name for the theatres owned by his new company, and decided that *Granada* was just right to convey the exotic and gay atmosphere that a theatre should have. All the company's theatres were thus renamed *Granada* in 1930, and the name was extended to the group's other activities – television, TV rental, motorway services and publishing among them. The company went public in 1935, and in 1948 applied for a licence to operate an independent television station. This was granted in 1954, with the result that, however geographically inappropriate, *Granada* TV has become firmly associated in the minds of television viewers with programmes emanating from Lancashire. The group branched out into publishing (*Granada* Publishing Co.) in 1961. As a name *Granada* has an apparent charisma which makes it a popular trade name: doubtless the associations with 'grand' and 'grandee' help, as well as Spanish glamour and even the success story of the *Granada* Group itself. An obvious example is the Ford *Granada* car, for several years one of Britain's most popular models.

Grape Nuts (breakfast cereal by General Foods) The cereal was the invention of Charles Post, who three years earlier had developed the 'food-cum-drink' which he was to market as *Postum* Cereal (which see). *Grape Nuts* was perfected in 1897 as a breakfast cereal made of baked wheat and malted barley. Post named it for its *nut*ty flavour and because he believed (mistakenly) that *grape* sugar – a familiar name for dextrose – was formed during the baking process. Like *Postum*, *Grape Nuts* was originally marketed as a 'health food'.

Graphophone see *gramophone*

Green Shield (trading stamps by *Green Shield* Trading Stamp Co.) The name was devised for the founder of the company, Richard Tompkins. He was aware that the American trading-stamp company, Sperry & Hutchinson, was known as 'green stamps' in the United States and so reasoned that if they wished to enter the UK market they would wish to retain this popular name here. With a view to forestalling this, he looked for a name that combined 'green' with some other favourable word. 'Green' was already known to be a popular colour with favourable associations among the public (spring, the countryside, youth, 'go', and the like), and the other half of the name was felt to be best embodied in 'shield', a word that had the required promotion association of security and strength. The name was registered in 1957, but not before the rights had been bought from a North London company already using it. In October 1980, however, the *Green Shield* stamp operation announced that it would have to close down.

Greyhound (bus transport company) The name is familiar to American road passengers for the long-distance coaches that travel over much of the country. The service originated in the transport provided in 1914 by a Swedish miner, Carl Wickman, to take miners to and from Hibbing and Alice, Minnesota, a distance of four miles. For this he used a seven-seater *Hupmobile*. The following year he extended the service, using bigger vehicles, to make America's first long-distance coach run – the ninety miles from Hibbing to Duluth, Minnesota. In these early days he painted the buses battleship grey because of the dusty road conditions, and the addition of extra seats in the vehicles made them look long and slim. One day, the story goes, an innkeeper commented to Wickman that the buses looked 'just like greyhound dogs streaking by'. Wickman adopted the name, and introduced the slogan 'Ride the Greyhounds'. (Pedants might point out that greyhound dogs are rarely grey and that their name derives not from the colour but from an Old English word meaning 'bitch'.)

Gumption (cleanser by Southon-Horton Laboratories) The product so named is manufactured and marketed by Southon-Horton Laboratories but the company *Gumption* Products is owned, as is the trade mark, by LRC Products. (Prior to 1980 *Gumption* Products was owned by Kelsey Industries, a firm that before 1947 was known as Industrial Engineering) 'Gumption' is a colloquial word, originally Scottish, for common sense or courage, and no doubt the product was so named with reference to such a phrase as 'use a little gumption'.

Gunk (degreasing compound by Fosmin Chemicals)   The product was launched in 1932 by the Curran Corporation in Mulden, Massachusetts, and the original licence in Britain was granted to Bennett (Hyde) Ltd in 1935 by what had become *Gunk* Laboratories Inc. in the United States. (*Gunk* is currently manufactured in Britain by Fosmin Laboratories under licence from the Radiator Specialty Co. of Charlottesville, North Carolina.) The name is thus of American origin, and became popularised in Britain during the Second World War by its use on aircraft located at American air bases in England. As a slang word, 'gunk' is a term for a variety of viscous or liquid substances, and can be used, reasonably derogatorily, of anything from an excess of eye shadow ('too much eye gunk') to waste matter blocking a pipe ('all that gunk down the plug-hole'). As applied to the dirt deposited on engines the name may be a portmanteau blend of *g*rease and j*unk*, suggested by other slang words such as 'gook' and 'gunge' and expressions of disgust such as 'ugh'.

Guy (commercial vehicles by *BL*)   The name is that of the founder of Guy Motors Ltd who first manufactured the trucks, Sydney S. Guy.

 HAG (decaffeinated coffee by Coffee HAG (UK))   The inventor of a process for manufacturing decaffeinated coffee was the German industrialist, Ludwig Roselius (1874–1943), who in 1906 founded a company to market the new product, Kaffee-*H*andels-*A*ktiengesellschaft ('Coffee Trading Company'). The initials of this gave the name of the product – in German Kaffee *HAG*. As an English word, of course, 'hag' has unfortunate connotations, but presumably the use of the word 'Coffee' before the abbreviation helps to dispel any doubt or adverse association regarding the product. The headquarters of the German company in Bremen are situated in Hagstrasse. (In German *Hag* means 'hedge', which is a fairly neutral word to be associated with coffee.)

Hai Karate (after-shave by Unicliffe)   The name was based on the 'machismo' association of 'karate', with Hai added as an arbitrary

Japanese-sounding word. But perhaps the inventors of the name knew that *hai* is in fact Japanese for 'amusement'? It also, of course, suggests 'high'.

Halex (table-tennis balls by *Halex* Table Tennis)   The name has its origins in a business arrangement made in 1877 between an industrialist, C.P. Merrian, and an inventor, Alexander Parkes. The latter's company had pioneered the manufacture and marketing of a new plastic material, *celluloid* (which see). For twenty years Merrian's company worked side by side with Parkes's firm, making coloured *celluloid* play balls from his materials. These balls were made in sizes of one inch, one and a half inches, and two inches, with the one-inch ball being the forerunner of the table-tennis ball as it is known today. Just before the turn of the century the two firms decided that they must respectively move to larger premises, and Merrian's firm moved to a site just outside London (now actually in London, just north of Walthamstow) called Hale End. The products made on this new site bore the trade name derived from it, *Halex*. The name is an effective one, with the suffix '-ex' having the literal sense 'out of' (out of Hale End) and the word as a whole perhaps suggesting 'hale', a desirable association for a product used in a vigorous sport.

Hambros (merchant bank)   At first sight the name appears to be devised from some *bro*thers whose initials were *H.A.M.* In actual fact the bank, a family one and officially an 'accepting house', was founded in 1839 by a Dane so named. The Hambro family has its origin in Calmer Levy, a German Jew, who in 1779 applied for his licence as a tradesman. He wanted to change his name to Hamburg, his native city, but the authorities became confused over the spelling so he opted for Hambro, an easier version. The British branch of *Hambros* was established in 1912 as the British Bank of Northern Commerce. In 1920 it merged with C.J. Hambro as *Hambros* Bank of Northern Commerce and the following year became *Hambros* Bank.

Hamlet (cigars by Gallaher)   The association is presumably meant to be a literary one, from Shakespeare. But the link seems a random one – what possible connection can there be between the 'prince of Denmark' and a cigar?

Handy Andies (paper handkerchiefs by Bowater-Scott Corporation)   Doubtless the name derives from the same source as *Andrex*, with 'Handy' denoting both 'useful' and '*hand*kerchief' and equally matching 'Andies' to form a satisfying (although not original) jingle name. Compare the next entry.

Handy Andy (household cleaning liquid by *Unilever*) The name was registered in 1946, and has the connotation of 'useful', 'usable by hand', as well as being a familiar nickname and literary name (the hero of Samuel Lover's novel so titled, published in 1842). *Handy Andy* the product was first introduced to Britain in 1959.

Harp (lager by *Harp* Lager) The origin of the name lies in the trade mark of the founder member of the company, Arthur Guinness Son and Co. Guinness is an Irish firm and the harp is the traditional Irish folk instrument. The harp, as a pictorial trade mark, was adopted by Guinness in 1862 and registered in 1876. Guinness introduced *Harp* lager on the market in Ireland in 1960.

Harpic (lavatory cleanser by Reckitt & Colman) The name may suggest 'harp' or 'harpy' (the rapacious monster in classical mythology with a woman's face and body and a bird's wings and claws), but such associations are false! It in fact derives from the name of its inventor who first sold it in London in the 1920s, *Har*ry *Pic*kup. *Harpic* was registered as a trade name by the *Harpic* Manufacturing Co. in 1924 and was acquired by Reckitt & Colman in 1948. Its popularity in the pre-war years led to some generic use of the name to apply to any brand of lavatory cleanser.

Hawker Siddeley (aircraft and manufacturer) The first half of the name may be thought to be a reference to the bird (as in the Harrier VTOL aircraft). It in fact comes from the name of Harry Hawker, who was chief test pilot in 1910 to Thomas Sopwith (famous for his Pup, Camel, Triplane and One and a Half Strutter aeroplanes). At the end of the First World War the *Hawker* Engineering Co. was formed, taking its name from Harry Hawker who was later killed testing a racing aircraft. The second half of the name comes from John Siddeley (later Lord Kenilworth) who before the First World War had started up his motor car business, the Siddeley Autocar Co., which merged in 1919 with another firm initiated by Sir W.G. Armstrong to form a name familiar in the early days of motoring, Armstrong-Siddeley. The *Hawker Siddeley* Aircraft Co. (now *Hawker Siddeley* Group) was thus formed in 1935 to merge many famous names of early flying and motoring days: *Hawker* Aircraft, Gloster Aircraft, A.V. Roe & Co. (see *Avro*), Armstrong Whitworth Aircraft, Armstrong Siddeley Motors, Air Service Training, and High Duty Alloys.

90

Hedex (analgesic tablets by Sterling Health Products)   The suffix '-ex' is intended to mean 'out of', i.e. the product takes the ache out of your head. However, *Hedex* actually sounds like 'headaches' (much as *Earex* sounds like 'earaches'), and as such is a name that might be liable to misinterpretation (a product usually provides something: does this one provide headaches?). In practice, of course, such an association is overruled by logic: no patent medicine would be designed to *give* you a headache, the name must therefore mean that it relieves one. In other words, and ignoring the significance of the suffix, which must escape many people anyway, the product is *for* headaches – '*Hedex* for headaches', in fact.

Hermesetas (soluble tablets by Crookes Anestan)   The first part of the name derives from the Swiss manufacturers, *Hermes*. The ending '-etas' is an unusual one, but does not appear to have a special significance. Perhaps it is a variant of the Latin ending '-itas', as in *sanitas*, 'health'.

Hillman (car and manufacturer)   As with a number of car names, *Hillman* suggests the character or performance capability of the vehicle. It is not a noted hill climber, however, but derives its name from William Hillman, who began his career manufacturing bicycles in the 1870s. Later he concentrated on medium-sized cars for the popular market, the most popular being the *Hillman* Minx, first produced in 1931, with a new model introduced in 1959 and this model in a new shape appearing in 1967. The company passed to *Chrysler* UK.

His Master's Voice (*gramophone* records by EMI Records)   The famous name, with the equally popular picture of a dog cocking an ear in front of an early hand-wound *gramophone*, originated with The *Gramophone* Co. The story behind the picture really is a story behind a picture. In 1899 Francis Barraud, a professional artist, visited The *Gramophone* Company's premises in London to ask if he could borrow a brass horn for a picture he was painting. Some years before he had painted a picture of his fox-terrier, Nipper, listening to an Edison *phonograph*, and had called the picture 'His Master's Voice'. (Nipper had earlier belonged to Francis's brother Mark, a theatre scenery painter, who died in 1886.) Now a friend had suggested to Francis that he should update his picture by substituting a new brass horn for the old black japanned one in the original painting. The picture was duly amended, and when Barraud returned the horn the managing director of The *Gramophone* Co., William Barry Owen, offered to buy the painting if Barraud would delete the Edison *phonograph* and paint in instead an 'Improved

91

Gramophone'. He did so – although the original can still be discerned under the addition. The *Gramophone* Co. paid £100 for the painting and replaced their original trade mark, an angel writing on a disc with a quill, by 'His Master's Voice', with the picture first appearing on their record labels in 1909. Some years later Barraud was given an annuity of £250 by the company. He died in 1924. Nipper, who had died in 1897, also appeared in a pictorial advertisement for Reid's Stout, where he was shown sniffing at a glass of beer, with the caption below running, 'What is it that master likes so much?' Barraud's original painting – he made several subsequent copies – hangs in the boardroom of EMI Records.

Hitachi (electrical and industrial machinery and manufacturer) The name is a Japanese one – not a personal name but that of the fishing village of Hitachi (now a coastal city) north-east of Tokyo where an engineer, Fusanosuka Kuhara, organised a mining company in the nearby hills in 1904. Kuhara was joined by a friend, also an engineer, named Namihei Odaira, who set up a repair shop for imported machinery in the mining site. In 1910 the two men established their own machinery building company under the name of *Hitachi* Seisakusho, today better known as *Hitachi* Ltd.

Hoechst (pharmaceutical products and manufacturer) The company was founded by four people – two chemists and two salesmen – in the town of Höchst, west of Frankfurt, Germany, in 1863, with their initial equipment amounting to 'a small boiler and a three horse-power steam engine'. The name is coincidentally German for 'highest', an extremely favourable connotation! The town itself, however, is on a plain and so not 'high' at all. The spelling *Hoechst* is an acceptable German alternative avoiding the awkward umlaut.

HONDA **Honda** (motorcycle and motor vehicle and manufacturer) The firm was established as the *Honda* Motor Cycle Co. by the Japanese engineer Soichiro Honda in 1948 in Hamamatsu, originally to convert surplus army engines to power bicycles. *Honda*'s most popular motorcycle, the 50cc C-100 with 'step-thru' frame, known in Japan as the Super-Cub, was first introduced in 1958.

 Hoover (vacuum cleaner and manufacturer) One of the best known of household names. William Henry Hoover (1849–1932) was not the inventor of the vacuum cleaner, but an American businessman who foresaw the sales potential of a new type of cleaner constructed by one J. Murray Spangler, a caretaker in an Ohio department store. Hoover persuaded Spangler to sell his rights to the invention, and in 1908 the *Hoover* Suction Co. produced the first *Hoover*, which sold for 70 dollars. Four years later, *Hoover* vacuum cleaners were being exported to Britain – where the machine had basically been invented by Hubert Cecil Booth in 1901. It is a pity that Spangler's name has now been forgotten: a 'Spangler' vacuum cleaner would have a name that would create several favourable associations ('sparkle', 'spangle') that *Hoover* can never have.

Horch (car and manufacturer)   Although German 'horch!' means 'listen!', the name is not a parallel to *Audi*. It is that of a German engineer, August Horch, who set up a company in 1899 to make engines. He built his first car in 1903, and from small, commonplace cars expanded to produce big, fast ones. Horch's company merged with *Audi*, *DKW* and others to form the Auto-Union consortium in 1932. Its last cars were made in 1938.

Horlicks

Horlicks (malted milk drink by Beecham Group)   The name is not a concocted one but a surname – that of James Horlick (1844–1921), an English pharmacist, who after qualifying in 1869 formulated an artificial infant food which he named 'Horlick's Food'. In 1873 he joined his mechanic brother, William, in America and they formed a partnership to manufacture the food. 'Malted Milk' was patented in 1883 and two years later the *Horlicks* Milk Co. was established with James Horlick as president and William as secretary. Around 1890 James returned to England and established a London branch. This moved to Slough in 1906. In 1945 *Horlicks* Malted Milk Co. (England) acquired – unusually – the American business and the company remained in the family until 1969 when it passed to Beecham.

Hotpoint (domestic electrical equipment and manufacturer)   It may well happen that when a company expands and extends its range of products its original name may appear quite unsuitable. This happened with *Hotpoint*, who began with electric irons (that got *hot* at the *point*), and eventually came to manufacture *Hotpoint* refrigerators! The firm's origins lie with the man who invented the iron with the hot point so that his wife could iron frilly ruffles and pleats. This was Earl Richardson, a Californian meter reader, who designed the iron in 1903. The following year Richardson formed the Pacific Electric Heating Co., which became the *Hotpoint* Electric Heating Co. in 1911. Seven years later this company merged with the American firm of General Electric. The British branch of the company was formed in 1920 as the *Hotpoint* Electrical Appliance Co.

Hovis

Hovis (wholemeal brown bread and manufacturer)   The bread started its life as 'Smith's Patent Germ Bread' in 1887, the year in which it was patented by Richard Smith, a Staffordshire miller. In 1890 a competition was held for a better name for the bread. This was won by a Mr Herbert Grime (who apparently was awarded the prize only ten years later). He took the Latin words *hominis vis*, 'strength of man', and contracted them to *Hovis*. The name was registered the same year, and the *Hovis* Bread Flour Co. was formed in 1898. In 1918, by special resolution, the company name was shortened to *Hovis* Ltd. In its early years the name appeared in advertisements with a tilde over the 'o' (i.e. as Hōvis) to indicate that the word was an abbreviation. It is not clear if Mr Grime's Latin phrase was a quotation from a classical author. Plautus and Livy write of *vis hominum*, but this means 'a quantity of men', not 'force of men'. The name is part of the parent group RHM (Ranks *Hovis* McDougall).

HP

HP (sauce by *HP* Foods)   It cannot be confirmed that the letters in fact stand for 'Houses of Parliament', although this is the popular theory, due to the photograph of these famous buildings on the label. Records show that a Mr Sampson and a Mr Moore first made *HP* sauce in Birmingham in the 1870s, and that they had purchased the name from a Mr Garton of Nottingham, who had been producing 'Garton's HP Sauce'. Could the letters have stood for something else, such as 'high power' or even 'horse power'?

Humber (cars by *Humber* Motor Car Co.)   The cars owe their name not to the river Humber but to Thomas Humber, designer of one of the earliest and best British bicycles, dating from 1868. Still manufacturing bicycles, Humber's company was absorbed in 1896 by the financial promoter H.J. Lawson, British inventor of a rear-driving machine (patented 1876) that was the forerunner of the modern safety bicycle. Four years later a re-formed *Humber* company began to make light cars, and from 1905 the name became associated with solid but conventionally designed touring cars. The company passed to the Rootes group in 1928.

Humbrol (brush and spray enamels and manufacturer)   The company was founded in Hull (on the river Humber) by a Mr Barton in 1919, and originally made oil products. The name is thus a combination of '*Humber*' and '*oil*'. The brand name was first used in 1935. In the mid-1940s the original company name of The Humber Oil Co. was changed to *Humbrol*. Many people living in Hull refer to the company by a name that reflects the old and new titles, calling the firm 'Humbroil'.

Hupmobile (cars and manufacturer)   A decidedly perky name for a car. Rather disappointingly, it is that of two brothers, Louis and Robert Hupp, who in 1908 formed the Hupp Motor Car Corporation in the United States and gave their name to their new car. The company never fully recovered after the Depression, and the last *Hupmobiles* were made in 1941.

Hush Puppies (shoes by Lilley & Skinner)   The name was registered in 1961 by the Wolverine Shoe and Tanning Corporation, an American company. It clearly conjures up softness ('Hush') and suppleness ('Puppies'), yet to many Americans a hush puppy is a type of cornmeal bread shaped into small cakes and fried in deep fat. But perhaps this was an additional deliberate homely association? (The bread is so named, apparently, since when thrown to hungry barking dogs with the cry, 'Hush, puppies!', it will effectively silence them!)

Hygena (kitchen furniture and manufacturer)   The derivation must obviously be 'hygienic', with the awkward spelling of the standard word simplified and modified to form a trade name. There is also a classical allusion, for Hygeia was the Greek goddess of health.

Ibcol (aromatic disinfectant by Jeyes Group)   The name is an abbreviation of *Ib*betson *Co*mpany *L*imited, the firm that formerly manufactured the product. It was acquired by Jeyes in 1955.

Idris (soft drinks and manufacturer)   The name is the surname of the company's founder in 1873, T.H.W. Idris. Idris is also the name of the legendary Welsh giant whose chair was supposedly sited at the top of the mountain called Cader Idris. This association – for those who are aware of it – serves to give the name a somewhat lofty connotation. (Though presumably the surname comes from this Welsh name.)

Imp (soot destroyer by Gourmet & Co.)   The product derives its name not from 'imp', although this is a good association conjuring up a small-sized yet busy thoroughness, but from 'improved'. The name was registered in 1898.

Imperial Leather (toilet soap by Cussons, Sons & Co.)   Should the name be 'Imperial Lather'? Apparently not. The story goes that a perfume with an aroma of leather was specially devised in the 1780s by a London perfumier, Bayley's of Bond Street, for a Russian count Orlof. The name chosen for the fragrance was 'Eau de Cologne Imperial Leather Russe'. In 1938 this name was used as a basis for the new fragrant toilet soap produced by Mr Cusson, founder of the present manufacturers.

Ind Coope (brewery)   The two names suggest beer and brewing (*India Pale Ale*, for example, or 'cooper'). In fact they are the surnames of two brewers. Edward Ind purchased the Star Inn and its brewery in Romford, Essex, in 1799. In 1845 he was joined by W.O.E. Coope and his brother George. After various mergers involving the formation of Allied Breweries in 1961, *Ind Coope* came to operate in south-east England with its centre in the company's brewery in Romford – where the business had started nearly two centuries before.

Indesit (refrigerators and manufacturer)   The name is an Italian acronym for *Ind*ustria *E*lettrodome*s*tici *Ita*lia, 'Italian Domestic Appliances Industry'. The company so named is based in Turin and Naples, with the name used internationally.

India Pale Ale (beer by *Bass* Charrington and other breweries)   *India Pale Ale*, or IPA, owes its name to the day when brewers apparently put a certain brew of pale ale into casks and sent it by ship to India – and back. Such a procedure was supposed to give the ale a maturity and quality superior to other ales. But the explanation of the name is suspect, and a much more likely origin of the name lies in the beer, East *India Pale Ale*, that was developed in the eighteenth century for export to British soldiers and administrators in India. Whether *Bass* Charrington or McEwans or some other brewery were the first to use the name seems in doubt, and the Brewers Society record that no less than six brewers claim to have originated IPA.

Innoxa (toilet preparations and manufacturer)   An association with 'innocuous' is correct. The founder of the company, the French dermatologist F. Debat, was not satisfied with the standards of safety offered by cosmetics at the time and so incorporated the Latin tag *primum non nocere*, 'first do no harm', into the name of his products.

Instant Whip (easy-to-make dessert by General Foods)   The prod-

uct was first named – and still is in the United States – *Jell-O* Instant Pudding. The name was changed for the British market, since *Jell-O* was not a name known in the UK. *Instant Whip* first went on sale in 1954.

Intourist (Soviet foreign travel agency)   The name might seem to imply an agency for tourists who come *in*to the USSR, or perhaps one designed for the *in*ternational *tourist*. In fact the prefix 'In-' derives from the Russian word *inostranny*, 'foreign'. *Intourist* was originally organised in 1929 with its head office in the Metropol Hotel, Moscow. It caters not only for foreign visitors to Russia but Soviet citizens wishing to travel abroad.

Iron Jelloids (iron tablets by Beecham Group)   The tablets contain, among other ingredients, ferrous sulphate. This supplies the first word of the name. The second word, with its '-oid' suffix, points to the consistency of the tablets – 'jelly-like'.

Ivory (soap by Procter & Gamble)   The name was launched in 1879. The soap itself was 'launched' when, by accident, a workman in Procter & Gamble's plant at Cincinnati let a machine introduce minute bubbles of air into a batch of soap – thus producing a soap that floated! The new soap, dead white in colour, proved very popular, but remained without a name until the company's senior partner, Harley Procter, heard a sermon in church in which was quoted a line from Psalm 45, 'All thy garments smell of myrrh, and aloes, and cassia, out of the ivory palaces, whereby they have made thee glad.' *Ivory* thus became the name of the new floating soap.

Izal (disinfectant by Sterling Health)   The name is said to have been devised by the company's advertising agent, T.B. Browne. How he arrived at it is not recorded. But a story also runs that the actual formulator of the product, a Mr J.H. Worrall, invented the word as an anagram of the name of his favourite sister, Liza. Later, however, he apparently denied this origin, saying that he had no such relative. Be that as it may, the name itself was first registered in 1893 for *Izal* Disinfectant, which had been previously sold as Thorncliffe Patent Disinfectant.

J

JAEGER　**Jaeger** (knitwear and manufacturer)　The story of *Jaeger* begins with Lewis Tomalin, a London accountant, who had married a German and could speak the language well. In 1880 he came across a book called 'Health Culture' by Dr Gustav Jaeger, Professor of Zoology and Physiology at Stuttgart University. The book's main thesis was that human beings would be healthier if they dressed in clothes made entirely of animal hair, and especially wool. Tomalin was inspired by the idea, and translated the book. Public interest in Jaeger's theories and subsequent demands for clothing of this type prompted Tomalin to open the first *Jaeger* shop – in Fore Street, London, in February 1884. Further, and as a tribute to the Jaeger ideal, Tomalin started a company with two associates. When his shop opened it bore the imposing legend over the door, 'DR. JAEGER'S SANITARY WOOLLEN SYSTEM'. The business expanded, and branched out into clothes of all kinds and styles, but it was only in the 1950s that the company eventually broke with the original animal-fibre doctrine. Synthetics had come to stay. 'Jaeger' is the German for 'huntsman' – perhaps not such an inappropriate association for a firm that based its ideals on the benefits that animals can offer man. To English eyes the name resembles 'Jaguar', which can also be helpful.

Jaguar (car by *Jaguar Rover Triumph*)　In September 1935 the name *Jaguar* appeared on a car for the first time, with the introduction of the SS *Jaguar*. The 'SS' may have been near-arbitrary, standing for anything from Super Sports to Super Sexed, but is generally thought to have indicated the *S*wallow *S*idecar Co., a firm founded in 1922 by a motorcycle enthusiast, William Lyons, to produce sidecars. By 1930 the company had moved on to manufacturing cars, a progression reflected in its change of name to SS Cars Ltd in 1934. And so the *Jaguar*. But why *Jaguar*? It is recorded that William Lyons had a list of over 500 fast-moving animals. Of these – and apparently for no special reason – the name of the jaguar was the one that appealed to him for the new car, and seemed best suited for its low lines and powerful performance. (The 'SS' prefix was to prove disadvantageous during the Second World War, and was dropped after it.) As a prestige car the *Jaguar* soon acquired its own affectionate nickname, the 'Jag'.

Jeep (utility vehicle by *Jeep* Corporation)　The usual explanation offered for this well-known name is that it derives from the initials

'G.P.', standing for 'general purpose' (vehicle). But things are not quite so simple. The vehicle was designed in July 1940 by Karl K. Pabst, consulting engineer of the Bantam Car Co., of Butler, Pennsylvania, in response to an invitation from the US Army for a military general-purpose vehicle. Both Ford of Detroit and Willys-Overland Motors submitted a prototype vehicle in November 1940, and the following summer the Willys model was accepted as the standard, with orders being placed with both firms. The Ford vehicle had the code letters GPW, standing for 'General Purpose-Willys', and Ford, therefore, claim the name derives from this. Sources at the *Jeep* Corporation, however, express doubt about the validity of this, since the name existed in the 1930s as a comic-strip character invented by Segar who 'could do almost everything'. (The creature was supposed to have made a sound 'jeep'.) It thus seems more likely that this versatile comic-cartoon character provided the name for the vehicle, rather than the initials – which may have been used by Ford but were never part of the designation of the model as issued by Willys-Overland Motors. The vehicle was in fact also known by a number of other names in the early years, as 'Bantam', 'Peep', 'Blitzbuggy', 'Jitterbug', 'Beetlebug', 'Iron Pony', 'Leaping Lena', and 'Panzer Killer'. The name itself was first registered as a trade mark in November 1940.

Jell-O (gelatin dessert by General Foods)   In 1897, Pearl B. Wait, a cough medicine manufacturer in LeRoy, New York, began to produce a type of gelatin dessert. His wife, Mary, coined a name for it, presumably basing her choice on 'jelly' or 'gelatin', with the 'O' ending then common for names of food products. (The dessert itself had been first patented even before this, in 1845, but was not produced in any quantity until 1897.) It was *Jell-O* (the firm) and *Postum* Cereal that formed the nucleus of what was to become the General Foods Corporation in 1929. See also *Instant Whip*.

Jiffy (padded bag by Jiffy Packaging Co.)   The aim of the bag is to wrap something quickly and easily – in a jiffy, in fact. 'Jiffy' itself, meaning a very short time, dates back as a slang term to the eighteenth century.

Jubilee (hose clip by L. Robinson & Co.)   The clip was first registered in the United Kingdom on 8 February 1929 – when there does not seem to have been any notable jubilee (the silver jubilee of the reigning monarch, George V, was six years later). Presumably, therefore, the name is a standard prestige one, with associations of importance and 'occasion'.

K (shoes by *K* Shoes) The initial is that of Kendal, the town in Cumbria, where in the early 1850s a leather merchant, named Robert Somervell, and his brother made uppers for the bespoke shoemakers of the district. About ten years later they began making shoes themselves, and for identification used to mark their products with the letter 'K' when sending them to outworkers for finishing. The name was registered in 1875, and *K* Shoes would appear to be the only company in Britain having a single letter registered as a trade mark in this way.

Kadett (car by *Opel*) The name suggests a 'younger' or 'cadet' model, but since *Kadett* in German means specifically 'officer cadet' or 'midshipman' the association is a prestige one.

Kalamazoo (business systems and manufacturer) The firm is a British company, originating as a Birmingham jobbing printers (Morland and Impey) in 1895. So why the name of the city in Michigan, USA? The name was adopted from that of a loose-leaf binder brought back from Kalamazoo by one of the company's founders, the company then obtaining the sole right to manufacture and sell this outside the USA. The firm itself was renamed as Kalamazoo in 1943.

Kardomah (coffee houses by Trusthouse Forte) The exotic name came to THF from a Liverpool tea and coffee importer and blender who set up his business in 1844.

Kayser Bondor (stockings and manufacturer) The firm began its career in 1928 as The Full-Fashioned Hosiery Co., with its first brand name, 'Fulfa', registered the following year. In 1931 a new brand name was registered – *Bondor*, derived (somewhat capriciously) from the French words *bon d'or*, 'good as gold'. In 1936 The Full-Fashioned Hosiery Co. joined forces with the American firm of Julius *Kayser* and Co. as *Kayser-Bondor* Ltd, this selling company manufacturing and distributing goods with the *Kayser* name in the UK. Ten years later, in 1946, The Full-Fashioned Hosiery Co. changed its name to *Bondor* Ltd. *Kayser Bondor* acquired the *Kayser* name from Julius Kayser and Co. in 1955 – and was itself taken' over by Courtaulds in 1966.

Keds (canvas shoes by US Rubber Co.) The manufacturers had wanted to name the shoes 'Peds', but this came too close to other brand names. After consideration, they decided to settle for 'the hardest-sounding letter in the alphabet', 'K'. This was in 1916. The name was registered the following year. For another American name that set store by the special value of 'K', see *Kodak*.

Kelly (doll by Marks & Spencer)   Originally, the designers of the doll considered 'Michelle' (a 'natural' for the store that sells *St Michael* branded goods), as well as the less prestigious 'Shelley'. But both names were already registered. After further discussions, 'Sally' was proposed – but this, too, was already booked. So with half an eye on Kelly Garrett of 'Charlie's Angels' (the TV American girl detectives), and secure in the knowledge that if a name appears hundreds of times in the telephone directory no one can register it, they made *Kelly* their final choice.

Kelvinator (refrigerator and manufacturer)   The name is based on that of Lord Kelvin (1824–1907), the English physicist, who first propounded 'open-cycle' refrigeration in 1852 and so paved the way for the development of the appliance. The suffix '-ator' presumably represents 'refriger*ator*'.

Kensitas (cigarettes by Gallaher)   To most British smokers, and certainly to Londoners, the name will suggest 'Kensington', one of the capital's fashionable districts. And this indeed is the name behind the name of the company that was established in 1898 by Julius Wix, a continental immigrant, who manufactured cigarettes for John Barker of Kensington. But why *Kensitas*? One explanation is that a foreign employee of Julius Wix telephoned a broken English order for 'John Barker of Kensitas'. Another traces the name to 'Ken Bar', an abbreviation used for designating manufactured articles by John Barker. A third theory is that there seems to have been a religious brotherhood named 'Kensitas' in Kensington. The firm of J. Wix & Sons was acquired by Gallaher in 1961.

Kent (cigarettes by D.J. Lorillard)   The name derives not from a place Kent – either the English county or the American city in Ohio – but as a token of respect for the former president of the manufacturers, Herbert A. Kent.

Kenwood (electric food mixers by Thorn EMI)   The name is indeed Ken Wood, the company's founder having been Kenneth Wood, who established the manufacture of electric mixers in Britain in 1947.

Kestrel see **Penguin**

Kia-Ora (soft drinks by Cadbury *Schweppes*) The name is Maori for 'good health'. The product has Australian links, since it was first produced (originally as lemon squash) by a farmer's son, John Dixon of Sydney, who had started a business as a seller of ice and soft drinks in 1896. *Kia-Ora* was marketed in Britain by a partner, A.H. Gasquoine, in 1913, and the company of this name was formed in 1929.

Kirbigrip (hair-grip by Newey Goodman) The name comes from that of the original manufacturers, Kirby, Beard & Co., who, although founded in 1743, registered *Kirbigrip* only in 1926. It was in the 1920s, the era of the Eton crop and bobbed hair-style, that there was a sharp drop in the demand for hairpins, and the *Kirbigrip* was invented to meet the demand of the wearers of the new short hair-style. (*Kirbigrips* are sprung, unlike traditional hairpins.)

Kit-Kat (chocolate-coated wafer biscuit by Rowntree Mackintosh) The product was named 'Chocolate Crisp' when first launched in 1935, becoming *Kit-Kat* in the late 1930s. The exact origin of this name is uncertain. A famous club of Whig politicians, The Kit-Kat Club, existed in the eighteenth century. It was named after one Christopher (or Kit) Cat, who kept a pie-house where the club met. But what connection could there be between a political club and a wafer biscuit, other than a name of prestige value? Perhaps the name has additional favourable onomatopoeic qualities that help: *Kit-Kat* suggests a dry, soft snapping or cracking, as of the biscuit being broken or bitten off. Or is this too fanciful?

Kiwi (shoe polish by *Kiwi* Products) Another unlikely association – a flightless New Zealand bird and a shoe polish! But in this case the origin is known. The name has a domestic origin. The shoe polish so named was originally marketed in 1906 by one William Ramsay in Melbourne, Australia. Ramsay called the polish *Kiwi* in honour of his wife, née Annie Elizabeth Meek, who was a New Zealander (born in Oamaru, South Island) and whom he married in 1901. The company's records indicate that Annie Ramsay was a source of inspiration and energy to her husband, so that he named his product after the bird that was one of the national symbols of her native country. ('Kiwi' is the nickname for a New Zealander.)

Klaxon (horn or warning hooter and manufacturer) The name was originally a United States trade mark – that of the firm who manufactured the horn, apparently about 1910. The derivation of the word remains rather obscure. It could be partly arbitrary, partly onomatopoeic. Or does it perhaps come from the French *claque*,

102

'clap' and *son*, 'sound'? (The verb *claquer* means to make a dry sound of some kind, as to 'crack', 'click', or 'slap'.) In his etymological dictionary *Origins*, however, Eric Partridge derives the name from Greek *klanxo*, 'I will make a loud noise'.

KLEENEX   **Kleenex** (cleansing paper tissue by Kimberly-Clark) One of the best known trade names – and sometimes used generically to apply to any paper tissue, of whatever make. The origin would seem obvious: 'clean' with the suffix '-ex'. This is undoubtedly the basic sense. The initial 'K', too, has not only desirable trade name qualities (see *Kodak*) but also an appropriateness for the product of a firm whose own name begins with 'K'. (The '-ex' is presumably 'out', 'away from'.) *Kleenex* tissues, when they first appeared on the market in the United States in 1924, were produced by a separate sales company, International Cellucotton Products Co. of Neenah, Winnebago, Wisconsin. At this stage they were 'absorbent pads or sheets (not medicated) for surgical or curative purposes in relation to the health'. Names ending in 'x' were fashionable in the 1920s. Among others of this period are *Lux*, *Celotex*, *Pyrex*, and *Cutex*.

Knight's Castile   **Knight's Castile** (toilet soap by *Unilever*) The magic in the name is not as great as it might seem. The soap was introduced in 1919 by John *Knight* & Co., which subsequently became part of Lever Brothers. *Castile* soap is a standard name (not a trade name) for a white or mottled soap made with olive oil and soda, such soap being originally made in Castile, Spain. The name has incidental superior connotations of chess: 'knight' and 'castle' are both important pieces in the game.

Kodak (photographic products and cameras and manufacturer) A trade name that is as well known internationally as *Coca-Cola*. The two names, in fact, appeared within two years of each other: *Coca-Cola* in 1886 and *Kodak* in 1888. *Kodak* as a name has no meaning: it is not intended to suggest any word (as 'code' or 'compact'), nor does it derive from any word. It was invented by the American photographic pioneer, George Eastman, who patented it on 4 September 1888. Fortunately for posterity, Eastman has recorded the reasoning that prompted him to choose this particular name. He chose it, he says, 'because I knew a trade name must be short, vigorous, incapable of being misspelled to an extent that will destroy its identity, and, in order to satisfy trademark laws, it must mean nothing. The letter K had been a favourite with me – it seemed a strong, incisive sort of letter. Therefore, the word I wanted had to start with K. Then it became a question of trying out a great number of combinations of letters that made words starting and ending with K. The word *Kodak* is the result.' It has been pointed out that the name is additionally onomatopoeic – it suggests the clicking of a camera's shutter. It may also be relevant that 'K' was the first letter of Eastman's mother's family name. The name has sometimes been used generically in a number of languages for a camera. This prompted the *Verband Deutscher Amateurphotographen-Vereine* ('Joint Society of German Amateur Photographic Associations') to issue the following warning (in German) in 1917: 'Whoever speaks of a *Kodak* meaning only a photographic camera in general is not mindful of the fact that he is damaging the German industry in favour of the Anglo-American by the widespread use of this word.' George Eastman also invented the name of one of *Kodak*'s most popular cameras, the *Brownie*.

Kolynos (toothpaste by International Chemical Co.)   The name was coined around the turn of the century by or for one Dr N.S. Jenkins, who developed the formula for the original toothpaste. The name comprises the Greek elements *kolouo*, 'I limit', 'I check' and *nosos*, 'sickness', 'disease'.

Konica (cameras by Konishiroku UK)   The name is simply a contraction of *Koni*shiroku and '*ca*mera', with the '-ca' ending fairly common for camera names, as with *Leica*.

Kosset (carpets by *Kosset* Carpets International)   The name would appear to be a commercial spelling of 'cosset', the carpet thus being one that pampers your feet, and presumably your house generally.

Kotex (sanitary towels by Kimberly-Clark)   As with *Kleenex*, the initial 'K' may be a link with the name of the manufacturers. Otherwise the name would seem to be almost arbitrary, with no specific origin. A connection with 'coat' is not likely. Perhaps here the suffix is not '-ex' but '-tex', denoting 'textile' or 'texture'. *Kotex* towels were introduced by Kimberly-Clark in 1920. The company was, however, embarrassed at being associated with such a personal product and set up a separate sales firm, International Cellucotton Products, to market it (see also *Kleenex*).

KP (nuts and crisps by *KP* Foods)   The letters stand for *K*enyon *P*roducts. Kenyon Son and Craven were producers of confectionery and nuts in Yorkshire. The firm was acquired in 1968 by United Biscuits.

Kraft (food products by *Kraft* Foods)   The name is that of the first manufacturer of processed cheese, James L. Kraft, in Chicago, 1903.

104

The name is a good one – perhaps almost too good for processed cheese – in that it suggests both 'craft' and German *Kraft*, 'strength'.

Kruschen ('health salts' by *Aspro*-Nicholas)   The product was first marketed in the late nineteenth century, and was originally manufactured by E. Griffiths Hughes, who also made *Rennies*. The name resembles a surname, but seems in fact to be a concocted word. *Kruschen* 'salts' were based on the medicinal properties of creosote, the German for which is *Kreosot*. Could the name be a kind of jocular diminutive of this, '*Kreosotchen*'? Until the Second World War the name had an umlaut ('Krüschen'), presumably to give it a kind of special linguistic 'status'.

Kwells (travel-sickness tablets by *Aspro*-Nicholas)   A dose of the tablets 'quells' travel sickness, claim the manufacturers. The 's' indicates a plural rather than a verb, however. (One such tablet would be a 'Kwell'.)

L

Lada (car by Volga Automobile Works)   The Russian car is manufactured in Tolyatti (formerly Stavropol) on the river Volga. The river is reflected in the logo of the vehicle, which depicts a boat. The name, however, does not derive from the Russian poetic word *ladya*, 'boat', but from a folk word meaning 'beloved' or 'dear one'. In the USSR the car's native name is Zhiguli, derived from the hills so called bordering the Volga not far from the city of manufacture. The car is known as *Lada* abroad since it is a simpler name in most languages and also since in some languages 'Zhiguli' has undesirable connotations. In English and French, for example, it resembles 'gigolo', and in Arabic can suggest similar sounding words with meanings such as 'fake' and 'ignoramus'. In Scandinavian countries, moreover, the sound 'zh' (as in English 'pleasure') does not exist. The name is also the standard Russian diminutive of Vladimir, which doubtless helps the car's popular image.

Ladybird (children's books by *Ladybird* Books)   The name was presumably chosen for the cheerfully coloured insect, a familiar creature in children's tales and rhymes ('Ladybird, ladybird, fly away home', and so on). It was first registered in the United Kingdom in 1915.

105

Ladybird (children's wear and manufacturer)   There is no legal link between this firm and the foregoing. In this case the name and device (similar to that of *Ladybird* Books) was apparently chosen as the result of a dream by an ancestor of Eric Pasold, the founder, with his brothers Rolf and Inigo, of what was to become the parent company of *Ladybird*, Pasolds Ltd. The insect has associations of brightness and friendliness that are appropriate both visually and verbally for a firm that manufactures colourful designs and garments for children.

Lagonda (car by *Aston Martin Lagonda*)   The name comes from Lagonda Creek, Ohio, the home of Wilbur Gunn, an American who decided against a possible career as an opera singer in favour of manufacturing tricars at Staines, Middlesex. His first four-wheeled cars appeared in 1907. The Italian flavour of the name – it is a near anagram of 'gondola' – make it suitable for a large, luxury car of international standing. In 1947 *Lagonda* ceased its independent existence and became part of the David Brown empire, together with *Aston Martin*.

Lambretta (motorscooter by Innocenti)   The Innocenti company was set up in Milan in 1933. Two years after the Second World War the firm's factories were rebuilt in the district of Lambrate (named after the river so called) in Milan, and the district's name passed in diminutive form to the motorscooter.

Lancia (car and manufacturer)   The name is that of the car's first manufacturer in 1908, the Italian racing driver, Vincenzo Lancia. The car's emblem, depicting a standard mounted on a lance, makes a play on Lancia's name (*lancia* is the Italian for 'lance'). The name itself, suggesting streamlining and speed, is coincidentally very suitable for a distinctive car.

Land-Rover (four-wheel drive vehicle by *Jaguar Rover Triumph*)   The first *Land-Rover*, produced in 1948, was designed to provide farmers with a cheap, rugged vehicle that could travel virtually everywhere over their *land*. It was so popular that within a year it had overtaken *Rover*'s saloon-car sales and by 1951 was outselling *Rover* cars by two to one. Much of the design of the *Range Rover* was based on that of the *Land-Rover* – whose name seems just right for a cross-country vehicle.

Largactil (anti-depressant drug by May & Baker)   As with many drugs, one might suppose a meaningless, concocted word or one comprising the names of chemical agents. However, *Largactil* in fact derives from two French words, *large activité*, 'broad activity'. These words were chosen to express the essential feature of the main ingredient of the drug, chlorpromazine, which is the 'extreme diversity of its pharmacodynamic activities'. The name was first registered in Britain in 1953.

Lec (refrigerators by *Lec* Refrigeration)   The link with '*elec*tricity' is an apt one, but fortuitous. The name derives from the initials of the original company, the *L*ongford *E*ngineering *C*ompany, formed in 1942 in premises on the Longford Road, Bognor Regis, Sussex. In 1946 the company moved to larger premises in the same town and abbreviated its name.

Lego (toy building bricks and manufacturer)   Not 'leggo' ('let go'), and only by chance the Latin word for 'I read'. The name was devised for children's wooden toys built in the 1930s by a Danish carpenter, Kirk Christiansen, from the Danish *leg godt*, 'play well'. The *Lego* brick was introduced on the market in the early 1950s. The name is a good international one – short, easy to pronounce in different languages, and easy to remember – and the product is called by this name in all the countries in which it is marketed. A 'town' constructed of *Lego* bricks near the company's head factory in Billund, Denmark, is named Legoland (also a registered trade mark).

Leica (camera by Ernst & Leitz)   The name, which inspired a number of other camera names ending in '-ca', comes from the manufacturer, *Lei*tz Gesellschaft, of Germany, plus '-ca' for '*ca*mera'. The camera was first produced in 1924. The film critic C.A. Lejeune, reviewing the film version of John Van Druten's play, *I Am a Camera*, in 1952 (the play itself being based on stories by Christopher Isherwood, with its title a quotation from his *A Berlin Diary*), gave the trade name prominence by her pithy summary of the performance she attended: 'Me no Leica'.

Lemon Hart (rum by United Rum Merchants)   The name is actually that of a person. Lemon Hart was a wine and spirit merchant of Penzance, Cornwall, in the latter half of the eighteenth century. He obtained his rum from trade with the West Indies: Penzance, in extreme south-west England, was one of the nearest landfalls in the days of sailing ships. It is known that Hart, who died in 1845, was Jewish, so presumably his unusual first name was an anglicisation of a name such as Lehmann. The association of rum and lemons, however, is not an unattractive one.

Lenor (fabric conditioner by Procter & Gamble) The name was chosen for its connotations rather than its direct meaning. It aims to suggest softness, hinting at words such as 'lenitive', 'lenity', 'lenient' (all from Latin *lenire*, 'to soothe'), and also, no doubt, 'lanolin' (from Latin *lana*, 'wool') and even 'languid', 'linen', 'lint', and 'laundry'. The name would have many of these connotations in a number of European languages. Procter & Gamble did, however, once receive a letter from a Welshman saying that he was puzzled why a fabric conditioner should be called by a Welsh name that means 'man of letters' (*llenor*). In fact 'Y Llenor' was the title of a Welsh literary journal published from 1922 to 1951.

Lesney (toys by Matchbox Toys) The name suggests 'Leslie' or 'Lesley' – and this in fact is the substantial derivation, from the three joint founders of the company in 1947, *Les*lie Smith, Rod*ney* Smith (no relation), and Jack Odell. *Lesney*'s best known product has been its 'Matchbox' toys, or diecast metal model vehicles.

Letraset

Letraset (transfers and manufacturer) The product was introduced by John Davis and Frederick Mackenzie of London in 1963. If you buy a sheet of letters to transfer on to other surfaces, you have a 'letterer set'. This presumably is the origin of the name.

Levis (jeans and manufacturer) Jeans of this type, with their characteristic rivets, were first made in 1850 by a Bavarian immigrant to the United States, Levi Strauss. It was the time of the Gold Rush, and many enterprising tailors were making tents and wagon coverings with their cloth for the use of the miners. It was a miner, in fact, who suggested to Strauss that he could fulfil a demand by making hard-wearing trousers. His jeans were the result. The rivets were added in 1874, originally because of a joke about a prospector whose trousers were taken to be riveted by a blacksmith since he carried rock specimens in his pockets.

Leyland see **BL**

Liberty (London store) The history of the famous store originates with Arthur Liberty, who owned a draper's shop in the High Street, Chesham, Buckinghamshire, in the first half of the nineteenth century. His son, Arthur Lasenby Liberty, born in 1843, opened his first London shop in Regent Street in 1875. For a store renowned for its Art Nouveau styles and designs the surname is coincidentally just right. (Indeed the Italian term for Art Nouveau actually is *stile Liberty*.) See also the next entry.

Liberty Bodice (foundation garment by R. & W.H. Symington) Symington's made an agreement with *Liberty* & Co. in the 1900s to use the name for corsetry in general and for the *Liberty* Bodice in particular. The garment had a unique strapping arrangement and was so popular in its early days that several manufacturers attempted to copy it and as a result were involved in litigation. The Bodice, whose name would seem in the circumstances to be as inappropriate as it was appropriate for Arthur Liberty's firm, was discontinued in the 1960s. (The garment was originally worn mainly by young children: a 'button-front' ladies' version of it is still marketed, mostly for the elderly, by Symington's.)

Librium (tranquilliser drug by Roche Laboratories) The name is a purely invented word, first patented in the United States in 1960. Although having no meaning, *Librium* nevertheless suggests both 'liberation' and 'equilibrium', which for a drug that relieves stress symptoms are helpful associations.

Lifebuoy (soap by *Unilever*) The toilet soap was introduced in 1933. The original soap appeared for sale in 1894, as a successor to William Lever's first soap, *Sunlight*. It was a carbolic household soap containing a germicide, with a name chosen to suggest safety (from disease). Both the household and toilet varieties are still marketed.

Lilia (sanitary towels and belts by *Lilia*-White) The suggestion of 'lily-white' is coincidental, since the name indicates a merger in 1958 of *Lilia* Ltd and other manufacturers of sanitary protection products including Arthur Berton, who produced Dr White's looped towel. (There was in fact no Dr White – the name was chosen to suggest a combination of medical reliability and purity.) The *Lilia* towel was originally marketed by a firm named 'Sashena', the letters standing for such words as *sa*fe, *se*cure, *hy*gienic, and the like. This was renamed *Lilia* Ltd in 1948. See also the next entry.

Lil-lets (sanitary tampons by *Lilia*-White) The product was introduced in 1954 by *Lilia* Ltd. The suffix '-lets' is intended to denote a diminutive, referring to a small-size 'towel'. (The usual form of this suffix is '-ette', as in kitchen*ette*. It can also apply to a girl or woman, as usher*ette*, drum major*ette*, as well as to a material or fabric, as stockin*ette*, georg*ette*, satin*ette*. All three uses would seem to be appropriate, although this particular form of the suffix is a rather clumsy one.)

109

Li-Lo (airbed and inflatable rubber mattress and manufacturer) The name presumably originates from a person's ability to 'lie low' in the bed, and also for the mattress's ability to 'lie low' in the water. The word has tended to be used generically (as 'lilo') for any make of such bed or mattress. Perhaps the suggestion of 'Lido' and the seaside is at work here. The name was first registered in 1936, when the bed was manufactured by P.B. Cow & Co. (see *Cow Gum*).

Linguaphone (recorded language-learning courses and manufacturer) The name is a classical hybrid, with Latin *lingua*, 'tongue', 'language', and the Greek element meaning 'sound' taken from *gramophone*. It arose in London in 1904 as a language-teaching system, using *gramophone* records and textbooks, devised by an émigré Russian, Jacques Roston. The name was registered in 1925. *Linguaphone* is an effective name in several languages, especially ones having a stock of classical words and roots. In Russian the name came to be used generically (*lingafon*) for any language course on records, and produced the standard term for 'language laboratory' – *lingafonnaya laboratoriya*.

linoleum (floorcloth of canvas with coat of oxidised linseed oil) The word derives from Latin *lineum*, 'flax', and *oleum*, 'oil'. The product, patented by F. Walton in 1860 and 1863, was originally a trade name, but was taken off the Trade Marks Register in 1878 since it had become a household word and was the only practicable way of describing the substance. Compare *Cellophane* and *gramophone*, among others.

Lion Brand (stationery by John Dickinson) The name originated in India in 1880. The manager of the Calcutta branch of John Dickinson recognised that many potential customers were illiterate and so put a heraldic lion of different colours (crimson, primrose, brown, blue, black and green) on the labels of different grades of paper. For a cheaper range he used a deer. (But did not the uncertain market potential of writing paper among an illiterate population disturb him?) In 1910 the company adopted the lion as an all-purpose trade mark in Britain, and in 1927 it used the *Lion Brand* symbol on products generally. After its merger with E.S. & A. Robinson in 1966, John Dickinson restricted the use of the symbol and the name to its stationery range.

Lirelle (polyester fibre by Courtaulds) The name is an invented one, with no special meaning. Even so, it suggests 'lyric' and has a suffix that suggests femininity (compare *Courtelle*, on which, presumably, it is based).

Listerine (antiseptic and disinfectant by Warner-Lambert) The antiseptic owes its name to the English surgeon who introduced the use of antiseptics, Sir Joseph Lister (1827–1921). The product was developed in 1879 by one of the founders of William R. Warner & Co., the American pharmacist, Jordan W. Lambert, who based his antiseptic on the earlier formula by Lister. It was reported at the time that Lister was not happy about having his name used in this way and that he objected to it. His objections, however, were of no avail. The common trade-name suffix '-ine' here would seem to mean 'of the nature of', or just 'based on' (i.e. Lister's antiseptic).

Longines (watches and manufacturer) The name is not that of the founder of the Swiss company, familiar to the public through its timing of international sports events, but of the village near St Imier in Switzerland where Ernest Francillon and Jacques David opened their watch factory in 1867.

Long Life (lager by *Ind Coope*) Rather a good name, since it can be taken on any or all of several levels. The lager will keep well (it has a long life if unopened); it may help its consumer to have a long life; it wishes you the traditional toast, 'Long Life!' The name may additionally refer to the extended cans in which the beer is sold. Finally, the name is agreeably alliterative.

Lotus (sports car and manufacturer) The name was devised by the firm's founder, Colin Chapman, who chose not to reveal the reasons that prompted his choice. Having an association with exotic flowers, the name is obviously a prestige one. Until the precise origin of the name is revealed, however, one can only speculate what actually prompted the racing driver's choice.

Loxene (medicated shampoo by Reckitt & Colman) The name would seem to be a blend of 'locks' and the suffix '-ene', the latter simply meaning 'product' or perhaps suggesting 'clean'.

Lucky Strike (cigarettes by American Tobacco Co.) The name was originally used in 1856 by Dr R.A. Patterson of Richmond, Virginia, for a sliced plug tobacco. The time was that of the Gold Rush, so a 'lucky strike' was what all prospectors sought. The American Tobacco Co. reintroduced the name for their blended tobacco in 1916 and cigarettes in 1917 – the latter in answer to Reynolds's *Camel*.

Lucozade (tonic drink by Beecham Group)   The name is derived from 'glucose', the product's chief constituent, with the ending '-ade' suggesting 'lemon*ade*' or some similar fruit drink. *Lucozade* was developed by William W. Hunter, a Newcastle chemist, at the shop of W. W. Owen and Son in the 1930s. Hunter's daughter had contracted jaundice, a disease prevalent at the time, and he was prompted to formulate a carbonated drink containing as much glucose as possible, flavoured with orange and lemon oils. He sold the product to Beecham in 1938.

Lufthansa (commercial airline)   The name of the chief German airline derives from *Luft*, 'air' and *Hansa*, an Old High German word meaning 'association' (as in the Hanseatic League, a medieval association of North German cities, notably Lübeck, Hamburg and Bremen, who monopolised trade with the Baltic).

Lurex (plastic fabric containing a metallic thread by The *Lurex* Co.)   The name is of American origin, and was first registered in the United States by the Dobeckmun Co. of Cleveland, Ohio, in 1945. The exact origin is not recorded, but presumably the name was chosen to suggest 'allure', rather than 'lurid', with the common trade-name suffix '-ex'.

Lurpak (butter and manufacturer)   Is the butter packed in a *lu*rid pack or an al*lur*ing pack? The latter would be an attractive suggestion but it may not be the correct one. Perhaps, since the butter is of Danish origin, the origin lies in the *lure* or *lur*, which was a long curved Bronze Age trumpet that is still used in Scandinavian countries for calling cattle. At any rate, some such instrument is shown on the packs of *Lurpak* butter.

Lux (soap and soap flakes by *Unilever*)   Perhaps a near perfect trade name – short, distinctive, ending in 'x', and suggesting 'light' (Latin *lux*) and 'luxury'. *Lux* flakes were inaugurated in 1899, the same year as *Monkey Brand*. Initially, they were marketed as 'Sunlight Flakes', but this name was not popularly received, so the following year they were renamed *Lux*. The name seems to have been suggested, as *Sunlight* was, by William Lever's patent agent in Liverpool, W.P. Thompson. Scarcity of raw materials caused the withdrawal of *Lux* flakes in the Second World War, but they were reintroduced in 1947. *Lux* toilet soap was first introduced in 1928.

Lyons Maid (ice cream and manufacturer)   A fairly obvious but quite neat pun ('Lyons made'). The origin of the name is more specific than might be supposed, however, since it combined the firm J. *Lyons* with the name of their top-selling ice cream product in 1955. This was Pola *Maid*, an ice cream manufactured in 'pole' lengths before being sliced and packed. The association with cinema usherettes selling ice cream, and with femininity generally, gives *Lyons Maid* an added attraction.

Lysol (disinfectant)   The name, which is now on the *British Pharmacopoeia*, originated as a trade name in 1891, from Greek *lusis*, 'loosening' plus the ending '-ol' meaning 'oil'. The substance is a mixture of creosote and soft soap, used as a disinfectant. The 'loosening' refers to its solubility in water.

Mace

Mace (food products by *Mace* Marketing Services)   The name is neither an acronym nor a personal name. *Mace* Marketing Services was founded in 1960 as an association of wholesalers and independent grocery shopkeepers to meet increasing competition from multiple supermarket chains. The symbol chosen for the group, and represented pictorially on its products, was the mace – the staff of office of the Speaker in the House of Commons. *Mace* Marketing saw in this the symbol of independent authority. Presumably the undesirable association with Mace, the trade name of the riot control spray, was regarded as being too American-oriented to have any effect on purchasers of the British group's products. A suggestion of the other 'mace', meaning the spice got from nutmegs, could on the other hand be favourable.

Mac Fisheries (fish and fresh-food supermarket chain by *Unilever*)   In 1919, Lord Leverhulme, as a philanthropic gesture, decided to assist the development of the Scottish isles of Lewis and Harris. He bought a herring-drifting firm called Bix and then purchased about 300 shops in which to sell the fish they were supposed to catch. What could these shops be called? Lord Leverhulme considered several names, among them 'Silent Deep', 'Island Deep', 'Lipsco' (*L*ewis *I*sland *P*reserved *S*pecialities *C*ompany), 'Silvascale', 'Wavecrest', 'Deepcast', 'Snack', 'Shoal', and 'Siren'. The basis 'Mac' for a name was then suggested to him, and he at first considered prefixing each type of fish with this, as 'Mac Herring', 'Mac Cod', 'Mac Lobster'. Fortunately, Leverhulme did not take this absurd idea any further, but instead used the typically Scots element for the shops alone. Thus after a very short period as 'The Island

Fisheries', '*Mac Fisheries*' was incorporated in 1919 with its head-quarters in London. A small but important point is that the two parts of the name are separated as two words (i.e. are not written as 'MacFisheries'). For this reason the name preceded all Scottish surnames starting with 'Mac-' in the London telephone directory. (A further development of the name was Mac Markets, the super-market chain.) By 1980, however, *Mac Fisheries* retail shops were becoming commercially unviable and *Unilever* began to close them.

Macleans (toothpaste by Beecham Group) In spite of good as-sociations with 'clean', the name is actually that of Alex C. Maclean, a New Zealander. First emigrating to America to work as a salesman for *Spirella* corsets, Maclean established his own business manufac-turing products for chemists in England in 1919, these being sold under the chemists' own names. In 1927, the chemist working for Maclean, Walter McGeorge, formulated a pink peroxide toothpaste which was so popular that a white version was produced. This was sold as 'Maclean's Peroxide Toothpaste'.

Magnetophone (tape-recorder) The *Magnetophone* was the name given to the first tape-recorder using plastic tape. This was produced by the German firm of AEG (*Allgemeine Elektrizitäts-Gesellschaft*, 'General Electric Company') in Berlin in 1935. The name – in German spelled without the final 'e' – derives from '*magnetic*' (tape) and the Greek element '-phone' based on *gramophone* or some similar instrument with this ending. The name has never become generic in English, where it is used to apply specifically to the German machines. In many other languages, however, the word is some-times used generically to mean 'tape-recorder', as French *magnéto-phone*, Russian *magnitofon*, and German itself *Magnetophon* (although the alternative German name *Tonbandgerät* is also widely used). Eighteen *Magnetophones* were recovered by the Allies from the AEG plant in Berlin at the end of the Second World War, and every tape-recorder developed since 1945 can be regarded as a descendant of these captured German machines. The *Magnetophon* is still pro-duced by AEG-Telefunken.

Magraw (cars by *Vauxhall* Motors) The name is the surname of a *Vauxhall* car dealer (K.J. Motors/Magraw Engineering) who also markets a conversion of the Cavalier as the 'Centaur'.

Maltesers (chocolate-coated confectionery by *Mars*) The associ-ation must be with 'malt' rather than with 'Maltese', the reference being to the flavour of the confectionery. The name also suggests 'melt', which is attractive advertising, and rather more learnedly,

114

'honey' (via Latin *mel* or Greek *meli*, *melitos*), also a favourable connection. By a coincidence the first two and last two letters of the name spells *Mars*!

Mandrax (sedative drug by Roussel Laboratories)   The name was devised, as is the case with a number of drugs, to have no meaning or special significance. The association, however, must be with 'mandrake', all the more since this is a 'drug-like' plant with narcotic properties. The name was first registered in Paris in 1963. In the late 1960s a colloquial form of it, Mandy (or mandy), became current among drug addicts – usually in its plural form of 'Mandies'. (This may have been partly prompted by the girls' name.) In some countries the name is slightly modified – as 'Mandrox', 'Mandrix', or 'Mandrex' – because of pre-existing trade marks.

Mansion (floor and furniture polish by Reckitt & Colman)   The name was first registered in 1908 by the Chiswick Soap Co., and is said to have been inspired by Chiswick House, a mansion near the original manufacturing site (see *Cherry Blossom*). It is also, of course, a prestige association, implying that the polish is suitable for the best of houses.

Manta (cars by *Opel*)   The *Manta* is a sports car, and its name is an exotic one, deriving from the fish so called, the manta or devil ray, renowned for its strength, speed and aggressive appearance. The name is thus a highly effective one, and suitably 'international' in form, but perhaps the association is almost too exotic? It will be lost on someone who has not even heard of the fish. (The word can be found, however, in most dictionaries.) And perhaps even the wrong association could be made, as with 'mantle' or 'mantra'.

MARATHON   **Marathon** (chocolate-coated bar containing peanuts, nougat and caramel by *Mars*)   The name has favourable allusions: to the Greek classical race, to an Olympic runner in the long-distance race so called (who needs strength and stamina, which the product purports to give you), to the 'staying power' needed for this race (which the product itself has – it lasts long). Apart from such connotations, the name is an attractive one in itself, soft and 'toothsome', which is just right for a confection. It also, of course, blends well with the company's best known product, *Mars*.

Marlboro   **Marlboro** (cigarettes by Philip Morris)   Although an American company, Philip Morris began as a British firm, with Philip Morris himself opening a shop in Bond Street, London, in 1847. By 1885 he was selling tobacco brands named 'Blues', 'Cambridge' and

115

'Derby' and cigarettes named 'Marlborough' (sic). The aristocratic theme is the common link here, of course, suggesting the titles of dukes and earls and 'blue blood'. (Marlborough College, the English public school, was probably not a link. The school is a relatively late foundation, 1843.) In 1924 the cigarette was launched in America under the shorter name *Marlboro*. Its specific promotion was originally as a cigarette for ladies (it had a red filter tip – 'a cherry tip for your ruby lips'), but was subsequently marketed as very much a man's cigarette, with a cowboy, 'Marlboro Country' promotion. The latter campaign may wrongly suggest that the association is with an American place so called, notably Marlborough (also actually spelled Marlboro), Massachusetts.

Marley (thermoplastic tiles by The *Marley* Tile Co.) The company's head office and works is at Riverhead, near Sevenoaks, Kent. *Marley* Lane, after which the tiles are named, is a road forming part of the medieval Pilgrims' Way from London to Canterbury also in Kent, at Lenham, south-east of Maidstone. The association with 'marl', the clayey soil from which roof tiles used to be made, is a fortuitous one.

Marmion (industrial cleanser by Procter & Gamble) Literary trade names are not common. One noted example is *Bovril*, another is *Marmion*, from the hero of Walter Scott's poem of the same name (in full 'Marmion, A Tale of Flodden Field'). The name was first registered in 1888 for a brand called 'Stanley's Marmion Flakes'. It was reregistered in 1923 and *Marmion* Granules, the industrial cleanser, is still made by Procter & Gamble at their Manchester works. The association is presumably one of strength and vigour, while the name's literary origin gives it a good status value.

Marmite (yeast extract and manufacturer) *Marmite* was first manufactured in England in 1902. Its name, however, is French in origin, since *marmite* is the French word for a type of cooking pot or stew pan (represented pictorially on the product's label). The actual French word seems to derive from a former name of a cat, meaning something like 'Purring Puss' – not a bad link-up for a name whose two 'Ms' already give it a 'lip-smacking' flavour.

Mars (chocolate covered bar with toffee-like filling and manufacturer) The name is most familiar in the nicely rhyming 'Mars bar'. Its derivation is not Mars the planet or Mars the Roman god of war but a family name: the firm was set up in England in 1932, as Mars Confections Ltd, by Forrest Mars, an immigrant American. The celestial and classical suggestion is strong, however, if only on account of two other products of the company, Milky Way and *Marathon*.

Martini (vermouth by Martini and Rossi)   The name is that of the Italian manufacturers. The vermouth so called was advertised in the American magazine *Puck* as far back as 1894. The first dry *Martini* is said to have been concocted by an American bartender, Jerry Thomas, at the Occidental Hotel, San Francisco, California, in 1860.

Marzine (anti-travel sickness tablets by Burroughs Wellcome & Co.)   The American version of the name is Marezine, which indicates its origin a little more clearly: from Latin *mare*, 'sea', and pipera*zine*, one of its main chemical ingredients. The name was registered by The Wellcome Foundation in 1954. In the *British Pharmacopoeia* the drug is called cyclizine hydrochloride.

Maserati (car and manufacturer)   The name is that of six Italian brothers, Carlo, Bindo, Alfieri, Mario, Ettore, and Ernesto, all of whom except one (Mario) were involved in the motor industry. Carlo was the first to build a car, the 'Carcano', in 1897, after which he worked for *Fiat*. Alfieri developed the 'Diatto' car for competitions from 1922. When he gave up racing, the other Maserati brothers brought out the first car under their own name. In 1948 Bindo, Ernesto and Ettore left the company to make the *Osca* (from the initials of *Officine Specializzate Costruzione Automobili* ('Specialised Automobile Construction Works'), whose emblem carries the words *fratelli Maserati* ('Maserati brothers').

Master McGrath (pet food by General Foods)   The name is that of a legendary champion Irish greyhound owned by Lord Lurgan, which won the Waterloo Cup in 1868 and has since had its exploits retold in a ballad popular among Ulster singers. The pet food so called was manufactured at Portadown, Northern Ireland, by Windsor Foods Ltd, founded in 1960, until this firm was acquired by General Foods ten years later. The dog food was subsequently launched throughout the United Kingdom following a television advertising campaign featuring a 'talking' dog.

Matsushita (electrical products by *Matsushita* Electric Industrial Co.)   The name is that of the founder, the Japanese businessman Konosuke Matsushita, who set up the firm in Osaka in 1918. ('Matsushita' is said to be Japanese for 'under a pine tree'.) The company has five main brand names: *National, Panasonic,* (sometimes used together, as *National Panasonic*), *Technics* and *Quasar. National*

117

was chosen by Mr Matsushita as being relevant in many countries, while at the same time pointing to one particular nationality; *Panasonic*, first used in 1955, applies mainly to audio equipment, radios, television sets, and the like, and is mock-classical for 'sound everywhere', or 'all sounding'; *Technics* dates from the early 1970s, and is used only for top-class hi-fi equipment with the suggestion of high *techno*logy; *Quasar*, used only in the United States and Canada, was inherited when *Matsushita* acquired a television manufacturing company of this name.

Max Factor (cosmetics and manufacturer)   The name, suggesting something like 'maximum factor', is actually that of the Polish immigrant to America in 1904, Max Factor, who established the firm in St Louis, Missouri, in 1909, having opened a perfume and theatrical make-up shop at the St Louis World's Fair in the year of his arrival. The United Kingdom branch of *Max Factor* opened in Bond Street, London, in 1935. Of all personal names providing the best associations for a trade name, this must be one of the most favourable. Factor is a Jewish vocational surname meaning originally 'agent'.

Maxwell House (instant coffee by General Foods)   The creator of *Maxwell House* coffee was Joel Owsley Cheek, originally a travelling salesman with a grocery firm. Cheek became specially interested in coffee, and set up on his own in 1882 to search for an ideal blend. He eventually achieved one that satisfied him, and offered it to one of America's top-rank hotels, the Maxwell House at Nashville, Tennessee. Soon the guests, it seems, were singing the praises of the new 'Maxwell House coffee', and thus the trade name was born. In Britain, *Maxwell House* ground coffee was first manufactured by Alfred Bird (see *Birds Eye*) in 1944, and the instant variety launched exactly ten years later. (This was the powdered coffee; the granules came in 1970.) A brand of instant coffee that never got off the ground was Maxim. This was launched by General Foods into a test market in 1969 but was dropped when the relatively high price discouraged wide sales.

Mazda (electric light bulbs by Thorn Electrical Industries)   The name was first used by the American General Electric Co. in 1909. It was suggested to them by Frederick P. Fish, a Boston lawyer and ex-president of the American Telegraph Co. After considering 'Apollo', 'Jupiter', and 'Jove', Fish decided that *Mazda*, the Persian god of light, was a more suitable name for the new tungsten incandescent lamp. (The full name of the ancient Zoroastrian deity is Ahura Mazda, meaning literally 'lord wisdom'.)

118

Mazda (cars and manufacturer)   There is no connection between this name and the foregoing. It is a corruption of the name of the founder of the Toyo Kogyo Co. in 1921, the Japanese businessman Matsuda. No doubt, however, the company welcomed the favourable if coincidental 'god of light' association. The first *Mazda* car appeared in 1935. The name is a good one for both cars and lamps, being easy to pronounce, containing an exotic letter ('z'), and in English also suggesting 'amazing' and even 'master'.

Mecca (entertainment and catering company)   Unless an acronym, the name must surely derive from the Saudi Arabian city, Mecca, the centre of pilgrimage of Muslims, as used in a popular sense to mean a place that attracts a number of visitors. As a trade name, it is short, easily spelt and pronounced, and at the same time on the exotic side (because of its religious, historical and geographical associations).

Meccano (children's miniature metal construction kit by General Mills UK)   The product was invented by Frank Hornby, of Hornby trains fame, in Liverpool in 1901. Originally the kit was called 'Mechanics Made Easy' but this was streamlined to *Meccano*, a more international-looking name, in 1907. The company also introduced another well-known toy name, *Dinky Toys*, in 1932. Both names were taken over by Lines Brothers, and in 1971 by Airfix Industries, after Lines Brothers got into financial difficulties. In 1979, owing to continued difficulties, Airfix announced that it would have to close the Liverpool works where *Meccano* had been manufactured since 1907. The kits are now manufactured in France.

Meggezones (throat pastilles by Plough (UK))   The name is a modification of the original firm founded in 1796 by a Mr Meggeson. The company specialised in cough and cold lozenges, syrups and medicated confectionery, all of which it introduced in the early nineteenth century. An advertisement in the *Chemist and Druggist Supplement* as late as May 1947, shows *Meggezones* and Meggeson Dyspepsia Tablets featured side by side, both as products of Meggeson & Co. Ltd.

melamine (type of plastic)   The name is not a trade mark, even though sometimes spelled with a capital letter. In the sense of 'plastic used for crockery', *melamine* dates from the early 1940s. The name itself was devised in 1834 by the German chemist, Baron von Liebig, famous for 'Liebig's extract of beef'. He based it on his own name, Melam, for a distillate of ammonium thiocyanate, in which the '-am' presumably derives from '*ammonium*' and the 'Mel-' may

119

either derive from Greek *melas*, 'black', referring to the colour of the substance at some stage of manufacture, or else be arbitrary. The name *melamine* is also used for *melamine* resin, or a material made from this resin, and this, strictly speaking, is the laminated plastic used for table tops and other hard surfaces.

Meloids (throat lozenges by The Boots Co.)   Meloids are small, black pastilles, and their colour gives their name, since Greek *melas* means 'black'. The '-oid' suffix may have little significance, but could simply mean 'in appearance', 'seeming' (see paragraph 8 of Appendix I, p. 199).

Meltonian (shoe-care products by Reckitt & Colman)   The name was first registered in 1921, and originally belonged to a manufacturer in the Melton Mowbray area of Leicestershire. By good fortune for him, the name has aristocratic associations, since not only is the area round Melton Mowbray hunted by three leading packs, the Quorn, Belvoir and Cottesmore, but the *Meltonians* were also an aristocratic hunting fraternity who used to come up to Melton Mowbray from London at weekends for 'sport'.

Mercedes (cars by *Mercedes*-Benz)   In 1899, Emil Jellinek, an Austrian financier and diplomat, who had been buying *Daimler* cars in increasing quantities for motor races, entered one of his cars in the 'Tour de Nice' in France under the pseudonym of 'Herr Mercedes'. The name was the Christian name of his ten-year-old daughter, as well as an aristocratic one in Spanish circles. The *Daimler* won, and the following year the manufacturers adopted the name for further models of the car, including ones specially made for Jellinek. These new models, which Jellinek said he was prepared to buy, and for which he arranged to have the sole rights of sale in Austria, Hungary, France, Belgium and America, were to be sold in these countries as the *Mercedes*. In all other countries the car was to be known as the 'New *Daimler*'. The *Mercedes* name soon became the only one, however, by which the car was known in any country. In 1925 the interests of the two firms of *Daimler* and Benz (the latter founded by Carl Benz in 1886) united as *Daimler*-Benz. After 1926 the separate *Mercedes* and Benz marques were discontinued in favour of *Mercedes*-Benz. Jellinek's second daughter was called Maja, a name used for a car popular with European royalty designed by *Porsche*. Like the *Jaguar*, the *Mercedes* is a sufficiently glamorous car to deserve an affectionate nickname, the 'Merc'.

Merrydown (cider by *Merrydown* Wine Co.)   The business was founded in 1946 by Ian Howie and Jack Ward. The two men produced the first 400 gallons of cider in the garage of Jack Ward's house in Rotherfield, East Sussex. Having no name for the embryo company they adopted the name of Jack Ward's house, 'Merry-down'. This was no doubt originally chosen for its agreeable local associations – Sussex is famous for its South Downs. The name, an unusual transfer from house name to trade name, is an apt one for a drink associated with rural England.

Metamec (clocks and manufacturer) The name derives from the two words '*meta*ls' and '*mech*anics'. The company was founded in 1923 by a Mr G.B. Jenkins, presumably as a more general engineering business, since clocks were not manufactured by the firm until 1943.

Metatone (tonic medicine by Warner-Lambert) The product would appear to have been launched shortly after the First World War. The second half of the name is presumably 'tone' or 'tonic', with the first half perhaps the Greek element *meta*-, 'change'. The name as a whole could thus suggest a 'change of tone'. Or does 'Meta-' point to 'metal', since the product is an iron tonic?

Methedrine (stimulant drug by Burroughs Wellcome & Co.) The name derives from *meth*yl and the last six letters of *Benzedrine*. The drug is actually methamphetamine hydrochloride, and was first used widely in the Second World War by the German army to counter fatigue among its troops on missions where little sleep was possible.

Mettoy (toys by *Mettoy* Playcraft) The name is an abbreviation of '*met*al *toy*', such toys being the company's original specialisation. Among the firm's best known toys are the *Corgi* range.

MG (car) The initials stand for *M*orris *G*arages. In these garages, set up by William Morris (later Lord Nuffield) in Cowley, near Oxford, as a retail outlet for the cars that bore his name, the manager was Cecil Kimber. Kimber began rebodying standard Morris models in 1922 and gradually established the *MG*. (The first models were named 'M.G. Super Sports' and were modified Morris Oxfords.) In 1929 *MG* had outgrown its premises and so moved to nearby Abingdon, where the first of a long line of *MG* Midgets were produced. This car, the first cheap and practical sports car, had a name that in turn, perhaps coincidentally, reflected the company name since 'Midget' contains both 'M' and 'G'. In 1961 the company produced the best-selling sports car, the MGB, with the 'B' of the name for BMC (the British Motor Corporation), of which MG was by then a part. In 1968 *MG* became part of British Leyland (see *BL*). (The early *MG*s had an MG registration, although this actually emanated from a London licensing authority, not an Oxford one.) In 1980, however, *MG* ended production of the famous car when bids by a consortium led by *Aston-Martin* to save it failed. Even so, the name was revived by *BL* in 1982.

Milk of Magnesia (antacid medicine by Sterling Health Products)   The name was registered in the *Trade Marks Journal* in 1880 by Charles Henry Phillips, a manufacturing chemist of New York. *Milk of Magnesia* is a homely name for a white suspension of *magnesium* hydroxide in water.

Milo (milk drink by The Nestlé Co.)   Although suggesting 'milk', the name is in fact that of a famous Greek athlete in classical times. *Milo*'s claim to fame is that he apparently carried a four-year-old bullock for 40 yards or more, then killed it and ate it in one day. On another occasion it was recorded that he supported the roof of a collapsing building in which Pythagoras was teaching, thus enabling the learned mathematician to escape. (The Greek sculpture known as the *Venus de Milo* in the Louvre, Paris, is nothing to do with this Milo. The statue was found in 1820 on the island of Melos, the French for which is *Milo*. Even so, the classical association may help the *Nestlé* product.)

Milton (antiseptic fluid by Richardson-Merrell)   The only association seems to be with the poet Milton – hardly likely for a medical commercial product. Yet apparently the original inventor of *Milton* in the early twentieth century was actually reading the poet at the time of his invention!

mimeograph (duplicating machine for producing copies from a stencil)   The name was first used in 1889 for a duplicator invented by Thomas Edison in association with Albert Dick, a lumberman. Its origin lies in the Greek words for 'imitate' (as in 'mime') and 'writing' (as in 'telegraph'). The name became generic in 1948.

Mini (car by Austin Morris)   The famous little *Mini* car has changed its management several times. First produced in 1959 by Austin, it later belonged to Morris, BMC, British Leyland, Leyland Cars, *BL*, *BL* Cars and eventually Austin Morris. It was the first of a range so called, and doubtless the actual name *Mini* contributed to the fashion for 'mini-' things (as *mini*cabs and *mini*skirts) in the 1960s. In 1978 Austin Morris held a naming contest within the company for a new *Mini* launched in October 1980. The choice was

122

between '*Mini* Maestro', '*Mini* Metro', and '*Mini* Match', which were the eventual shortlisted names from an original list of 8,500 names, including 'Mini-Two', 'Maxim' and 'Mini-Mite'. The winner, by a close head, was '*Mini* Metro', for which name there were 8,599 votes. ('*Mini* Maestro' received 8,332 votes and '*Mini* Match' only 2,793.) John Murphy, head of Novamark International, the London trade name creators, saw the name Metro as rather 'towny' for a car that was designed to be more than just a town car.

Minimax (fire extinguishers by Chubb & Son)   The origin is obvious, but what was the precise indication intended in the name? '*Mini*mum' trouble but '*max*imum' efficiency? '*Mini*mal' size but '*max*imum' effectiveness? Or perhaps there is some other derivation after all?

Minolta (cameras by *Minolta* Camera Co.)   The name is an acronym, deriving from '*ma*chine', '*in*strument', '*optical*', and *Ta*jima, the latter being the name (Tajima Shoten) of a Japanese wholesale firm dealing in silk fabrics run by the father of Kazuo Tashima, the founder of the *Minolta* Camera Co. An involved name, therefore, but a reasonably mellifluous one.

Mirro (cleaning powder by Procter & Gamble)   A well-known name with a well-known suffix. The basis of the name must be 'mirror', which in fact already contains the 'o' that is this suffix. The name itself is today much less apt than it was when the product was first marketed, since many modern cooking utensils either need no scouring or are coated with a special 'non-cleanable' surface anyway.

Mr Kipling (cakes by Manor Bakeries)   The name was one that was found to have the 'right consumer associations'. There was no real Mr Kipling to lend his name to the cakes that were first sold in the late 1960s. *Mr Kipling* was created as a 'master baker' who baked traditional-style cakes having a home-made appearance. One obvious association is of course with Rudyard Kipling, but such a connection, it seems, is merely a coincidence. Doubtless the actual sound of the name, beginning with the high-value 'K', prompted the choice – it actually sounds something like 'cake' and 'cooking', and suggests a simulated action ('kipling') of a succulent baking process. Manor Bakeries are a company set up by Ranks *Hovis* McDougall to manufacture and market the *Mr Kipling* range of cakes.

Mitsubishi (car and manufacturer)   The Japanese name basically

123

means 'three diamonds' (i.e. three rhombus shapes), this suggesting
three actual diamonds and giving the company's symbol of three
equilaterally placed diamond shapes. The business originated as a
local shipping service in 1870 named Tsukumo Shokai. After a
series of name changes (Mitsukawa Shokai, *Mitsubishi* Shokai, *Mitsubishi* Kisen Kaisha, Yuben Kisen *Mitsubishi* Kaisha) and a merger
with Kyodo Unyu (as Nippon Yusen Kaisha) the Mitsubishi company was established in 1836.

Mobil (petroleum products by *Mobil* Oil Co.)   The American trade
name began its life in England, where 'Mobiloil' was known to have
been available in 1899. Records regarding the etymological origin
of the name are vague but the source would seem to be 'mobile'
(or perhaps some Latin word denoting moving, as *mobilis*, 'easy to
move'). The 'mobility' applied to the new horseless carriages, which
the product lubricated. Mobiloil was registered as a trade mark for
lubricating oils in the United States in 1920. In England the name
Mobil was registered for lubricants at least as early as 1954, with
Mobiloil having been registered for lubricating oils in the United
Kingdom in 1924. Although *Mobil* is available in Mobile, Alabama,
there is no connection between the two names: the city was named
for an Indian tribe (whose own name apparently meant 'canoe
paddler').

Mogadon (tranquilliser and sedative drug by Roche Laboratories)   Like *Librium* and *Valium*, the name is an arbitrary one, with
no specific meaning. It was first registered in Britain in 1956. Like
all arbitrary names, however, it's bound to have associations, helpful or otherwise, with standard words and names. In this case it
suggests either 'moggy' (a cat) or, more exotically, the Moroccan
city of Mogador (now Essaouira). But perhaps cats and dreams of
a warm seaside city are suitable associations for a drug that assists
the restless to sleep at night.

Monkey Brand (scouring soap by *Unilever*)   The name – and the
soap – was introduced in 1899. William Lever acquired it by purchasing the American soap firm of Benjamin Brooke & Co. of
Philadelphia. The 'monkey' image of the soap was presumably to
arrest attention. Early advertisements showed a clothed monkey
seated by the roadside in the guise of a pavement artist, holding
out a frying pan for 'My Own Work'. (Packets of the soap itself
showed a monkey admiring its reflection in a brightly scoured pan
– undoubtedly one scoured with *Monkey Brand* soap.) An early verse
of doggerel likewise promoted the creature, whose advertisement
was designed by one G.E. Robinson in 1901:

124

In costume quaint, with pan in hand,
He would appear in antic pose,
And sing the praise of Monkey Brand,
That brightens homes, but *Won't Wash Clothes*!

Monkey Brand produced two offspring: 'Refined Toilet Monkey Brand' (which could even be used 'occasionally' as a dentifrice), and *Vim*, which went on the market in 1904.

Monotype (printing machine and manufacturer)   The *Monotype* machine, used in printing, produces *type* in individual characters (i.e. 'mono' or single characters). These characters are built up one by one until a line is completed. The name dates back to at least 1893, when the machine belonged to the Lanston *Monotype* Machine Co. of Washington, DC. In this year it was on display at the World's Columbian Exposition in Chicago, held to mark the 400th anniversary of the discovery of America.

Morgan Crucible (industrial materials and components and manufacturer)   The business was founded in 1856 by five Morgan Brothers, with the last member of the family to work in the company being Lord Reigate (John Vaughan-Morgan), born 1905. The company's first principal products were *crucibles* (refractory ceramic pots for melting metal in a furnace) for its non-ferrous foundries, and although it now produces a wide range of industrial products, the company is still the largest producer of foundry crucibles in the world.

Moskvich (car by AZLK)   The name of the Russian car means 'Muscovite'. The works that produces it was known until 1969 as the MZMA, initials standing for the Russian words for 'Moscow Factory of Small Cylinder Capacity Automobiles'. Since 1969 the works has been known as the AZLK, or 'Moscow Automobile Factory Named for the Lenin Komsomol'. The *Moskvich*, which is based on the *Opel Kadett*, was first mass produced in 1947.

Mothaks (moth repellent by Thompson & Capper)   The suffix of the name is interesting, and presumably is a variant of '-ex'. Perhaps 'Mothex' as a name was already registered? Or possibly the suffix was deliberately chosen to suggest 'axe'? The product would thus be one that fells or 'axes' moths – a powerful and attractive image!

Motobécane (mopeds and manufacturer)   The name derives from the two French slang words *moto*, 'motorcycle', and *bécane*, 'bike'. The firm of this name was established, as was Motoconfort, in the

1920s. In 1930 the two companies combined as *Motobécane* and became the world's largest manufacturer of mopeds and bicycles. In 1949 the firm launched its well-known *Mobylette* moped, whose name suggests a small (or feminine) motorbike while hinting also at the company name.

Moussec (sparkling wine by Reckitt & Colman)   The name seems to be a combination of French *mousse*, 'froth', and *sec*, 'dry'. These words in turn suggest terms applied to vintage wines, as *mousseux*, 'sparkling', and *sec*, 'dry' (but of champagne meaning 'of medium sweetness'). *Moussec* is commonly regarded as a champagne substitute but officially is a 'British sparkling wine'.

Mu-cron (nasal decongestant by International Laboratories)   The name is based on '*mucu*s', 'ch*r*onic', and 'de*con*gestant'. It was first registered in Britain in 1959.

Mum (deodorant by Bristol-Myers)   Presumably the name points to 'mum' (suitable for mothers) and 'keep mum' (will keep secret any body odour).

Muzak (system of piped music by Rediffusion)   The name was first registered in the *Trade Marks Journal* in 1938. It was devised, apparently, by combining *Kodak*, one of the best-known trade names of the day, and 'music'.

Nabisco (cereal foods, cake mixes and biscuits and manufacturer)   The name is an acronym of *N*ational *Bis*cuit *Co*-pany. This was formed in the United States in 1898 and the name *Nabisco* was first registered there in 1901. In 1971 the official company name was changed to *Nabisco* Inc. In Britain *Nabisco* Foods Ltd was the name assumed in 1956 by the *Shredded Wheat* Co.

Nardil (anti-depressant drug by William R. Warner & Co.)   The name is a random one, having no special significance. Nevertheless, it suggests either some kind of flower (a combination of a narcissus and a daffodil?) or some creature in an SF story. There could perhaps be an association with some sort of mystic force here (flower power?) which might be appropriate for the product. Internationally it is a good name to pronounce and remember.

126

Nationwide (building society) The society was formed in 1884 and was originally named the Co-operative Permanent Building Society. Because of muddled associations with the Co-operative Society, however, and uncertainty among members of the public with regard to the society's business policies, including doubt whether its services were available to everyone or not, the name was changed in 1970 to *Nationwide*. This new name was intended to emphasise the unrestricted nature of the society's savings and mortgage services.

Nembutal (hypnotic and sedative drug by Abbott Laboratories) This drug name is not an arbitrary one, as many are, but derives from the original chemical name of the substance: *n-e*thyl-*m*ethyl-*buto*barbitone. The suffix '-al' was allocated in the United States to denote a barbiturate (as in Veron*al*). The drug addict's slang term for it is 'nembie' or 'nebbie'. *Nembutal* was introduced to medicine in 1930.

NESCAFÉ **Nescafé** (instant coffee by The *Nestlé* Co.) *Nescafé* was the first brand of instant coffee, made in Vevey, Switzerland, in 1938 after eight years of research. Its name is a blend of *Nestlé* and the French for 'coffee', *café*.

Nestlé **Nestlé** (food products and manufacturer) In spite of the cosy, homely suggestion of 'nestle' and 'nestling' – an association put to pictorial use on the product labels – the name is the surname of the founder of the business in Switzerland in 1866, Henri Nestlé. In English-speaking countries the name is pronounced 'nestle'.

Nikon (cameras and photographic equipment and manufacturer) The name originates from the optical company founded in Japan in 1917, Nippon Kogaku KK. In 1932 this company produced camera lenses named Nikkor, and in 1948 its first 35mm camera named *Nikon*. From 1959 Nippon Kogaju became increasingly known throughout the world by this abbreviated name, formed from letters of its original name, which is still its official title (which means simply 'Japan optics company').

Nivea (skin cream by Smith and Nephew) The name originated in Germany with a company called Beirsdorf who manufactured the original cream. *Nivea* would appear to be based as a name on the Latin for 'snowy', *niveus*, feminine *nivea*, referring to the coolness of the cream and especially its ability to keep the skin snowy white. Beirsdorf also set up a factory in England to make *Nivea*, with the company name being diplomatically changed in the Second World

127

War to Herts Pharmaceuticals Ltd. Subsequently, the firm was acquired by Smith and Nephew (makers of *Elastoplast*) who continue to market *Nivea* under the company name of *Nivea* Toiletries.

No Name (tobacco by John Player)   The tobacco was originally blended and manufactured from an old recipe for the sole use of a director of the Imperial Tobacco Co. The unusual name derives from the fact that originally *no name* or publicity were given to the tobacco, but a demand for it prompted its devotees to style it themselves – as *No Name*.

Norvic (shoes by Norvic Securities)   The name is based on the Latin *Norvicensis*, 'of Norwich', in standard abbreviated form. The firm's headquarters are at Norwich, where the company was founded in 1846.

Novocain (local anaesthetic drug by *Hoechst*)   The drug was perfected by Alfred Einhorn and first registered as a trade mark in 1905. The name derives from Latin *novo-*, 'new' and 'co*caine*' – although it is actually a form of procaine, not cocaine. The word is sometimes spelt with a small 'n' and with a final 'e'.

NSU (cars and manufacturer)   The typically English abbreviation (suggesting National Students Union or some organisation on similar lines) actually comes from the German town of *N*eckars*u*lm, south of Stuttgart, where a firm was set up in 1873 to make knitting machines. The first *NSU* car was built in 1906. This was the Pipe, made under licence from Belgium. Today the company, *NSU* Motorenwerke AG, still offers a car of foreign origin as well as its own designs, with the model under licence now from *Fiat*.

nylon (synthetic plastic fibre)   Here is one of the most famous and interesting trade names of all: not a trade mark, yet protected by patent; having no significance, yet thought by many to have a definite meaning; a unique word, yet itself producing many similar names. The word was coined in 1938 by the Du Pont company as a generic name. The letters of the name are stated to have no significance, etymologically or otherwise, yet there must even so be a link with *rayon*, which predated it. There would also seem to be an even more basic link with the word 'cott*on*'. The Du Pont archives reveal that other names were suggested for the new manmade fibre, among them such contrived proposals as 'Duparooh' (from '*Du P*ont pulls *a* rabbit *o*ut *o*f a *h*at'). Many attempts have been made to explain the 'nyl-' element, the most common being

128

that these letters derive from *N*ew *Y*ork and *Lon*don. (One outlandish and mildly outrageous explanation of these letters was that they derive from an exclamation made by one of the chemists working on the product – '*N*ow, *y*ou, *l*ousy *o*ld *N*ipponese!') The official chemical name for *nylon* is polyhexamethyleneadipamide, referred to as polymide. The material exists under various trade names, among them American Anzo, Caproian, Crepeset, *Enkalon*, Shareen, Antron, Cordura, Nomex, Astroturf, Ultron, and Ayrlyn, and British *Bri-Nylon* and Celon. The name itself has spawned *Dacron, Orlon, Dralon*, French Crépon, East German Dederon, and Russion kapron, ilon, and meron. (Some of these are registered trade marks, as *Orlon* and *Dacron*.) In spite of the arbitrary nature of the letters 'nyl-' they do in fact suggest 'vinyl' – although there is no vinyl in *nylon*. The most popular use of the name was in the 'nylons' that were stockings made of *nylon* and a prized luxury in the Second World War.

O'Cedar (polish by The *Prestige* Group)   Presumably the name is meant to suggest a polish that gives a shine like that of cedar wood ('o'cedar'), this particular wood being chosen not only for its sheen and 'classiness' – it is used for cabinet-making as well as for building – but also for its fragrance. The polish, thus, will give the wood to which it is applied an image of 'looks good, smells good, *is* good'!

Odeon (cinemas by The Rank Organisation)   The business of *Odeon* Theatres Ltd was founded in 1933 (the first *Odeon* cinema was opened in Birmingham this year also) by Oscar Deutsch. Deutsch apparently chose the name because not only was it the Greek word for 'theatre' (in Greek *oideion*) but it also reflected his own initials. This original company assumed the name of *Odeon* Cinematograph Holdings Ltd, and in 1937 a new company of *Odeon* Theatres Ltd was formed. This was forerunner of The Rank Organisation (named after Lord Rank who acquired control of *Odeon* Theatres in 1941). The name is equally famous, but for different reasons, in Paris, where in 1797 the *Odeon* Theatre (*théâtre de l'Odéon*) was founded on the site of a monument to the original Greek theatre built in Athens for musical competitions. It was this Paris theatre that in turn gave its name to *Odeon* records, which were produced from 1903 by the International Talking Machine Co.

Odo-Ro-No (deodorant by *Colgate-Palmolive*)   A name that is both a fairly playful pun ('odour? oh no!') and at the same time suggestive of the nature of the product (a deodorant).

OK (sauce by Reckitt & Colman)   The name would appear to be simply recommendatory – the product was (and is) 'OK'. But perhaps the letters originally stood for something else, or at least hinted at other words?

Oldsmobile (car by General Motors)   On the face of it an unhelpful name for a new car. It derives, however, from the name of its creator, Ransom Eli Olds, who first produced his famous 'curved dash' runabout car in 1901. Olds was the American president of the Reo Motor Car Co. from 1904 to 1924, with this company's name (and that of its cars) deriving from his initials.

OMEGA **Omega** (watches by SSIH (UK))   The name was the code name for a new design of watch movement produced in 1894 by Louis Brandt et Fils, the founders of the Swiss company which became *Omega*. The name is a more or less standard prestige one, having classical connotations and perhaps, as the last letter of the Greek alphabet, suggesting a product that is the 'last word' in technology or progress.

Omo (detergent powder by *Unilever*)   The name was first registered in 1908, originally for a water softener. It seems to be quite arbitrary, formed from letters of the alphabet that in this combination produce a memorable shape. In his book *The Naked Ape*, Desmond Morris points out that the word is a 'threat-face brand name' that catches the eye. (The two 'Os' represent eyes, and the central 'M' a hooked nose or beak.) Possible associations with 'homo(sexual)' do not appear to have adversely affected the name or the marketability of the product, since there is no obvious link between the sexual proclivity and the washing powder that was introduced in 1954.

Opel (car by General Motors)   Just as the name *NSU* first appeared on knitting machines, so *Opel* was first to be seen on sewing machines – although somewhat earlier, in 1862. The first car of the name was produced in 1898. Adam Opel was a German engineer who founded the firm that began with sewing machines and went on to produce bicycles, refrigerators, air compressors and . . . the *Opel* car, whose name coincidentally but agreeably suggests 'opal' and even 'pearl'. The company was taken over in 1929 by General Motors.

130

Optrex (eye lotion and manufacturer)   The '*opt*ical' connection is the obvious one, with the standard trade name suffix '-ex'. Perhaps the French origin of the name accounts for the added letter 'r' (or possibly a name such as 'Optex' was already registered). The preparation was initially introduced in France in 1928 by a M. Rosengart, who was the poor-sighted son-in-law of M. *Famel*. *Optrex* was first registered as a name in Britain in 1931.

Orlon (acrylic fibre by du Pont de Nemours)   Like *Dacron*, the name seems to be arbitrary, with, however, the '-lon' no doubt deriving from *nylon*. The name has been used as a racehorse name, since it punningly suggests a winner ('all on' to win).

Osmiroid (pens by E.S. Perry)   The name suggests 'osmosis', perhaps with reference to the manner in which the ink passes through to the nib. The manufacturing company's chairman Mr G.W. Nockolds denies this connection, however, and gives the derivation of the name from another trade name used by the company, 'Iridinoid'. This itself is based on 'iridium', the metal frequently used in the small ball that is welded on to the end of a nib. *Osmiroid* is based on the name of a metal whose chemical and physical properties are very similar to iridium – *osm*ium. Even closer to the trade name is the alloy of osmium and iridium called *osmir*idium. The '-oid' suffix indicates a kinship or similarity, as with *celluloid* (like cellulose). For a similar name compare *Platignum*.

Ostermilk (milk preparation for babies by Farley Health Products)   Dried milk was first introduced into Britain in 1904 by *Glaxo*, who four years later booked an advertisement to promote their product on the entire front page of the *Daily Mail* (27 May 1908). In 1929 *Glaxo* changed the name of their dried milk to *Ostermilk* to denote the addition of 'Ostelin', a *Glaxo* vitamin D product (now no longer manufactured in Britain) whose own name presumably derives from *osteo-*, the Greek element meaning 'bone'.

Ovaltine (malt food drink by Wander)   The product was first launched in the nineteenth century in Berne, Switzerland, by Dr George Wander. It was originally marketed as 'Ovomaltine', the name consisting of a Latin element meaning 'egg' (*ovum*) – compare *ab ovo*, 'from the egg' – plus 'malt' and the suffix '-ine'. This name, however, proved difficult to register in Britain, so it was shortened to *Ovaltine*. In 1935 the 'Ovaltiney Club' was first promoted on Radio Luxembourg. This was a 'secret society' for children, with its own badges, rule books and secret codes, and even produced its own comics, the *Chuckler* and the *Dazzler*. The club's song, *We are*

131

the Ovaltineys became one of the most popular of pre-war jingles, and by 1939 there were an incredible 5 million active members. The regular Sunday evening programmes came to a halt when Radio Luxembourg closed down at the outbreak of the Second World War, but started up again in 1946, to continue for a number of years. (Wander Ltd, who still produce *Ovaltine*, incorporated the *We are the Ovaltineys* song in their TV commercials for the product in 1975 and again in 1980.)

Owl (pen nib by Macniven & Cameron)   see **Pickwick**

Oxo (beef extract by *Brooke Bond Oxo*)   Whether suggesting noughts-and-crosses or a 'threat-face brand name' (as Desmond Morris sees it – see the similar *Omo*), *Oxo* must be one of the neatest and aesthetically most satisfying of all trade names by its mere appearance. Its origin as a word is fairly transparent, from 'ox' with the popular nineteenth-century suffix '-o'. *Oxo* was registered as a name in 1899, having apparently originated as a semi-serious abbreviation for dried meat in granular form that was being exported to Europe from *Fray Bentos*. (*Oxo* itself was a development of Liebig's 'Extract of Meat', which was first produced in 1847 in Munich as 'extractum carnis' by the German chemist, Justus von Liebig.)

Oxydol (washing powder by Procter & Gamble)   The obvious association is with 'oxygen', thus with purity and freshness. The '-ol' suffix usually means 'oil', which does not seem appropriate here. Perhaps the name as a whole derives from some chemical, as 'eth*oxy*lat*ed* alcoh*ol* sulphate', a foaming agent used in liquid detergents. Or, more generally, the reference may be to an *oxid*ising bleach for whitening and cleaning fabrics. *Oxydol* was withdrawn in 1973 after 42 years on the market.

Ozalid (drawing office equipment and materials and manufacturer)   The name derives from one of the company's products, coated materials. The precise origin is in the diazo-sensitised coating applied to paper and film for use in drawing-office print-rooms: *Ozalid* is 'diazo' reversed with the letter 'l' inserted. The first rolls of *Ozalid* paper were manufactured in 1926. In 1976 *Ozalid* (UK) Ltd was formed as a result of the merger between *Ozalid* Co and Nig *Banda*. The name has generally suitable chemical associations, suggesting 'ozone', 'oxalic' and similar words.

Palitoy (toys by General Mills UK)   The name nicely conjures up 'pally toys' but in fact derives from the founder of the company A.E. Pallett. When application was first made to register the name around 1934, however, permission was refused on the grounds that there was a remote Indian village called Pali and that '*Palitoy*' could be taken to mean that the toys were actually made in this village. Even so, the company persisted in its use of the (unregistered) name so that in about 1939 they were actually allowed to register it.

Palmolive (soap and toiletries by *Colgate-Palmolive*)   The name derives from the palm and olive oils contained in the soap first manufactured in Milwaukee in 1898 by the soapmaker B.J. Johnson. (Palm oil from the flesh of palm fruits was used for slow lathering soaps; oil from the nut of the palm fruit gave the kernel fat for quick lathering soaps.) Olive oil was used for 'soft' soaps. The original business of *Colgate-Palmolive* was founded in 1806 by William Colgate, an English-born soap manufacturer who was brought to America as a child. His grandson, Samuel Morse Colgate (1862–1930), became chairman of the consolidated *Colgate-Palmolive*-Peet Co. The full name was the result of the merger after the First World War of the three soap businesses: those of William *Colgate*, B.J. Johnson, and the Peet Brothers.

Pan (books by *Pan* Books)   The ultimate origin of the name is the Greek mythological god Pan. Towards the end of the Second World War the English writer and illustrator, Mervyn Peake, gave a small pen-and-ink drawing of the god Pan to Alan Bott, the managing director of the Book Society and the Reprint Society. Bott was at the time thinking of starting a paperback publishing company as soon as the war was over but was stuck for a suitable name. He did not want to have a bird (because of *Penguin*) or an animal (because of the American kangaroo logo for Pocket Books), so had to try elsewhere. Sitting at his desk and pondering on the problem he found himself gazing at Mervyn Peake's little picture – and there, in the god *Pan*, was the name he had been seeking. *Pan* Books were actually founded in 1944.

Panadeine Co (analgesic tablets by Winthrop Laboratories)   The tablets comprise a combination of *Panado*l, Winthrop's brand name for paracetamol, introduced by them in the late 1950s, and cod*eine*.

The detached suffix 'Co' stands not for 'company', as in many trade names, but for chemists' Latin *compositus*, 'compound'.

Panasonic (electrical products by *Matsushita*)   see **Matsushita**

Pan Yan (pickle by Rowntree Mackintosh)   The name, in spite of its oriental look, has no actual meaning. It was chosen as the result of a competition among the employees of a London-based food manufacturer, Maconochie Brothers, in 1907. Rowntree Mackintosh acquired this company in 1967.

Parker Knoll (chairs and settees by *Parker Knoll* Furniture)   The name is a combination of the surnames of a German furniture manufacturer, Willi Knoll, and an English counterpart, Tom Parker. Willi Knoll came to England in 1930 to find a British manufacturer to take up his method of springing chairs by means of horizontal steel tension springing. Tom Parker was by chance visiting Heal & Sons of Tottenham Court Road, London one day when he saw a sample chair frame that had been submitted to Heals by Knoll. Tom Parker admired the new springing method, and sought out the maker, Willi Knoll, at the latter's London hotel. A few days later an agreement had been made between the two men for Tom Parker's firm of Frederick Parker & Sons to begin production of such chairs under the combined name of *Parker Knoll*.

Parkray (heating equipment by TI *Parkray*)   The name is a blend of The *Park* Foundry (Belper) Ltd, who actually manufactured the convector open fire of this name that was launched in 1953, and this firm's parent company, the *Ra*diation Ltd Group. The second half of the name also, of course, suggests 'ray'. The name of the manufacturing company was changed to Radiation *Parkray* Ltd in 1961, becoming just *Parkray* Ltd in 1972, and finally, to reflect the link with the company's new holding company, Tube Investments, TI *Parkray* Ltd in 1977.

Parozone (household bleach by Jeyes Group)   The name was originally that of the manufacturers, the *Parozone* Co., now part of the Jeyes Group. The company was incorporated shortly after 1900 with a name designed to have connotations of good health and cleanliness, with the two elements of the name, 'par ozone', presumably suggesting a meaning of 'by the sea'. Certainly both the sea and bleach have a common link in chlorine.

Passat (car by *Volkswagen* (GB))   Like the *Scirocco*, the name is that of a wind. The word is German for 'trade wind', and is sufficiently

134

unfamiliar in English to make the name meaningless. This is hardly the hallmark of a good trade name.

Paxo (stuffing by RHM Foods)   Suggestions have been made that the name is somehow linked with the French word for 'Easter', *Pâques*, or the Latin for 'peace', *pax*. This seems rather unlikely, however, so perhaps the simplest bet is a derivation from English 'packs'? The best kind of stuffing must be one that 'packs' well.

Peacock see **Penguin**

Pelican see **Penguin**

Penguin (paperback books by *Penguin* Books)   The name is said to have come from a suggestion made by the secretary of the firm's founder in 1935, Allen Lane. 'Why not Penguins?', she said, when Lane was still stuck for a name, and he thereupon sent his office boy off to get one drawn. (*The Shell Book of Firsts* quotes Sir Allen Lane as choosing the *Penguin* device because it 'had an air of dignified flippancy and was easy to draw in black and white'.) Two years later Allen Lane was standing by a main-line station bookstall when he heard someone ask for a 'Pelican' book. Alarmed at the prospect of a close rival so named he decided to issue *Pelicans* himself. Afterwards came other paperbacks named for birds beginning with 'P': *Puffins*, *Ptarmigans* (no longer published) and, more recently, *Peregrine* and *Peacock* books. (That 'paperback' also begins with 'p' is an added link.) When *Penguin* Books merged with Longman in 1970 they renamed Longman Young Books also with a bird's name but not one beginning with 'p', as they were not paperbacks. Thus *Kestrels* originated.

Pentel (fibre-tip pen by Japan Stationery Co.)   The pen was the first fibre-tip type, marketed in 1960. The first half of the name is obvious; the second half presumably has its derivation but this is not immediately apparent.

Pepsi-Cola (cola drink by Cadbury *Schweppes*)   The second half of the name is not a registered trade mark (see *Coca-Cola*). The name as a whole was devised in 1898 by Caleb D. Bradham, a drugstore manager in New Bern, North Carolina. His new elixir was patterned after *Coca-Cola* and was intended to relieve dys*pepsi*a – hence the name.

Pepsodent (toothpaste by *Elida* Gibbs)   The name is reasonably transparent, originating from '*pep*permint' (not, presumably, '*pep*-

135

*s*in') and the Latin 'tooth' element found in '*dentist*'. The *Pepsodent* Co. originated in the USA and was acquired by *Unilever* in 1944.

Peregrine see **Penguin**

Permutit (water-softening systems by *Permutit*-Boby)   The obvious derivation would seem to be a word such as 'permutation'. This is not exactly how the name originated, however. It began as a trade name used by United Water Softeners Ltd who changed their company name to *Permutit* in 1937. The name itself is based on Latin *permutare*, 'to exchange', and refers to the basic chemical action involved in the process of water softening, that of ion exchange – the exchange or conversion of alkalis and acids that occurs in the presence of certain porous materials. The '-it' ending of the name is not a Latin verbal ending appropriate for this particular word – 'he (or it) exchanges', for example, would be *permutat*. The *Permutit* Co. merged with William Boby & Co., also producing water-softening equipment, in 1974 to become *Permutit*-Boby.

Persil (washing powder by *Unilever*)   The name is French for 'parsley'. A sprig of parsley was the trade mark of a Frenchman named Ronchetti who learned how to add bleach to soap in 1907. However, the name may also have been devised to suggest '*per*borate' and '*sil*icate', two vital ingredients of the new discovery. *Persil* was the first household detergent, manufactured in Germany by Henkel & Co. of Düsseldorf in 1907 and by Joseph Crosfield at his factory in Warrington, Cheshire, in 1909. Crosfield named his new product 'the amazing oxygen washer', since it liberated free oxygen in use. *Persil* Automatic for use in washing machines was first marketed in 1968.

Perspex (transparent thermoplastic by ICI)   The name was registered by ICI in 1935 and is based on Latin *perspicere*, 'to look through' (with *perspexi* meaning 'I have looked through'). The substance was also manufactured in Germany by Röhm & Haas GmbH, who, however, registered it (also in 1935) under the name of Plexiglass, as which it is known today in the USA.

PG Tips (tea by *Brooke Bond Oxo*)   The initials derive from an earlier name, *Pre-Gestee*, in turn a variant of the original name, Digestive Tea. Digestive Tea was introduced in the 1940s as a counter to *Typhoo*, who in their advertising claimed that *Typhoo* aided digestion. The British wartime Ministry of Food asked both companies to drop the reference to a medicinal benefit and as a result *Brooke Bond* coined the name Pre-Gestee, which suggests that the tea could perhaps be drunk before food was digested, while at the same time retaining a link with the earlier Di*gest*ve Tea. Pre-Gestee, however, is a clumsy name, and soon grocers and van salesmen were abbreviating it to 'P.G.' The company adopted this as the new official name of the tea, adding 'Tips' to refer to the tips of the tea leaves that produced the blend's distinctive flavour. (Tea that contains a large proportion of the leaf-buds in this way is known by tea-blenders as 'tippy'.) The fact that 'tip' also suggests the 'peak' or best part of something helps to give the name an added prestige value. Even the use of initials can suggest an intimate acquaintance of something important (as 'the MD' or 'I'll have a word with J.B.'). *PG Tips* has become popularly associated with its 'chimps' tea-party' television commercials, the first of which appeared in Britain in 1956.

Phensic (analgesic preparation by Beecham Group)   The name seems to be based on one of the product's ingredients, '*phenac*etin'.

phonogram see **gramophone**

phonograph see **gramophone**

Phosferine (tonic by Beecham Group)   The product contains phosphoric acid, and this presumably explains the base of the name.

Photostat (photocopy)   The name is a registered trade mark, first originating about 1911. The '-stat' suffix is loosely based on Greek *statos*, 'stationary', the photocopy being a 'fixed' one of the original. More likely, however, the suffix was suggested by other scientific instruments and processes ending in '-stat', such as 'hydrostat' and 'thermostat'. The first such '-stat' appears to have been 'heliostat', a word first recorded in English in 1747 for a mirror turned by clockwork so as to reflect the light of the sun in a fixed direction, thus seeming to make the sun appear *stationary*. The name *Photostat* was sometimes used generically, but yielded after the Second World War to *Xerox*, also used as a general term (incorrectly).

Pianola (player piano)   The name is still a registered trade mark for a particular type of mechanical piano, although sometimes treated generically and spelled with a small letter. The instrument was patented by an American engineer, Edwin S. Votey, in 1897. Originally it was a 'push-up' device placed in front of a traditional keyboard. Later it was built into the action of a piano. The name seems to be a kind of mock-Italian diminutive of 'piano', on the lines of similar names ending in '-ola' (as *Victrola*). Other well-

137

known makes of player piano popular in the early twentieth century were the 'Ampico' (*A*merican *P*iano *Co*.) and 'Duo-Art'. The name has passed into the English language to mean 'easy task', but especially a bridge hand that needs no skill.

Pickwick (pen nib by Macniven & Cameron)   The lines 'They come as a boon and a blessing to men, The Pickwick, the Owl and the Waverley Pen' must be among the best known of all advertising jingles. As may be guessed, the firm that manufactured the *Pickwick*, *Owl* and *Waverley* pens was a Scottish one (indeed, as *Waverley* Cameron, still is). Messrs Macniven and Cameron established their business in Edinburgh in 1770. The first pen of the trio that they produced was the *Waverley* in 1863, at a time when the Waverley novels by Sir Walter Scott were popular. The *Pickwick* followed as another literary name – this time taken from Dickens's *Pickwick Papers*. The *Owl* is believed to owe its name to a contemporary literary magazine so called. During the Second World War an American service newsheet printed an up-dated version of the original advertising couplet: 'They come as a boon and blessing to men, The Blackout, The Torch and the cute little W.R.E.N.' (*Stars and Stripes* 4 October 1944.)

Pifco (electrical goods and manufacturer)   The name is an acronym for the original company founded by Joseph Webber in Manchester in 1900, the *P*rovincial *I*ncandescent *F*ittings *Co*mpany Ltd. This firm first made gas mantles before progressing to batteries and electric torches.

Plasticine (modelling material by Harbutt's *Plasticine*)   Yet one more name that is an actual registered trade mark yet frequently used generically and until recently even quoted in dictionaries with a small letter. The product was first manufactured by William Harbutt of Bath in 1897. The actual name derives from 'plastic' (in the 'moulding' sense, not the synthetic substance one) with the suffix '-ine' denoting either 'of the nature of' or a quasi-chemical material.

Platignum (pens by Mentmore Manufacturing Co.)   The name is, like *Osmiroid*, one that is suggestive of the metal used in the manufacture of nibs, in this case platinum.

Playtex (girdles and corsets and manufacturer)   The name seems to hint at two associations, '*play tex*ture' and 'latex'. The former points to the product's lightness and versatility – its wearer is free to play (or feel playful?) when wearing it. The latter association indicates the rubber material used in the manufacture of the product. (The combination of the two associations results in schoolgirl sniggers during geography lessons on rubber growing in South America.)

Plessey (telecommunications and electronics equipment and manufacturer) The name appeared for the first time in 1917 with a private company registered by a Mr Hurst Hodgson and a Mr W.O. Heyne. Among the original shareholders were two brothers, Raymond and *Plessey* Parker. The forename of the latter accounts for the company name, together with the coincidental fact that Mr Heyne's wife Elizabeth came from (or near) a village called *Plessey* in Northumberland. The name is a pleasant-sounding one (quite literally) and also has an agreeable French air. Indeed, the personal name and the place name may actually be of French origin.

Polaroid

Polaroid ('instant' cameras and manufacturer) The name ultimately derives from the trade name of a sheet material which *polar*ises light (because it is composed of long parallel molecules). *Polaroid*, however, is a trade name more popularly associated with the camera that uses a diffusion transfer process to produce finished photographs. This was the product of an American scientist Edwin Land – hence the full name of the camera, the *Polaroid* Land Camera, invented by him in 1947. *Polaroid* was founded in 1937. Dr Land stepped down after forty-three years as the company's chief executive officer in 1980.

Polo (peppermints by Rowntree Mackintosh) The suggestion of the name is an 'icy' or 'snowy' one suitable for a white peppermint (compare 'Fox's Glacier Mints'). The two 'Os' make the name visually attractive, and are reinforced by the well-known 'mint with a hole' catch phrase. There is an incidental prestige bonus in the association with the game of polo, implying that the mints are 'top-class' ones.

Polycell

Polycell (house decorating materials by *Polycell* Products) *Polycell* is the original name that produced *Polyfilla*, *Polystrippa* and many others. It was registered in 1953 and the word is based on the type of material in the product. This was sodium carboxy-methyl cellulose which consists of long chain molecules of cellulose, i.e. many cellulose units, or *Polycell* (*poly-* being the Greek element for 'many', as in 'polytechnic', a college that teaches many different technical subjects). The name *Polyfilla* (a *Polycell* 'filler') was registered in 1956. In Germany it is marketed as Moltofill and in Holland as Alabastine. Polyclens, a brush stripper, was registered in 1956,

139

Polypeel, for stripping wallpaper, in 1957, Polystrippa, a paint stripper, in 1958, Polyfix, for fixing ceramic tiles, in 1961, Polygrout, for grouting ceramic tiles (finishing them with a thin fluid mortar), in 1962, and Polytex, for renovating ceilings in 1974.

Polyfilla (wall-cavity filler by *Polycell* Products)   see **Polycell**

Pomagne (sparkling cider by Bulmer HP)   There is a similarity between this name and *Moussec* (perhaps intentionally?). *Pomagne* presumably derives from a combination of French *pommes*, 'apples', the product's basic ingredients, and 'champ*agne*'. Perhaps, too, the resemblance of the name to 'pomade', an elegant dressing for the hair to make it shine, is also deliberate? *Pomagne* is also a name that is nicely complementary to *Babycham*, since between them they give 'champagne'!

Pontiac (car by General Motors)   The name is that of the city in Michigan which was promoted by the *Pontiac* Co., itself founded in Detroit in 1818. Both city and company took their name from the Indian chief of the Ottawa tribe who in the two years of what became known as 'Pontiac's War' (1763–4) raised the whole western frontier against the British. He was defeated, however, since he did not win the support of the French, on which he had been counting. The *Pontiac* Co. began by manufacturing wagons, but in 1907 produced its first car, initially called the 'Oakland' for the county of which *Pontiac* city is the seat. In 1926 General Motors introduced a new car to their range of inexpensive, popular ranges and named it the *Pontiac*. The car was a six-cylinder one, which explains the legend that appears on the car's emblem below a head of *Pontiac* himself: 'Chief of the Sixes'.

Pony (barley wine by The Guernsey Brewery Co.)   The name was given by a founder director of the company who was an officer in the Hussars and a keen polo player.

Porsche (car and manufacturer)   The famous German sports car is named after Ferry Porsche, son of the Austrian designer, Ferdinand Porsche, who in the 1930s had been responsible for the *Volkswagen*. Ferry Porsche developed the sports car named after him from the *Volkswagen* design.

Post Toasties (breakfast cereal by General Foods)   In 1904 Charles William Post, who earlier had produced *Postum* cereal and *Grape Nuts*, came out with a brand of cornflakes named 'Elijah's Manna'. People liked the taste of the product, but not its name.

Indeed, when Post tried three years later to export the flakes to Britain the British government refused to allow the registration of such an esoteric trade mark. Post was therefore obliged to rechristen his products, and he thus called it *Post Toasties* – a name that, not just on religious grounds, must be seen to be much more effective.

Postum (cereal products by General Foods)   The name was first used for a 'food drink' (a cereal beverage) developed by the American, Charles William Post, while convalescing from a serious illness in 1894. Post soon started his own company, *Postum* Cereal Co., to manufacture other types of cereal, including *Post Toasties* and, in 1911, *Instant Postum*, a cereal-based night drink designed for people who could not, or did not like to, drink tea or coffee. Post died in 1914. In 1922 the name of his firm was changed to *Postum* Cereal Co. and seven years later the company became part of the newly formed General Foods Corporation. The '-um' ending seems to be an arbitrary suffix, perhaps meant to have classical associations (as in 'nostrum').

Pozidriv (machine screws by Linread)   The origin of the name is almost certainly '*po*sitive *driv*e'. The distinctive cross-shaped *Pozidriv* recess superseded the original Phillips recess, with patents for both being the property of the American company, Phillips International. The *Pozidriv* recess has now, in turn, been superseded by the Supadriv, a name of obvious meaning and the property of the engineering company, Guest, Keen & Nettlefolds.

Prestcold (refrigerators and manufacturer)   The company of this name was formed in 1934 as a division of the then Pressed Steel Co. (now Pressed Steel Fisher, the car body division of *BL*). Pressed Steel Co. pioneered the all-steel car body in Britain, borrowing their technique from an American company, E.G. Budd of Philadelphia. In the late 1930s Pressed Steel felt that they were well placed and well equipped to move into the growing market for domestic refrigerators: if they could press car-body panels, they could surely press the square cases of a refrigerator cabinet. The company therefore set up a production line at its headquarters at Cowley, Oxford, to make refrigerators, and named them *Prestcold*, this being a blend of *Pressed* Steel and 'cold'. Pressed Steel is still part of *BL*, but now manufactures only refrigeration compressors. For an apparently contradictory trade name for refrigerators, compare *Hotpoint*.

Prestige (kitchenware by The *Prestige* Group)   More than obviously a prestige name! The precise motivation for the name is not known.

141

Primus (oil stoves by Bahco Tools) The stove named 'Primus' was invented in Sweden at the end of the nineteenth century by a workman, F.W. Lindqvist. In 1889 a Mr B.A. Hjorth opened a tool and engineering shop in Stockholm and acquired the exclusive rights for the sale of Lindqvist's *Primus* stove. Then, in 1893, a young man named Soeren Condrup, a partner in a British firm, was on holiday with his wife in Norway and noticed Lindqvist's *Primus* stove in a shop. He was impressed with it, ordered 100 stoves, and with his partner secured the rights to act as sole selling agents for *Primus* stoves in the United Kingdom. (The initials of B.A. Hjorth and the first two letters of Condrup's name give the name of the present manufacturers, Bahco.) *Primus* is Latin for 'first', and the *Primus* stove was in fact the first practical wickless stove. The name is also, of course, a generally favourable or recommendatory one for a product that is reckoned to be 'first' of its kind in the market.

Printator (erasable writing pad by *Printator* Sales) The first part of the name is obvious. The suffix '-ator' would seem either to denote a word such as 'duplic*ator*' or to mean simply 'device' (as in 'pulverisator') and be a technical-looking alternative to '-er'.

Procea (bread by *Slimcea*) *Procea* bread originated in New Zealand in the early 1930s as 'Procera' bread. This name, still in use in Australia and New Zealand, hinted at the special patented *proce*ss used to extract gluten from flour. The process was brought to Britain by a laboratory under the charge of three doctors named Amos, Kent and Jones. They it was who decided to change the name to *Procea*. In 1958 the range of breads as sold by *Procea* Products Ltd was extended to include a *Procea* slimming loaf. This very soon became known as *Slimcea*. Eventually, the company became known as *Slimcea* Ltd and in 1975 was sold off to Spillers. *Procea* as a name has a vaguely foreign look. This is attractive rather than detractive.

Pro-Plus (stimulant by Ashe Laboratories) The product first came on the market in 1956, with a name chosen to suggest its purpose: it was *for more* energy in order to counteract fatigue. The name is loosely Latin based, since *pro* is 'for' and *plus* is 'more'.

Ptarmigan see **Penguin**

Puffin see **Penguin**

Put-U-Up (divan beds by Schreiber Furniture) The name has an obvious derivation – it can 'put you up' for the night on a sofa that has been converted into a bed, which 'you put up' quickly. It has, however, a tendency to be used generically for any make of 'convertible' and is sometimes seen spelt 'Put-You-Up'. Schreiber Furniture in fact registered the latter version of the name in the 1970s, not because they wished to protect it but because their advertising agents thought the original spelling was dated and had the wrong image. Even so, they still use the old form of the name which, until Schreiber took them over in 1967, belonged to the firm of Greaves & Thomas Ltd. In 1971 Schreiber were advised to place an advertisement in the *U.K. Press Gazette*. It read: 'PUT-U-UP is a Registered Trade Mark identifying articles of furniture made by Greaves & Thomas Limited, Edinburgh Way, Harlow, Essex. PUT-U-UP was first used by Greaves & Thomas in 1906 and was registered as a Trade Mark in 1924. Please remember that PUT-U-UP is a Registered Trade Mark.'

Pyrex (heatproof glassware by Corning) *Chambers Twentieth Century Dictionary* (new edition published 1983) has an entry for *Pyrex* giving the word's etymology as Greek *pyr*, 'fire', and Latin *rex*, 'king'. However, Clarence R. Patty, Jr, director of patent operations for the parent American company, Corning Glass Works, writes that 'there is nothing in our files to indicate any element of support for this conjecture.' The name in fact originated in 1915 as a trade mark for heatproof baking dishes made of glass. The first item in the baking-ware line was a pie-plate, and so the first suggestion for a name for it was 'Pie Right'. But since Corning Glass Works had earlier taken to using names ending in 'x', a combination of 'pie' and 'x' was suggested and *Pyrex* was chosen 'purely on euphonious grounds'.

Quaker

Quaker Oats (breakfast cereal and manufacturer)   There seem to be two possible origins of the name. The first, and more likely, is that Henry D. Seymour, one of the founders of a new American oatmeal milling company, had been searching for a name for his business in a dictionary but had found nothing suitable. In an encyclopedia he came across an article on the Quakers and was struck by the similarity of the religious group's qualities and the desirable attributes of oatmeal – purity, honesty, strength, and manliness. The other story says that Seymour's partner, William Heston, had seen a picture of William Penn, the English Quaker, while walking in Cincinnati and being himself of Quaker ancestry had decided there and then that the 'quality' parallels were exactly right for him to adopt the name. Trade marks of religious origin are not common (see *Post Toasties*), and the name *Quaker Oats* inspired more than one law suit. In one of these the Society of Friends (the official name of the Quakers) even petitioned Congress in the United States to bar trade marks with religious connotations but were unsuccessful. The name was first used in 1877, with the original company name being the *Quaker* Mill Co., of Ravenna, Ohio. The company also manufactures pet foods and in 1970 acquired *Felix* Cat Foods Ltd of Biggleswade, Bedfordshire, who had been manufacturing dry cat foods for over thirty years.

Quink (ink by The Parker Pen Co.)   The name is a contraction of '*qui*ck-drying i*nk*'.

Quix (household detergent by *Unilever*)   Presumably the name derives from '*quick s*oap', '*quick s*uds', or just 'quick' alone with a semi-arbitrary 'x' ending.

Racal (radio communications equipment by *Racal* Electronics)   The name is derived from the Christian names of two of the original partners who founded the company in 1951, Sir *Ra*ymond Brown, who was head of Defence Sales for four years from 1966, and G. *Cal*der Cunningham.

Racasan (air fresheners and manufacturer)   The founder of the company was *R*obert *A*lan *C*handler, and its first product was *San*itary Fluid. This is the basis of the name, with the infix '-a-' presumably selected to match the two other 'a's'. *Racasan* ceased trading in 1977 and its employees were taken over by Odex Ltd.

Radox (bath powder and liquid by *Aspro*-Nicholas)   *Radox* first appeared on the market in the 1920s as a foot bath that allegedly '*rad*iated *ox*ygen'. In 1957 the name was transferred to a bath product.

Rael-Brook (menswear by *Tootal*)   The name is directly that of one of the company's original owners, Harry Rael-Brook. He, however, had formerly been Harold Sea*brook*, working in partnership with Mrs R.R. Is*rael* (as I. Israel & Sons), and together with Mrs Israel's son Hyman Usher Israel changed his name in 1955.

Range Rover (cross-country and road vehicle by *Jaguar Rover Triumph*)   The vehicle was first produced in 1970 and was conceived by Maurice Wilks who also originated the *Land-Rover*. The name actually derives from that of the *Land-Rover* and reflects the essential design of the vehicle enabling it to have cross-country ('range') ability while basically being suitable for road use. It was called the 'Road Rover' when still in the planning stage in the late 1950s. A rather finicky point is that *Range Rover* has no hyphen, whereas *Land-Rover* does.

Rawlplug (fixing devices by The *Rawlplug* Co.)   That the name suggests 'wall plug', the company's best-known product, is a happy coincidence. The actual derivation is from the name of one John *Rawl*ings, who in the early years of the twentieth century invented a brass cross-shaped plug to replace the traditional builder's 'wooden wedge between the bricks' on an occasion where the old method could not be used. He appreciated that his idea had potential, and evolved a fibre plug made of jute bonded with animal blood. The First World War delayed development of the *Rawlplug* so that the company was not formed until 1919.

Rayburn (cookers by *Glynwed* Domestic and Heating Appliances)   It seems that the name was introduced on the instigation of Mr W.T. Wren, the managing director of Allied Ironfounders who first produced the cooker. He took it from an American friend, a Mr Rayburn, whose name he felt was doubly appropriate for an appliance that both cooked the food and warmed the kitchen.

rayon (man-made fibre)   *Rayon*, or as it was formerly known, 'artificial silk', is the oldest of the man-made fibres. The word, which is a generic name, not a trade mark, was chosen by the National Retail Drygoods Association in 1924. The derivation seems to be either in the French word *rayon* meaning 'ray' or in an arbitrary word suggesting 'ray' (and perhaps influenced by 'cotton'). The 'ray' is the filament or extended fibre that is formed in the manufacturing process. *Rayon* as a term is now virtually obsolete in Britain, such words as cupro, modal or viscose being used instead. Among American brand names for different types of *rayon* are Enka, Jetspun, Fibro, Vincel, Avisco, and Fiber 40. A name derived in turn from *rayon* is *nylon*.

145

Rennies (antacid tablets by *Aspro*-Nicholas)   The name is that of the inventor of the tablets, a Yorkshireman called John Rennie. For some reason Rennie had chosen France as his sole marketing area, hence the French device 'Digestif Rennie' found on the packets. By what is obviously a coincidence, the name is used as an animal's pet name in the story *Rennie, the Rescuer* by Felix Salten, where Rennie is an Alsatian. In *The Pet Name Book* (Workman Publishing, New York, 1979) Sue Browder derives the name from a Gaelic word *raighne* meaning 'small, mighty, and strong' – an association that would doubtless please the manufacturers.

Rentokil (woodworm and dry rot eradication process and manufacturer)   The suggestion is certainly *'rent* to kill' but the name actually started out as 'Entokil', derived from Greek *entoma*, 'insects', plus 'kill'. 'Entokil Fluids' was the name given by Harold Maxwell-Lefroy, professor of entomology at Imperial College, London in the 1920s, to bottles of solution designed by him to exterminate the death-watch beetle then prevalent in Westminster Great Hall. When, however, application was made to register the name, permission was refused as there already existed a similar name. Thus an initial 'R' was added to produce *Rentokil*. The company itself was formed in 1927.

Revlon (cosmetics by *Revlon* International Corporation)   The name derives from that of Charles Revson, who founded the company in 1932, with the 'L' coming from the initial of one of his partners, Charles Lachman. Among the perfumes produced by the manufacturers is one called 'Charlie' (just as *Max Factor* have 'Maxi-Fresh' make-up and 'Maxi').

Rexine (artificial leather by ICI)   The product was originally manufactured by the British Pluviusin Co. in 1899, following a process devised in 1884 to produce 'leathercloth' by using a solution of nitro-cellulose and castor oil. The actual trade mark, *Rexine*, however, was the property of the British Leather Cloth Manufacturing Co., also founded in 1899. Yet another firm making *Rexine* was New Pegamoid, who first produced it in 1902. By 1925 all three firms had been acquired by Nobel Industries Ltd which the following year was itself merged into ICI. By 1939 the name had come to be written as 'rexine' (with a small letter) and used as a term for artificial leather or 'leathercloth'. The origin of the name is somewhat obscure, but a fair assumption is that it derives from Latin *rex*, 'king', plus the traditional trade name suffix '-ine'. The name remains the protected trademark of ICI.

Ribena (blackcurrant drink by Beecham Group) The name derives from the Latin botanical term for the blackcurrant, *Ribes nigrum*. The product was developed by H.W. Carter & Co. of Coleford, Somerset, in the late 1930s. During the Second World War *Ribena* was distributed free to babies, young children, and expectant mothers because of its high vitamin C content. This was something of a precedent for a branded product.

Rio Tinto-Zinc (mining and industrial company) The London-based parent company is the *Rio Tinto-Zinc* Corporation (usually abbreviated to RTZ) which has interests in almost every major metal and fuel – although rather less in zinc! It was formed in 1962 from the merger of the *Rio Tinto* Co. with the Consolidated *Zinc* Corporation. *Rio Tinto* had originally operated a copper-pyrites mine, near the town of Riotinto (now Nerva) in south-west Spain, where the river was polluted from the workings of the mines and so was named the *Rio Tinto*, or 'tinted river'. The mines were very old, and had initially been leased to a Swede named Wolters in 1725. In 1873 they passed to the British *Rio Tinto* Co. set up that year for the specific acquisition of the mine. (The workings were returned to Spanish control in 1954.) The Consolidated *Zinc* Corporation was established at Broken Hill, Australia, in 1905 to process the residues of silver, lead and zinc ore that had been discovered here twenty-two years before.

Rizla (cigarette paper and manufacturer) The product derives from the fine paper first manufactured by a Frenchman named Lacroix in 1796. From this developed so-called 'rice paper' used for rolling tobacco to make cigarettes. The name thus comes from the French for 'rice', *riz*, with the first two letters of the name of *La*croix. The correct trade name appears in the form *Rizla+*, where the cross (French *croix*) completes the name of the Frenchman.

Robbialac (enamel paint by Berger, Jenson & Nicholson) The name is ultimately from the Italian artist, Luca della Robbia, who as an apprentice in the fifteenth century began to model medallions in terracotta and evolved what came to be called the 'della Robbia glaze'. The secrets of his process were his alone, and even today the exact procedure for achieving his glaze has not been fully established. In the nineteenth century a paint manufacturer, John Charles Nicholson, was asked by one of his agents for a blue-white or off-white paint 'as in the della Robbia glaze'. In the course of his travels on behalf of his firm Nicholson had seen della Robbia's glaze when once visiting a church near Florence. He therefore knew what his agent was after. Some years later Nicholson perfected a new enamel paint and, recalling the agent's description, named it *Robbialac* for 'della Robbia', with '-lac' denoting a *lac*quer paint (compare *Brolac*, made by the same firm.) John Charles Nicholson was the son of the co-founder of Jenson & Nicholson, who merged with another company, Berger, to become Berger, Jenson & Nicholson in 1960. (William Nicholson had set up as a manufacturer of coach paints in 1821.) The name *Robbialac* is still used in many overseas countries but no longer in Britain.

Robin (starch by Reckitt & Colman) The bird could be said to have a 'crisp' image which is no doubt why its name was chosen in 1899 for the starch made by Reckitt & Sons. Moreover, animal and bird names were in something of a vogue at the end of the nineteenth century and beginning of the twentieth: compare *Lion Brand* (1880) and *Kiwi* (1906).

Rolex (watches by The *Rolex* Watch Co.) The company that became *Rolex* was founded in London by Hans Wilsdorf, whose choice of name resulted in an arbitrary word with no definite meaning. The name is quite suitable for a watch, however, suggesting 'rolling' and short enough to be conveniently placed on the dial. At the same time it is easy to pronounce and to remember. *Rolex* is said to be the first watch name to have the suffix '-ex'. Certainly *Timex*, for example, came much later. The *Rolex* Oyster waterproof watch was introduced in 1926, having a descriptive name.

Rollei (cameras and manufacturer) The German firm of Franke and Heidecke had made a stereoscopic plate camera called the Heidoskop, then a roll-film one called the Rolleidoskop. This in turn led to the Rolleiflex and Rolleicord, twin-lens reflex cameras. Their names in turn led to the shorter *Rollei*.

Roneo (duplicators and stencils by *Roneo* Alcatel) The *Roneo* continued the story of the *Cyclostyle* (see *Gestetner*). The germ of the name can be seen in the *Neo*-Cyclostyle, a pen patented by Gestetner in 1888 as an improvement on the original *Cyclostyle*. (It had an inclined wheel, whereas the *Cyclostyle* had a wheel at rightangles to the shaft.) The *Neo*- element, of course, is Greek for 'new'. In the United States the pen came to be called the *Neo*style at the request of Augustus David Klaber, Gestetner's agent in New York for *Cyclostyle* products made by Gestetner in London. In due course Klaber and Gestetner split, with Klaber registering the *Neo*style Co.

148

in New York in 1893. In 1899 Klaber was selling a duplicating machine called the Rotary *Neo*style. The following year he returned to London, where he had been born as the son of emigrants from Prague, and sought a simpler name for the duplicator. With his final choice of name still uncertain he registered three names as trade marks on 23 October 1901: Neoro, Nero and *Roneo* – the latter from *Ro*tary *Neo*style. Shortly after, his company changed its name to the *Roneo* Co. and the trade name was assured. The *Roneo* story does not quite end there, however, since a fourth name that Klaber registered in 1901 was Neostyle. Legally this was a risky thing to do since although he had devised the name himself in America, it derived directly from Gestetner's Neo-Cyclostyle. The two names were confusingly and misleadingly similar. Not surprisingly, therefore, Gestetner petitioned in 1903 for the removal of 'Neostyle' from the Register of Trade Marks. At first he lost his case. On taking the matter to the Court of Appeal, however, the decision against him was reversed and it was ruled that Klaber's mark should be removed from the Register. Some years later, after the 1905 Act of Parliament had revised the law so as to disqualify any descriptive word from being used as a trade mark, Klaber in turn brought a case against Gestetner and succeeded in having 'Cyclostyle' removed from the Register on descriptive grounds. Even so, the name was subsequently revived with the restriction that it could not be applied to wheel pens – that is, the very product for which the name had been chosen! At the end of it all, though, *Roneo* remains as a distinctive and somehow apt word for a duplicating process. Not only do its two 'Os' suggest a rotating motion, but the name has something of a Latin look. It also, of course, suggests 'Romeo'. In 1980 the business, formerly part of Vickers, was sold to Alcatel, a subsidiary of the French Compagnie Générale d'Électricité.

Ronson (cigarette lighters by *Ronson* Products) The company was founded in the United States in 1895 by Louis V. Aronson, from whose surname the trade name derives. In Britain the company was incorporated in 1929 as *Ronson* Art Metal Co., this being changed two years later to *Ronson* Products Ltd. In 1953 *Ronson* Furniture Ltd applied to use the name as a trade mark. This was naturally opposed by the cigarette-lighter manufacturers and the application was withdrawn the following year.

Ronuk (floor polish by Sterling Industrial) The name is something of a mystery. It originated in 1896 as the brand name of a polish-manufacturing company later acquired by Newton, Chambers Ltd, the previous owners of the Sterling Group. The polish so called was made by a Mr T. Horace Fowler who had an ironmongery store in Brighton. As for its origin, the gist of the story seems to be that it was the winning entry in a name-selection competition won by a retired army colonel who had served some time in India, and that the name means something like 'brilliance' in one of the Indian languages.

Rotodyne (helicopter by Westland Aircraft)   The name is sometimes used generically for a compound helicopter or 'convertiplane' – a helicopter that has short wings to provide most of its lift force. The *Rotodyne* was first produced by the Fairey Aviation Co. in 1957. Two years after Fairey was absorbed by Westland Aircraft in 1960, the craft was abandoned. (Only two were built as it was.) The name seems to be a combination of 'rotor' and 'dynamic', although it may well derive from 'aero*dyne*', a word used for any flying machine that derives most of its lift from aerodynamic forces.

Rover (car by *Jaguar Rover Triumph*)   The name was originally used for a tricycle produced in 1884 by a firm set up to manufacture pennyfarthing cycles and tricycles in Coventry in 1877. The business progressed, making first motorcycles, and then the first *Rover* cars in 1904. Two years later the firm, which had originated as a partnership between John Kemp Starley and William Sutton, became the *Rover* Co. The name was simply used descriptively, as suitable for a machine on which the rider could 'rove' the countryside and which was thus itself a 'rover'. In the course of time it was transferred from the car to both the *Land-Rover* and *Range Rover*. The *Rover* Co. merged with the Leyland Motor Corporation in 1967 (see *BL*).

Rowenta (household   electrical   appliances   and manufacturer).   Surely the name must derive from the girl's name Rowena? No – although the association is doubtless a favourable one for a domestic product. The name is actually formed from letters taken from the name of the founder of the original company in Offenbach-am-Main, Germany, in 1884 – *Ro*bert *Weintra*ud.

Royale (car by *Vauxhall* Motors)   The name is simply a prestige one – 'royal', with the added 'e' giving the word a French aristocratic touch, as well as suggesting a foreign glamour. (French words ending in 'e' have also a feminine connotation.)

RSVP (sherries by Showerings, Vine Products & Whiteways)   The name would seem to be derived from the initials of *S*howerings and *V*ine *P*roducts (who with Whiteways are known collectively as SVPW), with the initial 'R' added to suggest the 'classy' invitation (as if to a sherry party?). Vine Products was founded in London by two Greek brothers, Minos and Alexander Mitsotakis, in 1905, and in the 1930s registered the name 'VP' for its wines. In 1954 it acquired *Britvic* Ltd and in 1961 merged with Showerings and Whiteways Cyder Co. (see *Cydrax*).

Rufflette (curtain-styling products and manufacturer)   The name is chiefly associated with the curtain-heading tapes that enable the curtain to hang in pleats or gathers. This would seem to be the association produced by the name *Rufflette*, i.e. 'little ruffles', with the '-ette' suffix both diminutive and feminine (and French).

Ryvita (rye crispbread by The *Ryvita* Co.)   The name was devised in the mid-1920s from 'rye' and Latin *vita*, 'life', by a Mr Campbell Garrett, the first importer of Swedish crispbread into Britain. 'Vita' is a popular element for some of the older 'health' foods as *Bournvita* and *Vit-Be*.

Saab (car and manufacturer)   The name is formed from the initials of the *S*venska *A*eroplan *A*ktie*b*olaget ('Swedish Aeroplane Company') founded in 1937. For some older English-speakers the name might conjure up prestige associations with 'sahib', which could be a bonus from the manufacturer's point of view, even if a chance one.

Sabena (Belgian commercial airline)   Another acronym, this time from the *S*ociété *a*nonyme *b*elge d'*E*xploitation de la *N*avigation *a*érienne (literally 'Anonymous Belgian Society for the Exploitation of Aerial Navigation'). The company was set up in 1923 by SNETA, the Société Nationale pour l'Étude des Transports aériens ('National Society for the Study of Aerial Transport'). (An 'anonymous society' is French and Belgian legal jargon approximating to a 'limited company'.) The first official flight made by a *Sabena* aircraft was on 23 May 1923, when a Handley-Page single-engined aeroplane flew mail and goods from Brussels to Lympne, Kent, via Ostend. To English ears the name *Sabena*, perhaps because it resembles the girl's name Sabrina, sounds attractively melodious.

St Bruno (tobacco by Ogden's) Tobacco so named was first sold by Thomas Ogden in 1896. The exact reason for the choice of the name does not seem to be known, but in the 1890s saints' names were popular for a number of products (as the next entry). St Bruno himself was the founder of the order of Carthusian monks in the eleventh century. Tradition has it that monks grew tobacco at the monastery in Valdemosa, Spain. If so, this may be the origin of the name.

St Ivel (dairy products by *Unigate*) The strong suggestion, of course, is of 'St Ives', since there is no place called *St Ivel* in Britain, and no known saint of this name. The name is actually fictional. It is that of an imaginary monk who allegedly lived near the river Yeo which runs through Yeovil in Somerset. The Old English name of the river was Ivel (as the river Ivel in Bedfordshire is still called), and 'St Ivel' was invented by a Mr Barrett, director of Aplin and Barrett, a West Country cheese manufacturing firm, as an advertising gimmick around the year 1900. *Unigate*, who now produce *St Ivel* cheese, have one of their main centres in Yeovil.

St Julien (tobacco by Ogden's) The name of this tobacco is even less well documented than that of *St Bruno*. There seems to be no association with the wine-growing districts of France in spite of the French name of the saint. Indeed, which particular Julian (or Julien) is commemorated here – if any? Perhaps the name was chosen simply to match *St Bruno*, for *St Julien* tobacco came on the market about the same time as the other brand. Any saint's name is usually seen as a prestige name.

St Margaret (hosiery by Corah) The firm of Corah was founded at the Globe Inn, Silver Street, Leicester, in 1815. It was here that Nathaniel Corah first started out as a hosiery factor, since the Globe Inn was a recognised rendezvous for stockingers with goods to sell. The business grew, and after a number of developments (and the death of Corah) the firm finally moved to a plot of land near St Margaret's Church, in north-east Leicester, and here in 1865 the foundation stone for a large factory and warehouse was laid. It was this site that gave the company its brand name, *St Margaret*, which was first used that same year.

St Michael (products by Marks & Spencer) The first firm with which Marks & Spencer established a direct relationship was the hosiery firm of Corah (see last entry). In 1928 Marks & Spencer registered their own brand names for goods manufactured to their orders. A number of saints' names were considered to match *St*

152

Margaret, including 'St Joan', but the final choice of *St Michael* was made by the chairman, Simon Marks, in honour of his father, Michael Marks, who as a Polish refugee had first set up his stall on the open market at Leeds in 1884. This stall ('Marks' Penny Bazaar') was the nucleus from which arose Marks & Spencer, the company itself being created in 1926.

Sanatogen (tonic wine by Whiteways of Whimple) The product was patented in 1898. Its name would appear to be a pseudo-classical blend of some Latin word meaning 'health' or 'healthy' – perhaps *sanatio*, 'healing', or 'curing' – and some scientific word ending in '-ogen' as 'hydrogen', whose own suffix '-gen' means 'that which produces'. The name has long been associated with the anagrammatic *Genatosan* company, based in Loughborough.

Sanforized (pre-shrunk fabric and manufacturer) The name is derived from *Sanfor*d Lockwood Cluett (1874–1968), the American director of engineering and research of Cluett, Peabody & Co., a firm of shirt and collar manufacturers founded by George B. Cluett, originally from England, in 1901. Sanford Cluett was the inventor of the patented process of 'Sanforizing', basically by pushing back (compressing) a fabric that had been pulled out when it was under tension in the various stages of manufacture (weaving, bleaching, dyeing and printing). In English-speaking countries the name of the process is generally (and rather unusually) known in the past tense as *Sanforized*. In most European countries it is 'Sanfor' and in Latin America the trade name is 'Sanforizado'.

Sanyo (electrical goods by *Sanyo* Masubeni) The name of this Japanese company means 'three oceans', a name that presumably is designed to indicate its international image – the Atlantic, Pacific, and Indian oceans being the three principal oceans of the world. The company was incorporated in 1950.

Sarille (viscose *rayon* by Courtaulds) The name is simply an invented word, with no meaning. It is mellifluous enough, even sounding something like a girl's name, and its ending '-ille' suggests the French feminine diminutive suffix '-elle'.

Savlon (disinfectant and babycare products by Care Laboratories) The name strongly suggests French *savon*, 'soap', and also the name of the ICI subsidiary who produced it, Avlex. The name is still an ICI trademark.

Saxa (salt by RHM Foods) The origin of the name is uncertain, although we do know that it was first used in 1907. There could be a connection with Latin *saxum*, 'rock' (or with the plural, *saxa*, 'rocks'), since rock-salt is common salt in solid mineral form.

Saxin (artificial sweetener by Burroughs Wellcome & Co.) The derivation must surely be in 'saccharine', of which the name, first used in 1897, is a conventional contraction.

Saxone (shoes and manufacturer) This may be based on the surname Saxon, or rare name Saxone, or otherwise some kind of historical prestige name, presumably chosen to suggest toughness and a 'pedigree'.

Scalextric (model racing car systems by Hornby Hobbies) The origin of the name is in the range of model vehicles introduced in about 1950 by Minimodels. These were called 'Scalex', as they were made to no specific scale (i.e. were 'scale x'). An elec*tric*al system was introduced in 1957 and the name was thus expanded to the rather awkward *Scalextric*.

Scania (commercial vehicles and manufacturer) The name is a latinisation of Sweden's southernmost region, Skåne, which comprises the counties of Kristianstad and Malmöhus. Here in the town of Malmö, the English bicycle manufacturers, *Humber*, whose products were selling well in both Sweden and Denmark, set up a small factory in the 1890s. Originally the works was known as Swedish *Humber* AB, but just before the turn of the century it split from the parent company and began producing vacuum cleaners, paper machinery and gear wheels as well as bicycles. For its new independent activities it took the name Maskinfabrics AB *Scania*. As with many similar companies, production soon expanded and progressed to the manufacture of motorcycles and automobiles, the first *Scania* car being built in 1901. The following year they produced their first truck, the forerunner of the *Scania* commercial vehicles seen on the roads of many countries of the world today.

Schick (electric razors by Warner-Lambert) German *Schick*, 'elegance', or French *chic*, 'stylish' (both really the same word)? The answer is neither, since the name comes from a retired American colonel, Jacob Schick, who in 1931 first put on the market the electric razor that he had patented three years earlier. *Schick* shavers were originally produced by the American firm of Eversharp. The business was acquired in 1970 by Warner-Lambert. There could hardly be a more apt surname for a product!

Schweppes

Schweppes (soft drinks by Cadbury *Schweppes*)   Another happy coincidence. In spite of the obvious onomatopoeic possibilities of the name – just right for an effervescent drink, and exploited as such by the manufacturers – the origin is in the name of Jacob Schweppe, a German who settled in Geneva as a jeweller in about 1768. In 1780 he turned his attention to the manufacture of artificial mineral waters, and in 1792 went to London to start his business there. In 1798 he took three Englishmen into partnership and formed the firm of Schweppe & Co., which name lasted until 1834 when it was restyled as *Schweppes* Ltd. The company merged with Cadbury Brothers Ltd in 1969 to form Cadbury *Schweppes*.

Scirocco (cars by *Volkswagen* (GB))   The name is the actual word, Italian in origin (ultimately Arabic), for a special type of warm wind that blows from the Sahara across to Sicily and the south of Italy. For another wind-named *Volkswagen* car see *Passat*.

Scotcade (mail-order firm)   The company was founded in Britain in 1973 by an American marketeer, Bob Scott. Presumably the name is a blend of *Scott* and 'ar*cade*'.

Scotch (adhesive tapes by *3M*)   There is some mystique – and also something of a mystery – about the name, whose precise origin is a little uncertain. One thing is undisputed, however – neither the name nor the product has any connection with Scotland or the Scottish, except in the most indirect of senses. The story behind the name seems to run as follows. In the 1920s a fashion had grown for having cars painted in two tones, and *3M* had evolved a 2-inch-wide masking tape for use by car manufacturers when painting such cars. This was an expensive procedure, and some bright fellow hit on the idea of limiting the adhesive coating to just one quarter of a strip of each side of the tape, instead of covering the entire two-inch width. The tape, however, had a tendency to fall off, and car manufacturers and garage proprietors were as dissatisfied as before. At one garage, when the *3M* salesman called, he was told to 'take this Scotch tape back to those bosses of yours and tell them to put adhesive all over it – not just on the edges.' *3M* thus realised that 'stinginess' did not pay, and reverted to the full coating. When the salesman next called, and was asked if he was 'still selling that Scotch tape', he was pleased to be able to reply that he wasn't. Thus, it appears, the characteristics or meanness traditionally attributed to the Scots and resulting in the name of the people being used in this sense ('stingy') launched a trade name so well known that it has almost come to be generic.

Scotties (paper tissues by Bowater-Scott)   The tissues were first manufactured in the United States by the *Scott* Paper Co. and were first produced in Britain in 1957 by Bowater-*Scott* at their mill in Kent. Scott was the name of two brothers, E. Irwin and Clarence Scott, who founded the firm as a toilet paper manufacturing business. They began their career, however, by selling paper bags from a handcart in Philadelphia in 1879.

Seccotine (adhesive by Royal Sovereign Pencil Co.)   The adhesive – in fact refined liquid fish glue – seems to have originated in Germany in the second half of the nineteenth century where it was patented by an Irishman, John Stevenson. The original manufacturers of *Seccotine* were the Northern Ireland firm of McCaw, Stevenson & Orr, founded in 1878, with the product (and its name) passing much later to the English Royal Sovereign Group. It is one of the few trade names to have its entry and etymology – or a version of it – recorded in the last (1933) edition of the *Oxford English Dictionary*. There, with a note that it appeared in the Trade Marks Journal on 19 December 1894, the name is explained as 'apparently suggested by Italian *secco*, dry'. This, with the common trade-name suffix '-ine', would certainly seem to be not far short of the truth, although perhaps French *sec*, 'dry', may also have had its influence.

Securicor (security services and manufacturer)   Presumably the name is a blend of '*securi*ty' and '*corps*', with reference to the military-style uniform of the company's employees and the 'guardhouse' appearance of its vehicles.

Sellotape (adhesive tapes and manufacturer)   The word originated from another trade name, *Cellophane*, since this provides the cellulose base film for *Sellotape*. The initial 'C' was replaced by an 'S' so that the name could be registered as a trade mark. *Sellotape* was first marketed in Britain in 1937. The manufacturers are understandably anxious that the name should not be used generically (with a small letter) to apply to any brand of 'pressure sensitive' adhesive tape, as it is technically called. Their important rivals in this field, of course, are *3M* (see *Scotch* above).

Sensodyne (toothpaste for sensitive teeth by Stafford Miller)   The first half of the name refers to the *sens*itivity of the teeth; the second half suggests the 'dyne' or power (as in 'dynamo') that the toothpaste has to eliminate this sensitivity. The element 'dyne' is rather unusual for a pharmaceutical product: it is normally applied to some mechanical or electrical product, as *Rotodyne*.

Servis (domestic appliances and manufacturer)   This apparently illiterate spelling of 'service' may in fact have originated, according to one story, from the word so spelled by a works hand who had entered – and won – a competition held to choose a good brand name. The tale may well be apocryphal, however, and what is more likely is that the name was so registered in order to differ from an existing trade mark 'Service'. Or perhaps the 'phonetic' version of the word was selected deliberately to be neater and more memorable than the correct spelling. In any case, the name achieves the aim of suggesting the objective of the manufacturers and their appliances.

7-Up (soft drink by Cadbury *Schweppes*)   In the village of Price's Branch, Missouri, a Mr C.L. Griggs invented a popular orange drink in 1920 called Howdy. Aiming to improve on it, Griggs marketed another drink as Bib-label Lithiated Lemon-Lime Soda. The drink was tasty but the sales were bad (with that name, hardly surprising), so he tried to think of a better name. The story goes that after six tries he came up with '7-Up', and this was the name that made the drink the bestseller it is today. No doubt the association with the card game seven-up helps: in the game the trump card is a turned-*up* card and there is a fixed total of *seven* points to win.

Shell (petroleum and manufacturer)   The story of *Shell* began in the first half of the nineteenth century in the curio shop in East Smithfield, London, set up by a Jewish dealer, Marcus Samuel. Samuel's children had fastened seaside shells to their empty lunch boxes on returning from a holiday, and the dealer made up a number of such boxes and labelled them with the names of the resorts the shells had come from. For the more sophisticated demands of his lady customers he imported fancy polished shells from abroad. His shop soon became known as the Shell Shop, and business expanded rapidly so that by 1830 Marcus Samuel had built up an international trade in oriental curios and copra, as well as shells. When barrelled kerosene was added to his cargo list, the world-wide activities of the Shell Shop were consolidated as the *Shell* Transport and Trading Co. This was in 1897 when the firm had been taken over by Samuel's son, also called Marcus. (Marcus *père* died in 1870, aged 73.) The company adopted the scallop as its trade mark in 1904.

Shloer (apple juice by Beecham Products)   Presumably the name is a surname, perhaps that of the original manufacturer or producer?

157

Or could it simply be an onomatopoeic name, designed to suggest a drink that you can quaff or 'slurp'?

Shredded Wheat (breakfast cereal by *Nabisco*)   *Shredded Wheat* was the first ready-to-eat breakfast cereal, produced by one Henry D. Perky in Denver, Colorado, in 1893. After being marketed locally, Perky founded the Natural Foods Co. two years later and started to make the cereal on a factory scale at Worcester, Massachusetts. His idea for the cereal is said to have come from seeing fellow dyspepsia sufferers in a Nebraska hotel eating whole boiled wheat with milk for breakfast. Perky decided that such wheat would be more easily assimilated in 'shredded' form. In 1929 the National Biscuit Co. acquired the Canadian Shredded Wheat Co., including the operation in England established in 1908, the Shredded Wheat Co. of England. In 1956 the name of this English company, which had remained as part of the National Biscuit Co., was changed to *Nabisco* Foods Ltd. Meanwhile, back in about 1924, the name *Shredded Wheat* had been registered, but with the passing of the Trade Marks Act of 1938, which among other things banned the registration of descriptive words, an action was taken against the *Shredded Wheat* Co. to have the name removed from the Register. This action succeeded, with the result that in 1941 the National Biscuit Co. registered the name *Welgar* (from its English head office and works at *Wel*wyn *Gar*den City, Hertfordshire) and also that competitors began to produce their own brands of *Shredded Wheat*. The name has thus become common property in the United Kingdom, and packets of the cereal will state, in addition to the words *Shredded Wheat*, the name or trade mark of the manufacturers, so that the public will know whose brand they are buying. None of this would have happened, of course, if only Mr Perky had named the cereal after himself – and what a good name for a breakfast cereal 'Perkywheat' would have been!

Sifta (salt by RHM Foods)   The product was acquired by RHM Foods in the late 1960s. The name must surely derive from 'sift', implying that the salt has been carefully sifted or that it is suitable for 'sifting' onto food.

Silvikrin (hair dressing and shampoo by Beecham Group)   The name is a well-established one, dating back before the Second World War, although the shampoo *Silvikrin* was first marketed only in 1960. The origin remains uncertain, although it is known that the first half of the name has led some people to think that the product was one for grey or silver hair. The ending '-krin' must surely derive from Latin *crinis*, 'hair'.

158

Simca (car and manufacturer)   The French car owes its name to a French acronym, la *Société industrielle et mécanique des constructions automobiles* ('Industrial and Mechanical Automobile Construction Company'). This was founded in 1934 by an Italian, Henri-Theodore Pigozzi, to expand his activities as a distributor of *Fiat* cars in France. The first *Simca* cars were thus *Fiat*s. Only in 1951 did *Simca* produce a car that was markedly different from a *Fiat*: this was the model named the Aronde (an old French word for 'swallow'). The *Simca* company were subsequently taken over by *Chrysler*. As an acronym, the name is an internationally effective one, and additionally suggests to an English-speaker the nature of the product.

Sindy (dolls by Pedigree Dolls & Toys)   *Sindy* first went on the market in 1954. The name was chosen as the result of a street survey in which four possible names, together with a photo of the doll, were shown to little girls. *Sindy* was the favourite. In the survey, however, the name was 'Cindy', and as it was realised that this common name could not be registered as a trade mark, one of the directors of the manufacturing company, H.R. Lines, changed the 'C' to an 'S'. (Compare a similar device with *Sellotape*.)

Singer (car and manufacturer)   There is no connection with the Singer sewing-machine. The latter was invented and patented (1851) by Isaac Merrit Singer, the American businessman who founded I.M. Singer & Co. to manufacture his invention. The *Singer* car evolved in England from the Singer Cycle Co. founded in 1876 in Coventry by George Singer. Via motorcycles, the *Singer* Motor Co. was formed in 1903 to build automobiles based on the Lea-Francis design. The name was ultimately swallowed up in the Rootes Group. Yet *Singer* is not at all a bad name for either a car or a sewing-machine, suggesting a mechanical motive power that runs sweetly and smoothly.

Sirdar (woollen goods and knitwear and manufacturer)   The name at first sight looks like a concocted word or anagram. 'Sirdar', however, is the English word for the former title of the British commander-in-chief of the Egyptian Army. (The word actually derives from the Persian for 'head possession'.) In this case the reference is to Lord Kitchener, who was appointed Sirdar of Egypt in 1892. The company was formed during Kitchener's term of office, and the name is thus both commemorative and of aristocratic origin.

Škoda (motor vehicles and manufacturer)   The Czech name is that of the engineer, Emil Škoda, who founded the company as an engineering firm in Pilsen in 1869. The *Škoda* Works became famous for its manufacture of military equipment, especially artillery.

Skol (lager beer by *Ind Coope*) The name is a toast, from Danish *skål*, literally 'bowl', 'cup'. Compare *Long Life*.

Sleepeezee (beds and bedding and manufacturer) The origin is obvious ('sleep easy'). What is interesting about the name is its eccentric spelling, usually found with a 'one-off' shop (as 'Beezeebee' for a confectioner's or tea shop) rather than with a large company of some standing and repute, and its hidden pun – *Sleepeezee* is 'full of 'E's! It is certainly memorable, and perhaps, as a trade mark, something of a curiosity: what other name has six identical vowels? The name originated in about 1934.

slimcea **Slimcea** (slimming bread and manufacturer) The name is a 'spin-off' from *Procea*. *Procea* Products Ltd extended their range of loaves in 1958 to include a slimming loaf. This soon became known as a 'Slimcea'. *Procea* Products were taken over by the Cavenham Food Group, who extensively promoted the loaf, and eventually the company name became known as *Slimcea* Ltd. In 1975 it was sold off to Spillers.

Smarties (coloured chocolate-coated beans by Rowntree Mackintosh) There seems no doubt that the name is simply what it says, denoting a 'smart' kind of sweet (i.e. one that is bright, fresh, gay, fashionable, and all the good things that 'smart' is), with the suffix '-ie' denoting an affectionate diminutive. In the United States the *Mars* company acquired the rights to market *Smarties*.

Smash (mashed potato powder by Cadbury *Schweppes*) Although the obvious link is with 'mash', the name is a risky one, since 'smash' can have several undesirable connotations, such as motor accidents and shop-window ('smash-and-grab') raids. But presumably the association is intended to be with the colloquial 'smash' that means 'very good', as a 'smash hit'. The 'S', too, helps to reinforce the name of the manufacturer, Cadbury *Schweppes*. But even so, surely the product is not one that gives the consumer a potato that you 'break with a crushing blow' – for that is the dictionary definition of 'smash', and the basic meaning of the word. The one or two bonuses of the name seem to be easily outweighed by its many minuses.

Sobranie (tobacco and cigarettes by Gallaher) The firm was founded in 1879, and since then has been blending and manufac-
160

turing 'Balkan' cigarettes and tobaccos. The word is Bulgarian for 'parliament', and so would appear to be a prestige name. Gallahers took over the *Sobranie* interests early in 1980.

Solignum   **Solignum** (wood preservatives and manufacturer)   The name was first used in 1894. It has a genuine classical look, and the Latin for 'wood', *lignum*, can be easily spotted. But how about the initial 'So-'? This would appear to be intended to mean 'saving', 'preserving', and thus might be based on the distress signal '*SOS*'. On the other hand the Greek verb *sozein* means 'to save', and this would be a more fitting element to match the other classical half of the name.

   Sony (electrical equipment and manufacturer)   Many Japanese trade names turn out to be taken simply from the surname of a company founder or an inventor. *Sony* is rather different. When Japan's first transistor radio was produced by the Tokyo Tsushin Kogyo Kabushai Kaisha (company) in 1955 the directors understandably felt that they needed a much more 'streamlined' and international name for it than the full length company name. At first they considered 'TTK', which was certainly better, but there already existed a TKK (Tokyo Kyuko KK, or Tokyo Express Co.) which would be confusing. Earlier, they had used 'Tape-corder' for their tape recorder and 'Soni' (from '*sonic*') for this machine's tape. Considering 'Soni', the directors felt that this would probably be mispronounced in English, as 'so-nigh'. But the international (Latin) base '*son*', meaning 'sound', was good, and an alteration of the final 'i' to 'y' would suggest 'sonny', and give the name a homely, affectionate touch. If, however, the actual name was spelt 'Sonny' the Japanese would pronounce this as 'son-ny', and this might be associated with the Japanese word for 'loss', *son*. This would not do, since the radio was clearly intended to produce a profit! Finally the variant *Sony* was decided on for the transistor, and the name passed to the company as a whole in 1958.

Sorbo (sponge rubber by *Li-Lo*)   The derivation is almost certainly 'ab*sorb*', plus the once popular trade-name suffix '-o'. Although sometimes spelled with a small 's' (as in the *Concise Oxford Dictionary*) and used generically, there is no evidence that the name is not a registered trade mark. It would seem to have originated in the first half of the twentieth century, if not earlier.

Spam (tinned meat by George A. Hormel and Co.)   The name is a contraction of '*sp*iced *ham*'. The word was devised in 1937 when the American food manufacturers, George A. Hormel & Co., were looking for a name for their newly marketed cans of luncheon meat.

161

(They already produced pork shoulder meat in cans under the name 'Spiced Ham'.) A cash prize of 100 dollars was offered for the best suggestion of a name for the new product. 'Brunch' was suggested, and seriously considered, but '*Spam*', proposed by an actor-brother of a Hormel vice-president, was the easy winner. *Spam* has been manufactured in Britain for Hormel by Lovell & Christmas since about 1957.

Spar (food-chain stores) The letters are not those of an acronym. The company is of Dutch origin, and was started up by a wholesaler, A.J.M. Van Well, in The Hague in 1932. As his trading device, Van Well chose the symbol of a fir-tree, the Dutch for which is *spar*. The company has always promoted the fact that a similar-looking (but unrelated) Dutch word *sparen* means 'savings'. Such a 'value-for-money' association will be lost, however, on the very many non-Dutch-speaking *Spar* customers. True, some English-speakers may link the English word 'spar' with the fir-tree, and be linguistically correct in doing so, since the Dutch word and the English are closely related. But does this help to boost the company's sales significantly? *Spar* International was formed in 1948, and the company's first British branch opened up in the 1950s.

Spearmint (mint-flavoured chewing gum by The Wrigley Co.) The name – more correctly 'Wrigley's *Spearmint*' – is the standard word for a common garden mint (*Mentha spicata*) used to flavour the gum. (The 'spear' refers to the plant's sharply pointed leaf, not to its pungency.) The name was first registered in the United States in August 1907. The telegraphic address of Wrigley in Britain is 'Spearmint Plymouth'.

Spirella (corsets and fashionwear by The *Spirella* Co. of Great Britain) The base of the name is 'spiral'. Shortly after 1900 an American engineer, Marcus Beeman, was concerned that there was no flexible support that could be inserted in corsets. By bending a piece of wire backwards and forwards in a series of 'Ss' he devised a spiral stay which he called the '*Spirella* flexible stay'. Two of his associates were impressed with the device and began designing corsets on an anatomical basis, incorporating the *Spirella* stay. A few years later one of the two partners, a Mr Kincaid, came to England and set up the *Spirella* Co. of Great Britain in 1909. The '-ella' suffix, with its feminine and diminutive connotations, is found in a number of trade names for types of fabric and clothing for women: compare *Clydella* and *Viyella*.

Spontex (rubber products by Viscose Group) The name is of

French origin, and although the exact derivation is uncertain there must be a link with English '*sponge*' and '*tex*ture', doubtless via the Latin word for 'sponge', *spongia*, and the international suffix '-tex' to denote a material.

Spry (cooking fat by Van den Berghs & Jurgens)   Apart from the obvious good image of the name, suggesting a cooking fat that is 'lively' in the pan when heated, the word itself is vaguely suggestive of '*sp*utter' and 'fry', presumably a desirable sound-association!

Sqezy (dishwashing liquid by *Unilever*)   The freaky spelling of the name ('q' not followed by 'u') makes it memorable although in turn liable to mis-spelling (as 'Squezy', say). The meaning is obvious: the product is sold in squeezable bottles. *Sqezy* was introduced on the market in 1956 by *Domestos* Ltd as the first dishwashing product in a 'squeeze pack'. *Domestos* was taken over by *Unilever*, who still manufacture the liquid, in 1961.

SR (toothpaste by *Elida* Gibbs)   The initials stand for 'Sodium Ricinoleate', itself a trade mark for a cleaning agent made from an acid present in the castor oil plant (Latin *ricinus*). Gibbs *SR* tooth-paste was the first product to be advertised on British commercial television, on 22 September 1955.

Standard (cars by *Standard-Triumph*)   The *Standard* Motor Co. was founded in Coventry in 1903 by Reginald Walter Maudslay, a civil engineer. At Maudslay's request his consulting engineer, Alex Craig, designed 'a car to be composed purely of those components whose principles have been tried and tested and accepted as reliable standards.' ('In fact', added Maudslay, 'I will name my car the Standard car.') The first *Standard*, a single-cylinder six-horse-power model, never went into production: the first to be built was the two-cylinder 12/15 horse-power *Standard*, presented at the Crystal Palace Motor Show in 1904. In 1908 the company displayed the Union Jack on the car, the first time that this had happened, as a symbol of its all-British manufacture. (Was there something of a pun here – a standard on a *Standard*?) The flag was incorporated in the car's emblem in 1931. *Standard* also made power units for SS Cars Ltd (see *Jaguar*), thus prompting the popular idea that these initials stood for 'Standard Special' rather than 'Swallow Sidecar'. In 1945 the company purchased the goodwill of the *Triumph* Co., itself being taken over by the Leyland Group (see *BL*) in 1960. The last *Standard* car, an Ensign, was manufactured in 1963.

State Express (cigarettes by *Ardath* Tobacco)   The name was

163

registered at the time of the formation of *Ardath* by its founder, Albert Levy, in the late nineteenth century. He took it from the Empire State Express, then the world's fastest train, which ran from Buffalo to New York City. When travelling on this train Sir Albert, as he became, noticed that the engine number was 999. This inspired the numerical combinations used by him for a number of brands of cigarettes (see *Three Fives*). The British branch of *Ardath*, *State Express* of London, became part of British-American Tobacco (now BAT Industries) in 1925.

Steradent (denture cleaner by Reckitt & Colman)   A fairly transparent name, implying a product that cleans and *steri*lises *dent*ures. *Steradent* was first registered as a trade name in 1934.

Stergene (synthetic detergent by *Unilever*)   The name would seem to be a blend of '*steri*lise' and either 'hygiene' or some chemical term such as 'phos*gene*' or 'oxy*gen*'. The suffix '-gen(e)' means simply 'producing' in most trade names, so here perhaps 'producing a liquid that is sterilising'. (*Stergene* does in fact contain a bacteriostat, or ingredient that inhibits the growth of bacteria.) The word itself, perhaps coincidentally, somewhat resembles 'de*tergen*t', which is a bonus. *Stergene* was introduced in 1948.

Strada (car by *Fiat*)   The *Strada* was extensively promoted in Britain in 1979 as a car that was 'built by robots'. When launched earlier in Italy and other European countries it was named 'Ritmo', Italian for 'rhythm', 'pace'. In the United States and Britain, however, this name was found to produce a negative reaction – to an English ear it sounds like an awkward acronym of some kind – so the name in these countries was changed to *Strada*, which is simply Italian for 'street', 'road'. The link with 'autostrada', the Italian word for a motorway, is also helpful, of course.

Subaru (car and manufacturer)   The name is the Japanese for the Pleiades cluster of stars in the Taurus constellation. The cluster in fact contains several hundred stars but most people can only distinguish the six brightest with the naked eye – sometimes seven. These six stars represent the six companies which merged to form Fuji Heavy Industries in 1953 and are represented pictorially in the company's emblem. The first *Subaru* car was manufactured in 1958. *Subarus* were introduced to Britain in 1977.

Subbuteo (table football and manufacturer)   The unusual name has an unusual origin. In 1947 the founder of the company, Peter Adolph, wanted to name the game he had invented 'The Hobby',

164

after the type of falcon so called, but this word was descriptive and so could not be registered. Instead, he took the Latin ornithological name of the bird, *Falco subbuteo subbuteo*, and used that instead. It is an awkward name, both to spell and pronounce – even if it does partly suggest 'boot'. Perhaps 'Buteo', suggesting a 'mini-hobby', might have been better.

Sunbeam (car by *Chrysler* UK)   The history of the name is rather a complex one. The original *Sunbeam* was a bicycle, then a car first produced in 1901 by the *Sunbeam* Motor Car Co. After the Rootes Group had gained control in 1935 of the Clement-*Talbot* end of this company, the car was called the *Sunbeam-Talbot*. Earlier, however, both Clement-*Talbot* and *Sunbeam* had been taken over by Darracq, respectively in 1919 and 1920. The *Talbot* part of the car's name was gradually dropped, and finally disappeared in 1955. Then, since Rootes are mainly owned by the American *Chrysler* Corporation the car became the *Chrysler Sunbeam*. For more, see *Talbot*. The name itself is simply a bright, cheerful one.

Sunlight (soap by *Unilever*)   *Sunlight* soap was the first branded soap, produced by William Lever in 1885. Originally all Lever's soaps, made for him by a number of manufacturers, were branded *Sunlight*. Then, when Lever transferred his business to the purpose-built site and model village called Port Sunlight (south of Birkenhead, now in Merseyside) in 1888, he concentrated on his own brand of *Sunlight* soap. The name obviously conjures up brightness, health and cleanliness. For a similar name in a classical version, see *Lux*. (And for a similar purpose-built work-site to Port Sunlight, see *Bournville*.)

Suzuki (motorcycle and manufacturer)   The company that first manufactured motorcycles in 1952 was founded in Japan in 1909 as a textile-engineering business by Michio Suzuki. In 1954 it changed its name to *Suzuki* Motor Co. and expanded into cars, vans and motorboats as well as motorcycles. To an English-speaker's ear the name has an attractively feminine touch, suggesting 'Suky' or 'Susie'. Although this is apt for a lightweight bike, designed for a female rider, it is incongruous for some of the hefty 'superbikes' that *Suzuki* produce.

Swan Vestas (matches by Bryant & May)   There are two names to consider here. In 1883 the Liverpool firm of Collard & Co. introduced a new match brand named *Swan*. The name was doubtless chosen to represent elegance and neatness, and could be attractively illustrated on the box. This was also the time when animal and bird names were popular (compare *Robin*). In 1895 the American firm, The Diamond Match Co., acquired Collard, and although continuing to produce *Swan* matches introduced a different match in 1897 called *Swan* White Pine *Vestas*. The latter word was aimed at a market in which the traditional 'wax vestas' were declining – hence 'White Pine' (or wooden) *Vestas*. When Bryant & May amalgamated with Diamond Match in 1901 they took over the Liverpool production of *Swan* Vestas, as they were familiarly called, with the name being officially shortened thus in 1906. Wax vestas themselves ceased to be produced at the start of the Second World War. A vesta, originally 'vesta match', was a nineteenth-century match with a wax stem (later a short wooden match) that took its name from Vesta, the Greek goddess of the hearth, whose *vestal* virgins tended the sacred fire in her temple in the Forum. It was in effect a general trade name for such matches. In the children's novel *Holiday House* by Catherine Sinclair, published in 1839, 'Laura afterwards singed a hole in her muslin frock, while lighting one of the Vesta matches . . .' (Early wooden matches, by contrast, took another mythological name, Lucifers.)

Sweetex (artificial sweeteners by Crookes Anestan) The only mystery here is the '-ex' suffix. What does it denote? Hardly 'out'; perhaps '*ex*cellent'. Most likely it is arbitrary, simply added to a standard adjective to indicate a commercial product. *Sweetex* was first marketed in 1955, when the '-ex' ending was still going strong.

T

TALBOT **Talbot** (car and manufacturer) The name was reverted to in 1978 by the European interests of the *Chrysler* Corporation. It comes from the original French firm, Automobiles *Talbot*, of Suresnes, a suburb of Paris. The link is a historical one, for the Talbots were a Norman family of the English aristocracy, with John Talbot, first earl of Shrewsbury, being a famous English soldier who fought several times in the French wars from 1420 onwards. There were thus English *Talbot*s and French *Talbot*s, the cars of the French company being called Darracq in England to avoid confusion with the English cars, manufactured by the *Sunbeam* Motor Car Co. (See this name.) The immediate source of the name *Talbot* was the Earl of Shrewsbury and *Talbot*, a descendant of John Talbot. He was one of the financial backers of the French *Talbot* when it was called the

Clement-*Talbot*, being the French Clement car imported into England.

TAMPAX

Tampax (sanitary tampons and manufacturer)   The name is a blend of '*tamp*on' and 'packs' spelt phonetically. (The 'packs' presumably refers to the function of the tampon rather than the packet in which the product is sold.) The firm was founded in New York in 1936.

Tannoy (public address system by *Tannoy* Audio Communications)   Another near generic name applied to any make of loudspeaker relay system. It originated in 1922, when an English engineer, Guy Fountain, was looking for ways of simplifying the charging process required by lead-acid accumulators used to power radio receivers. Fountain produced a chemical rectifier using two different metals in a solution. One of the metals was a lead alloy and the other was tantalum, and when he began to market the materials Fountain coined the name *Tannoy* from a blend of both of these ('*tan*talum' and 'all*oy*').

Tan Sad (perambulators by *Tan Sad*-Allwin)   The company's original product was a motorcycle pillion seat called the '*Tan*dem *Sad*-dle'. Hence the name.

Tarmac (road-making materials and manufacturer)   The indirect source of the name is John Loudon McAdam (1756–1836), the Scottish engineer who was general surveyor of roads in England from 1827 and who introduced improved roads built of crushed stone and thus the word 'macadamised' to the English language. In 1901, when the search was on for even better road conditions, the county surveyor of Nottingham, E. Purnell Hooley, noticed that a patch of road near an iron works in Denby, Derbyshire, was quite dustless and unrutted by traffic. On enquiring the reason, he was told that the road had been accidentally covered in tar when a barrel fell off a passing dray and, in order to simplify matters, the tar had been covered with waste blast-furnace slag from the works. This gave Hooley an inspiration, and by April the following year he had obtained a patent for a method of mixing slag with tar. Hooley called the material *Tarmac*. In 1903 he formed the TarMacadam (Purnell Hooley's Patent) Syndicate Ltd, which name was mercifully shortened in 1905 to *Tarmac* Ltd. The name has come to be used at times for any made-up road surface, largely as a result of the runways built in the Second World War by the company as part of the large airfield construction programme ordered by the government.

167

Tcp

TCP (antiseptic fluid by Unicliffe)   The letters would seem to stand for a chemical, perhaps '*t*richloro*p*henylmethyliodosalicyl', although there is also a claim that the product was invented by one *Th*eodore *C*adwallader *P*arry.

Teasmade (automatic tea-making machine by Goblin Electrical Appliances)   The manufacturers had difficulty in registering the name in 1947 as it was descriptive. Descriptive, that is, if understood as 'tea's made', but not if seen as 'tea's maid'! Goblin purchased the invention from a Mr Thornton in 1936, when it was originally so called. During the period of difficulty regarding the registration, the then chairman and managing director of Goblin wanted to call the product 'Cheerywake', a name that was fortunately out-voted by the rest of the directors. In order to have the descriptive name accepted for registration, the firm distributed the product through leading stores such as Harrods and Selfridges until the time came when these stores accredited Goblin as the manufacturers of the appliance.

Technicolor (colour cinematography process and manufacturer)   The name is a blend of '*techni*cal *color*'. It dates back to 1917, when the *Technicolor* Motion Picture Corporation, an American company founded two years earlier, produced the first *Technicolor* film, *The Gulf Between*, in a two-colour additive system. The first three-colour *Technicolor* film was the Walt Disney animated short, *Flowers and Trees*, produced in 1932, and the process was used for the first time in a feature film, *Becky Sharp*, three years later. The name is sometimes mis-spelled by the English as 'Technicolour'.

Teflon (non-stick plastic material by du Pont de Nemours)   The name is a contraction of a chemical: poly*tetra*fl*uo*roethyle*ne*. This is a tough resin which has good resistance to heat. *Teflon* was first produced by du Pont in 1938.

Tern (shirts by *Tern*-Consulate)   The name is an 'image' one as well as being short and simple. The Arctic term is a bird famous for its lengthy migratory flights from Greenland and North America virtually to the Antarctic in the south. The *Tern* shirt is thus promoted as having an 'across-the-world' durability and marketability.

Terylene (synthetic polyester by ICI)   The derivation is not 'terry' towelling or the personal name Terry but the chemical name of the polyester which is made from an ester of *ter*ephthalic acid and eth*ylene* glycol. The name was first used in 1951.

Tesco (supermarket chain by *Tesco* Stores (Holdings)) For once the suffix '-co' does not mean 'company'. The name was chosen by the founder of the chain, Sir John Cohen (1898–1979). In the early stages of his business, John Cohen's tea was supplied by a man named (appropriately enough) T.E. Stockwell. *Tesco* derives from the latter's initials with the '-co' taken from Sir John's own surname *Co*hen. When the *Sunday Times* voted Sir John 'Personality of the Week' on the occasion of his eightieth birthday (8 October 1978), it mischievously interpreted the name as an acronym for '*T*o *E*clipse *S*ainsburys with *C*utprice *O*ffers'. The name is an effective one, easy to pronounce and remember, and with an international or even slightly exotic flavour to it. (To those who know the Scilly Isles it will probably suggest the name of the island famous for its sub-tropical gardens, Tresco. Such a holiday, sunny association can do the company nothing but good.)

Thames and Hudson (publisher) The British firm was founded in 1949 with offices in both London and New York. Initially the firm aimed at an English-speaking readership on both sides of the Atlantic, and so chose a name that would reflect this – the Thames and the Hudson are the rivers on which London and New York respectively stand. The 'east-west' theme is also seen in the company's colophon, which represents two dolphins, one facing left, the other right.

Thawpit (cleaning fluid by Sterling Industrial) The obvious association is with 'thaw' – but how can a cleaning fluid do this? But perhaps the name is a blend of two surnames, such as Thaw and Pitt or Pitman.

THERMOS **Thermos** (vacuum flasks and manufacturer) The famous name has an interesting linguistic and legal background. It was devised in 1904, as a straight borrowing of the Greek word for 'hot', *thermos*, by a resident of Munich, who had won a competition to name a new type of domestic vacuum flask, developed by Reinhold Burger. Three years later a group of English businessmen secured the patent rights to manufacture the flask for marketing in the British Empire, South America, and a number of other countries, and formed the company of *Thermos* Ltd, at the same time registering the name as a trade mark. In 1963, however, the name became legally generic in the United States as the result of an application made against King-Seeley *Thermos* Co. by the comparatively small company of Aladdin Industries. The English *Thermos* Co. was shaken by this decision, as were a number of other companies whose brand names were in danger of becoming generic (notably *Formica*), and ever

169

since has made increasingly strenuous efforts to protect the name. The fact remains that even so – and aided by the American legal verdict – the name is sometimes used for any brand of vacuum flask, in English and several other languages.

Three Candlesticks (stationery by John Dickinson Stationery)   The derivation of the name is unusual: it comes from an inscription on a token coin discovered in 1799 on the site of John Dickinson's office in the Old Bailey, London. On one side of the coin, which is about the size of a farthing, is the wording 'At the 3 Candlesticks'; the other side has the inscription 'In the Ould Baly 1649' and the letters A.I.K. The coin was subsequently identified as belonging to a merchant who gave such coins to his customers as small change for their purchases. Such a practice was common in the seventeenth century when there was a severe shortage of low-value coins and many traders issued 'token coins' to their own design, promising ultimately to redeem them for silver. The original 'Three Candlesticks' would presumably have been the inn where 'A.I.K.' carried on his trade. As a trade name it is impressive for its length, and although its associations are favourable they are perhaps more likely to be made with fashionable wining and dining in twentieth-century minds than with seventeenth-century trading. But no matter.

Three Castles (tobacco by Ogden's)   The name was suggested to the original manufacturers, W.D. & H.O. Wills Ltd, by a Mr G. Waterston of Edinburgh. He had taken the name from a line occurring in the first chapter of W.M. Thackeray's novel, *The Virginians*: 'There's no sweeter tobacco comes from Virginia, and no better brand than the Three Castles.' Thackeray, it would seem, had himself invented the name for use in his novel, which was first published serially in 1857–9. Wills introduced the tobacco brand of this name in 1877, following it a year later with a brand of *Three Castles* cigarettes.

Three Fives (cigarettes by *Ardath* Tobacco Co.)   The name is a brand of *State Express* cigarettes, appearing on the pack in numerical form ('555') as well as in words. The phrase goes back to the original State Empire Express train in which Albert Levy, founder of the *Ardath* Tobacco Co., used to travel. On one occasion he noticed that the engine number was 999. This prompted him to choose similar three-number names to be used for his State Express cigarettes. He thus registered '111', '222' and so on up to '999'. The whole series of nine brand names was in use until the 1950s, with

'555', or *Three Fives*, being the most successful – and also the only *State Express* brand marketed in Britain.

3M (adhesive tapes and manufacturer)   The reference is to the three 'Ms' of the *M*innesota *M*ining and *M*anufacturing Co., a firm set up in 1902 in Two Harbors on the shore of Lake Superior in Minnesota, to exploit corundum. The founders were five local citizens – a doctor, a lawyer, a merchant, and two railroad executives. The name is something of a misnomer, and has caused confusion. The intention of the five founders was in fact not to manufacture corundum but to mine it. Only in 1905 did the company begin to manufacture sandpaper and shortly afterwards ceased mining until 1930, when the name could be said to be accurate. (Even then, however, the mining was not of corundum but of quartz.) Further confusion is caused since the name suggests that the company is associated with Minnesota iron mining, which is not the case. This misunderstanding is not helped by *3M* employees themselves, who colloquially call their company 'The Mining'. Perhaps the relative anonymity of the abbreviation is the best way out of such misleading associations. One of *3M*'s best known products is *Scotch* Tape.

Three Nuns (tobacco by W.D. & H.O. Wills)   Yet another 'three' name. The origin of this particular one is disputed. It is known that the brand so-called was originally manufactured, some time before 1892, by Messrs J. and F. Bell, whose products were acquired by Stephen Mitchell & Son of Glasgow in 1904. Mitchells were in turn amalgamated with Wills in 1957. The name *Three Nuns* was apparently suggested by Hope Bell, the second son of James Bell, the original producer, for a tobacco that was smaller and lighter than a then popular brand of strong tobacco called 'Thick Black'. Bells also manufactured cigarettes called 'Three Bells', and perhaps the younger Hope chose his *Three Nuns* to match this while at the same time suggesting a more 'ethereal' tobacco than the strong 'Thick Black'. There is not normally a ready association between nuns and smoking, although if monks can grow tobacco plants (see *St Bruno*) why not nuns?

Tia Maria (coffee-flavoured liqueur by Booker-McConnell)   The words are Spanish for 'Aunt Maria'. The romantic story behind the name goes something as follows. In 1655 the Spanish grandees who had taken possession of Jamaica were obliged to flee before the invading forces of Cromwell's British expedition. Maria, the young servant girl employed by one such escaping family, had time to salvage only a few of her mistress's belongings, including a pair of black pearl ear-rings once owned by Queen Isabella of Spain and an ancient family recipe for a family cordial. In time Maria married a gallant British officer (who else?) and became the mother of a large family. When Maria's eldest daughter in turn married, her mother gave her the black pearls and the fading parchment recipe. The resulting cordial was named *Tia Maria* – 'Dame Maria' or 'Goodwife Maria', perhaps, rather than 'Aunt' – in memory of the servant girl's loyalty and devotion to the family. Nearly three hundred years later the recipe was rediscovered and adapted to make the liqueur so called.

Times Furnishing (furniture and manufacturer) The firm was founded at the time when *The Times* newspaper was selling an encyclopedia in instalments. The name 'Times' was thus adopted as a fairly arbitrary prestige choice. Many years later an Indian maharajah wrote to *The Times* to say how much he admired the newspaper and at the same time asked if he could have a catalogue of their furniture. A potentially hazardous legal situation had thus been created! Fortunately for the Jacobs brothers, who had started the furniture business, they had been using the name 'Times' for the statutory period of recognition, twenty-five years, so were not obliged to change it. Instead, they merely agreed to modify the name to The *Times Furnishing* Co. The company was taken over by Great Universal Stores in 1968.

Timex (watches by *Timex* Corporation) The American company was originally called the United States Time Corporation. Shortly after the Second World War the company's president, Joakim Lehmkuhl, decided the corporation needed a new basic product name which might eventually replace the corporate name. After rejecting many possible names he chose *Timex* as it was product-related and 'had a scientific overtone'. The name is thus a fairly standard one with a traditional suffix.

Tio Pepe (sherry by Gonzales, Byass) The name is very similar to *Tia Maria*. Presumably there is a story somewhere about a Spanish 'Uncle Pedro' or 'Old Pepe' who first blended this sherry or who had a special recipe for it.

Tizer (sparkling soft drink and manufacturer) The association intended must obviously be 'appetiser', with the short form of the name, especially one that has been deprived of its initial syllables in this way, suggesting a product suitable for children (who make similar words, such as 'tickly' for 'particularly'). The resemblance of the name to 'tiger' also helps to give the product a 'strong' image.

172

Toblerone (chocolate confectionery by Tobler)   The name is that of the Swiss manufacturer, with the ending '-one' an Italian suffix meaning 'big' (i.e. an augmentative). (Compare 'minestr*one*' which is a 'big' soup because thick and rich.)

Toledo (cars by *Jaguar Rover Triumph*)   The *Triumph Toledo* is named for the Spanish province and its capital, noted for its wealth of architecture and steel swords. Compare *Granada* (although not a *Triumph* model).

Toni (home perm by *Gillette* Industries)   The name was invented for Richard Neison Harris (known as 'Wishbone' Harris from his fondness for this part of a chicken) by a friend. Harris ran a beauty business in the 1930s in Saint Paul, Minnesota, called Noma, Inc. (This name came from one of its products: chemically activated hair-curling pads that needed *no ma*chines to generate heat for setting the curls.) He was trying to develop a method by which women could obtain a good, cheap permanent wave at home instead of having to sit for hours in beauty salons. Harris's first entry into this market, called 'Rol-Wav', was a failure. It was too cheap! He therefore worked on a better-class product at a higher price. And this was named *Toni*. Harris's friend chose the name, allegedly, since Harris was a graduate of Yale, a 'tony' university – i.e. one that had 'tone' or 'class'. The word is probably unfamiliar to many English people, and even Harris said he had never heard of it. Its association for most people will thus be a girl's name, Toni being an affected and/or fashionable form of Antonia. This link is exactly right for a home perm, of course. Indeed, the name is possibly even more effective today, with the increase in first names like Toni (Jodi, Judi, Sheri, Suzi), than it was when it first appeared in 1944. Never mind the 'tony' link, the name is on winning ground. The famous slogan, 'Which Twin has the Toni?', was invented in 1946 by Harris's elder brother Irving.

Tonibell (ice cream by *Lyons Maid*)   The name is that of a company that sold 'Toni's Cream Ices' from 1946 to 1960. Toni (unlike the previous entry) is here presumably an arbitrary Italian-sounding name, with 'bell' added to suggest a pedalling ice-cream vendor. *Tonibell* also conjures up Tinker Bell, the fairy in J.M. Barrie's *Peter Pan*. A happy bonus for a product whose consumers are largely children.

Tootal (menswear and manufacturer)   In spite of the obvious resemblance to 'total' – a good association for a firm offering a wide range of products – the actual origin of the name is one Edward

Tootal who joined an established clothing business in 1842 as a partner, this business having been first started in Manchester by a Mr Gardner in 1799. The rather frivolous link with 'tootle' probably benefits the name as a 'merry' association rather than a trivial one. The unusual surname, which appears in various spellings (Toothill, Tottle, Tutill and the like), seems to originate from some forebear who lived by a look-*out hill*.

Toshiba (electrical appliances and manufacturer)   The name is a contraction of the full title of the Japanese firm, the *To*kyo *Shiba*ura Electric Co. Shibaura is the region of Tokyo where the company's headquarters is located.

Toyota (car and manufacturer)   The firm was launched by a Japanese inventor name Sakichi Toyoda in the early 1930s when he turned over to his son Kiichiro, who was building a motor car, the patent of an automatic loom he had designed for a weaving company in Oldham, Lancashire, in 1929. The family were superstitious, however, and changed their name from Toyoda to Toyota, since 'Toyoda' requires ten characters in Japanese but 'Toyota' only eight – and eight for the Japanese is a lucky number.

Trac II (twin-blade razor by *Gillette* Industries)   The razor, which has two single-edged blades gripped by a plastic cartridge, was introduced in 1971. At first a name based on 'tandem' was considered for it, but legal advisers doubted that 'Tandem' could be registered as a trade mark. Also considered were 'Double Track', 'Dimension II', and 'Face Saver'. Eventually an acronym of '*t*win-blade *ra*zor and *c*artridge' was adopted. In 1977 the *Atra*, designed to supersede it, was introduced.

Transworld (paperback books by *Transworld* Publishers)   see **Corgi Books**

Trebor (confectionery and manufacturer)   The most casual crossword puzzler will immediately spot the reversal in the name. Who was this thinly disguised Robert? He could have been Robert Robertson, who got together with Sydney Marks and two other young men in about 1910 with the intention of starting up a business making boiled sweets to sell to East London retailers. All four were ambitious, but none was well off. The place that they were considering renting was thus a humble site – a row of little terraced houses in Forest Gate, London E7, named 'Trebor Villas'. This they rented for 25 shillings a week – which they regarded as costly – but the name, they felt, was propitious since it was Robert Rob-

174

ertson's own name spelt backwards. Thus *Trebor* was born. The company still possesses the name-plate of the original 'Trebor Villas', and some of the original houses still survive. It would be interesting to learn the identity of the original reversed Robert who gave his name to the villas.

Tricel (triacetate fibre by Courtaulds)   As with the names of a number of artificial fabrics, the derivation is from a chemical term, in this case *cel*lulose *tri*acetate. *Tricel* first appeared in 1954.

Tricity (cookers by Thorn Electrical Industries)   An obvious derivation, worth recording for its lack of deviousness or indeed ingenuity. The company that was one of the first manufacturers of electric cookers in about 1900 was originally named *Tricity* Cookers Ltd. The name can hardly suggest anything except 'electricity', in fact, although there is a token hint at 'city' or an appliance that has three main functions.

Triplex (safety glass by *Triplex* Safety Glass Co.)   The name was first used in Paris in 1909 for a non-shattering glass constructed of three layers – a 'sandwich' of glass containing celluloid. (The discovery of the non-splintering quality of the glass was the result of an accident six years earlier, when a French chemist, Édouard Bénédictus, dropped a glass flask formerly containing a solution of nitrocellulose and found that it did not break.) The derivation of the name lies in Latin *triplex*, 'triple', 'three-fold', while the 'triple x' suggestion of the word is used by the company as its trade mark ('**XXX**').

Triumph (car by *Jaguar Rover Triumph*)   The name began as a generally prestige name for bicycles manufactured in Coventry from 1889 by the *Triumph* Cycle Co. The company moved on to the production of cars after the First World War, with the first *Triumph* appearing in 1923. In 1939, after increasing financial problems, the company went into receivership but the *Triumph* name was kept alive during the war and after it was taken over by the *Standard* Motor Co. to form the *Triumph* Motor Co (1945) Ltd. One of the firm's most popular post-war cars was the little TR2, the initials standing for '*Triumph* Roadster'. In 1959 the structure of the company was changed and *Standard-Triumph* International was formed, this in turn merging less than two years later with Leyland Motors. In 1968 *Triumph* became part of the British Leyland Motor Corporation who as *BL* still produce it (in the company called *Jaguar Rover Triumph*). The car has no connection with the long-running *Triumph* motor-cycle, produced by Norton-Villiers from the early

175

1970s. After this latter firm closed down its plant at Meriden in 1973, however, the workers staged a sit-in. As a result the government-sponsored Meriden Motorcycle Co-operative was formed in 1975 and this continued to produce the bike.

Trubenised (fabric-fusing technique and manufacturer) The originator of a process for producing shirt collars (for example) that do not need to be starched was an American engineer, Benjamin Liebowitz. In the 1920s he developed the idea of textile 'spot welding'. This involved inserting an interlining of cotton with acetate yarns into a collar and fusing the resulting three plies together by means of a solvent and pressure. The result was a collar that retained its porosity and permeability, which was important for washing and wearing. At the time Dr Liebowitz was working for his father's firm of S. Liebowitz & Sons. The new fusing technique was however sufficiently important, it was felt, to justify the establishment of a subsidiary company. This was called the Essley Shirt Co., with the name derived from *S. Lie*bowitz. Finding the constraints of running a business rather tiresome, Benjamin Liebowitz set up a licensing business for his process by agreement with his family. This was the Trubenizing Process Corporation which was soon to produce the *Trubenised* semi-stiff collar. The name is thus an artificial verbal adjective formed from '*true*' and '*Ben*jamin'.

Trusthouse Forte (hotel and catering company) The firm originated in 1903 with the formation of Trust Houses, whose objective was to restore the standards of old coaching inns in Britain, many of which had declined with the coming of the railways. In 1970 the company, by then called Trust Houses Group Ltd, merged with Forte Holdings Ltd, the latter firm founded by Sir Charles Forte in 1935 as a catering interest. The name is often abbreviated to THF.

Tupperware (plastic houseware by The *Tupperware* Co.) The name suggests 'Cupperware', but the actual origin of the name is an American moulding engineer, Earl Tupper, who in the 1940s saw the possibility of using polyethylene for making bowls and other containers for food. *Tupperware* products were first introduced in the United States in 1945 by the Tupper Plastics Co. A special feature of the company is its *Tupperware* parties held to market the products in housewives' homes. Such parties were first promoted in America in 1946 and became so popular that in 1951 a special sales organisation, *Tupperware* Home Parties, was set up to run the home-based sales operations. This direct-sales method was brought to Britain in 1960, and *Tupperware* was first manufactured in England in 1963 at Wigan, Lancashire (now Greater Manchester).

Turtle Wax (car polish by Holt Lloyd International)   The name was devised by the founder of Turtle Wax Inc., Chicago, Benjamin Hirsch. Having begun by selling a car polish named 'Plastone', Hirsch was driving in the States when he stopped at a place named Turtle Creek. There he rested by a stream and was struck by the appearance of his reflection in the water. The combination of name and incident led him to think of a new name for his product, *Turtle Wax*. This, at any rate, is the story, the substance of which may well be true. The unusual name has resulted in supplies of turtles being offered to the company on several occasions. A former president of the company, Carl Schmid, used to refuse such offers politely and point out that the 'turtles' in *Turtle Wax* have the same relationship to the product as horses do to horseradish sauce.

TVR (cars and manufacturer)   The initials come from the first name of *Trevor* Wilkinson, the company's founder in the early 1950s. The three-letter initialism is in line with a number of similar car and motorcycle names, such as *BMW*, *DKW*, *NSU*, BSA, KTM and NVT.

Typhoo (tea by Cadbury *Schweppes*)   The name was the invention of a Birmingham grocer, John Sumner, who in 1863 was wondering what he could call a new brand of tea which seemed to relieve indigestion. He needed a distinctive name, one easy to pronounce, and a name that could be registered. After a number of ideas he eventually devised *Typhoo*. This has an oriental appearance suitable for tea ('typhoon') and together with 'Tips' or 'tea' was alliterative. The suggestion of 'typhoid' does not appear to have any ill effect on the popularity of the name or the product.

Tyrozets (antiseptic throat lozenges by Merck Sharp & Dohme)   The name derives from two of the product's ingredients, *tyro*thricin and benzocaine, with the 'z' of the name also suggesting 'lozenge'. The '-ets' suffix may refer to the manufacture of the lozenge by tabletting rather than moulding. Among earlier products of the company were 'Tetrazets', 'Tracinets', and 'Hydrozets', names that also strongly influenced *Tyrozets*. The lozenge was first marketed in 1949.

Ucal (pharmaceutical products by Macarthys Pharmaceuticals) The name is the acronym for *U*nited *C*hemists *A*ssociation *L*td, a firm taken over by Macarthys Pharmaceuticals Ltd of Romford, Essex.

Uhu (adhesive by Fismar) Not an acronym, not even a contraction, but the German word for the eagle owl! This bird inhabits the Black Forest where the German manufacturers of *Uhu* have their factory. The name has been in existence since about 1935, and is probably even better known in Germany than it is to English-speakers. Presumably the German name of the bird is derived from its call, just as 'peewit' and 'chiffchaff' are in English. The packaging of the adhesive has wording reminding the English-speaker how to pronounce the name ('yoo-hoo'). This is not the German pronunciation, which is nearer to 'oo-hoo'. The English pronunciation thus resembles the 'attention-seeking' cry sometimes spelt 'yo-ho'. For the product this self-advertising suggestion can be nothing but good. Moreover, like *Oxo*, the name is symmetrically satisfying to look at. *Uhu* is manufactured by the Irish firm of Fismar Ltd for the Beecham Group in Britain.

Umbro (sportswear by *Umbro* International) The manufacturing company is not on the river Humber but was founded in the 1920s by the H*umbr*eys *bro*thers, Harold and Wallace. (The latter was a silent partner, taking little or no interest in the firm.) The holding company of *Umbro* International and *Umbro* International (Footwear) is still called Humphreys Brothers Ltd. The footwear company markets products under the name *Adidas*.

Unigate (dairy and food products and manufacturer) The name reflects the merger between *Uni*ted Dairies and Cow and Gate, the former a practical name, the latter a romantic one. *Unigate* make *St Ivel* products.

Unilever (food products and detergents and manufactuer) The name unites the three companies of NV Margarine *Uni*e, Margarine *Uni*on, and *Lever* Brothers. NV Margarine Unie and Margarine Union were respectively the Dutch and British branches of the Dutch company Van den Berghs and Jurgens (itself a merger between two rival family businesses) formed in 1927. Lever Brothers was the English firm founded in 1885 by William Hesketh Lever

178

(1851–1935), later Viscount Leverhulme, and James Darcy Lever. (See *Lifebuoy, Lux, Sunlight.*) These three firms merged in 1930 to form *Unilever,* now a multinational organisation operating in over seventy-five countries. Operations in the United Kingdom are controlled by *Unilever* Ltd; operations outside Britain are controlled by *Unilever* NV, a Dutch company. Too many names beginning 'Uni-' could be a bad thing. Might there not already be several people who think that *Unigate* and *Unilever* are connected? The connotation of power behind 'lever' is no doubt of coincidental advantage to *Unilever.*

Uniroyal (rubber, plastic and chemical products and manufacturer) The original name of the firm founded in 1892 was the United States Rubber Company, or US Rubber in its short form. High feelings about the American involvement in Vietnam and the racial disturbances in Little Rock, Arkansas, in 1957 led to demonstrations against the company in some Latin-American countries. The 'nationalist' name was therefore changed to one that was universal and usable anywhere – *Uniroyal.*

Unitas (toilet fittings by Twyfords) The name almost certainly derives from Latin *unitas,* 'unity'. It was first registered in 1884 for a WC basin made in one piece, i.e. with an integral bowl and trap. Before this, the pan and trap had been manufactured in two separate parts. An unusual spin-off from the trade name has been the standard Russian word for a lavatory pan, *unitaz,* the altered spelling of the word being influenced by an existing Russian word *taz* meaning 'basin'. Thomas Twyford, the manufacturers of the articles, were already exporting washbasins and elementary-type closet pans to Russia in 1849, and the *Unitas* integral unit followed in due course.

Univac (computers and manufacturer) *Univac* started out as the Eckerts Mauchly Computer Corporation in the United States with a *Univac* computer. The latter name was an acronym for '*uni*versal *a*utomatic *c*omputer system'. In the early 1950s the corporation was taken over by Remington Rand and became the *Univac* division of this parent company. In 1955 the Sperry Corporation, formed by Elmer Sperry in 1905, merged with Remington Rand. The result was *Univac*'s parent group, the Sperry Rand Corporation. The correct title of the company is thus Sperry *Univac,* the 'Sperry' serving as a unifying name with Sperry Rand.

V

Valderma (antiseptic soap and cream by Reckitt & Colman)   The name was originally registered in 1940 by Dae Health Laboratories. The 'derma' element is undoubtedly derived from Greek *derma*, 'skin'. The initial 'Val-' directly suggests 'value', of course, but almost certainly derives from Latin *valeo*, 'to be strong', 'to be healthy'. Compare *Valpeda*.

Valium (tranquilliser drug by Roche Laboratories)   As with *Librium* and *Mogadon*, also made by Roche, the derivation is an arbitrary one, and the name has no meaning. The word is normally pronounced as 'valley' rather than as 'vale', which suggests that it may have connotations of 'value', 'valid', or even 'valour', in the public mind, rather than 'veil', say. It looks like a genuine Latin word (as does *Librium*), but the nearest Latin word to *Valium* is *vallum*, 'palisading', or *validum*, 'strong', 'powerful' – which could conceivably be a useful link. *Valium* was first produced in the United States in 1963.

Valor (oil heaters by *Valor* Heating Co.)   The name comes either from English 'valour' (or 'valor') or from the late Latin *valor*, 'strength'. Either way, it would seem to be simply a prestige name of a general nature. It was first popularised in 1890, when a Mr J. Wilson-Browne opened up a business in Birmingham to manufacture oil-storage containers. As a brand name for his products he used the trade mark of a small firm that he had taken over – a shield with the word 'Valor' written diagonally across it. The name and the device became the familiar insignia of the company that was founded in 1897 and that, after an abortive spell making bicycles, manufactured the *Valor* oil heater.

Valpeda (foot balm by Reckitt & Colman)   The name was based on an earlier name of the same manufacturing company, *Valderma*, with the 'peda' derived without doubt from Latin *pes, pedis*, 'foot'. *Valpeda* was registered as a name by Dae Health Laboratories in 1944, four years after *Valderma*. As with this other name, the 'Val-' element almost certainly means 'strong', 'healthy'.

Vanden Plas (car by *Jaguar Rover Triumph*)   An unusual name for a British car. It originated in Belgium, where a carriage-maker in Antwerp in the 1880s was Guillaume Van den Plas. The carriages

180

inevitably progressed to car bodies, but further advances were halted by the German invasion of Belgium in the First World War. Meanwhile in England, in 1913, a firm called Theo Masui Ltd, of Westminster, London, had changed its name to *Vanden Plas* (England) Ltd in order to build car bodies designed by Van den Plas under licence. When war broke out this company was taken over by the Aircraft Manufacturing Co. of Hendon and became committed to manufacturing aeroplanes. After the war *Vanden Plas* was resuscitated, moved to London in 1923, still making car bodies, and then, after another spell of involvement in aircraft work in the Second World War, became a subsidiary of Austin in 1946. The name then transferred to cars, with the 1947 Austin Princess becoming the *Vanden Plas* Princess and finally, from 1974, just the *Vanden Plas*.

Vaseline (petroleum jelly by Chesebrough-Pond's) There are two accounts of the origin of the name, both linked with the product's first manufacturer in about 1870, the American chemist Robert A. Chesebrough. The first, and more popular, is that Chesebrough devised the word from German *Wasser*, 'water', and Greek *elaion*, 'oil', thinking that petroleum was produced by the decomposition of water in the earth. The second, more homely version of the name, is that one day, when working in his laboratory and finding no empty beaker to hand, Chesebrough tossed out the flowers his wife had brought him from their *vase* and filled it with petroleum jelly. When he had perfected the process, there were several vases of jelly in the laboratory, and they inspired the name, with '-line' being the then popular suffix for medical products. The name has come to be used generically in French and German, and is sometimes treated generically in English, although in fact a registered trade mark in Britain.

Vauxhall (car and manufacturer) *Vauxhall* Motors is usually connected with the site of its headquarters, at Luton, Bedfordshire. The first *Vauxhall* car, however, was produced in 1903 in the Vauxhall district of south London, where originally, in 1857, a Scottish engineer named Alexander Wilson had founded the *Vauxhall* Ironworks at Lambeth. (Vauxhall itself was named after the 'Hall', or house, belonging to a Norman soldier here called Fulk or Falkes Le Bréant who, oddly, had in his day been Lord of the Manor of Luton.)

Veeto (depilatory cream by Reckitt & Colman) The name, when originally registered in 1922, belonged to a London firm called Tokalon Ltd, and was derived from the French *vite*, 'quickly'. (The

181

cream removed unwanted hair rapidly.) By 1961 the name had passed to Dae Health Laboratories, and in this year was changed to *Veet* 'O' – the 'O' standing for 'odourless'. When the property of Reckitt & Colman, this was finally streamlined to *Veeto*. The name also, of course, suggests 'veto' – 'no' to unwanted hair!

Veganin (analgesic tablets by William R. Warner & Co.)   An apparently arbitrary name – yet obviously suggesting 'vegetable', all the more since 'vegan' is a term sometimes used for a vegetarian. Yet the product does not appear to have any vegetable connection. (Its chief ingredients are *aspirin* and paracetamol.)

Velcro (fabric fastener by Selectus)   The name can be derived from English '*vel*vet *cro*chet' but in fact comes from the French equivalent, *velours*, 'velvet', *croché*, 'hooked'. *Velcro* the name originated around 1957 in Switzerland, where the 'touch and close' fastener, as it is called commercially, was invented by a Mr Georges de Mestral. The fastener consists of two *nylon* strips, one with a number of tiny hooks and the other with a corresponding number of small loops which the hooks grip when the two strips are pressed together. The 'Vel-' element of the name could be somewhat misleading, since the fastener is not made of velvet but, as mentioned, of *nylon*. Presumably its action suggests the smoothness of velvet, or its 'pile' is short and thick, as that of velvet is.

Velox (photographic paper by *Kodak*)   The word is Latin for 'swift'. *Velox* photographic paper can be developed under artificial light, which speeds the process up. Such paper was invented by L.H. Baekeland, better known for *Bakelite*, who in 1899 sold his *Velox* company and rights to George Eastman (see *Kodak*).

Vent-Axia (air-extraction units and manufacturer)   The company originally manufactured fans known as Axia Fans. These were axial fans, i.e. fans rotating on an axis (and not moving to and fro). The name was changed to *Vent-Axia* in 1936, with the first half of the name standing for 'ventilation'.

Vespa (motor scooter by Piaggio)   The Italian name means 'wasp'. The reference is not so much to the buzzing sound of the scooter but to its appearance: the rear end of the original *Vespa*, produced in 1947, did make it look like a wasp. The Italian manufacturers, Piaggio, went in for insect names. They also produced a three-wheeler car called 'Ape', Italian for 'bee', and an outboard motor named 'Moscone', 'bluebottle'.

Vick (vapour rub by Richardson-Merrell)   Who was Vick? Luns-ford Richardson, an American druggist in Selma, North Carolina, produced in the 1890s an embrocation using menthol which was then a novel external treatment for colds. He originally called it 'Richardson's Croup and Pneumonia Cure Salve', but understand-ably felt that a slicker and more marketable name was needed. He found it in his brother-in-law, Dr Joshua Vick, in whose drug store his career had begun. The name thus became first 'Vick's Salve', then 'Vick's VapoRub'. (Some accounts say that the name had also been suggested to him by a magazine advertisement for 'Vick's Seeds'.) 'Vick's VapoRub' was first sold in Britain in 1918. The manufacturing company, *Vick* Chemical Co., continued under this name until 1960 when it became a division of Richardson-Merrell. The vapour rub subsequently reverted to the name 'Vicks' rather than *Vick*, no doubt to reflect its origin more accurately.

Victory-V (lozenges by Barker & Dobson)   The name conjures up Churchillian images of the Second World War. The origin of the name, however, is not in call-signs and patriotic gestures but in a Bolton spinning-mill and a Scottish doctor. The doctor was Edward Smith, who in the mid-nineteenth century had compounded a loz-enge designed not only to relieve coughs and colds but also to settle upset stomachs. So great was the demand for the lozenge in Bolton, where Dr Smith worked, that he stepped up production and put it on the market as the 'Cough No More Lozenge'. In the process of expansion the doctor took over a bankrupt pharmaceuticals factory in Nelson, Lancashire, belonging to one Thomas Fryer, and in-stalled his younger brother there as manager. Back in Bolton one day, both brothers were on the trail for a more succinct trade name for their lozenges. Seeing a mill called the 'Victory Spinning Mill' Edward Smith told his brother: 'There's your name, William – Victory. How well it goes with Nelson.' He then named his product 'Victory Chlorodyne Lozenges' – in fact a misnomer, since they contained no chlorodyne. Aware of the anomaly, and also of the fact that because of its chlorodyne link the product might attract stamp duty, Smith dropped the word 'Chlorodyne' from the name and changed it to 'Linseed Licquorice V Lozenge Victory', placing the word 'Victory' last to make it proprietary. In 1911 the name was further streamlined to '*Victory-V* Lozenges'. Thus the alliterative phrase would appear to have originated some time before the Sec-ond World War and its extensive use by Churchill as a morale-raising device.

Victrola (*gramophone* by RCA)   The original manufacturing com-pany was incorporated in the United States in 1901 as the Victor

Talking Machine Co. (for the background to this, see *gramophone*). In 1906 the company produced a *gramophone* designed to look good as furniture, in a mahogany cabinet, and this was the *Victrola*. The concept of a combined *gramophone* and elegant piece of furniture proved popular, to the extent that imitation *Victrolas*, called 'Grafonolas', were subsequently produced by *Columbia*. The name seems to be a mock-Italian version of 'Victor', almost certainly influenced by the name *Pianola*, which had appeared nine years earlier. Based on the word *Victrola* in turn was 'Radiola', for an electric-recording *gramophone*, introduced in 1925, and the 'Electrola', an electrically operated *gramophone*. The *Victrola* was absorbed into RCA (the Radio Corporation of America) in 1929.

Vileda (cleaning cloths and manufacturer)   The arbitrary-seeming name derives from German *wie Leder*, 'like leather', the reference being to the company's principal product, a synthetic chamois window-cloth and car-cloth – which cleans like real chamois leather. *Vileda* the company is a German subsidiary of Bondina Ltd, itself a subsidiary of Carl Freudenberg GmbH who market the product world-wide.

Vim (cleansing powder by *Unilever*)   *Vim* was put on the market in 1904, initially with a good deal of misgiving about the choice of name which was 'thought to be too reminiscent of certain processed meat products'. (As a product, it was in fact an offshoot of *Monkey Brand* scouring soap.) One may like to see a classical origin of the name – Latin *vis*, *vim*, 'force', 'vigour' – but more likely is the English colloquial word 'vim' with the same meaning (and itself deriving from the Latin word).

Vimto (sparkling soft drink by J.N. Nichols (*Vimto*))   The original name of the drink was 'Vimtonic', i.e. a 'tonic' drink that gives you 'vim'. This was shortened some time ago to *Vimto*.

Virgin (*gramophone* records and manufacturer)   The name is typical of the 'counter-culture' movement of the 1970s. *Virgin* Records was founded in 1970 as a mail-order record company specialising in rock music. Its name, apart from any sexual connotations, must also have been chosen with the intention of denoting a 'virgin field' – that of mail-order rock records sold at a discount. ('Virgin' also implies 'innocence': ironically the name was apt for the new company, which went heavily into the red within a year of its launch.) The *Virgin* record label was introduced in 1973. An alternative name considered for the company, but wisely rejected, was 'Slipped Disc'.

Virol (malt tonic food by *Optrex*)   One of the most famous and most interesting of trade names, and one of the oldest. *Virol* was first produced experimentally in 1899, in the Old Street, London, factory of *Bovril* Ltd. As the demand for the product grew, *Bovril* formed a separate company, *Virol* Ltd, in the early 1900s. In 1920 the *Virol* production factory was moved to larger, more modern premises at Perivale, Middlesex. Some time before the Second World War *Virol* became associated with *Ambrosia*, and in order to create a product that would be a rival to *Horlicks* the joint venture produced '*Virol* and Milk'. This, however, proved expensive, and production ceased during the war. After the Second World War *Virol* changed hands more than once. Cavenham Foods took over *Bovril*, and therefore *Virol*, in 1971, but in 1977 sold *Virol* to Jenks Brothers of High Wycombe – who two years later sold it to *Optrex*. The name itself was created in the 'classical' period, and therefore might be supposed to originate from Latin *vir*, 'man' (or *virilis*, 'manly') with the '-ol' suffix denoting 'oil' (Latin *oleum*). The Latin word *vir* means not only 'man as opposed to woman' but also 'man as opposed to boy', and this distinction seems to support the origin of the name, since *Virol* was widely advertised as a suitable 'tonic' product for children ('Virol – Growing Boys Need It' was one popular slogan). But the fact that *Virol* was first made on the premises of *Bovril*, as an alternative product to *Bovril* itself, strongly suggests that the name is in fact a partial anagram of *Bovril*, with the 'virile' connotation a bonus. Whatever the truth of the case, no one seems to have been worried that the name might suggest 'viral'. But then, such an undesirable association would have been impossible, since the word 'viral' (as the adjective of 'virus') first appeared in English only as recently as 1950.

VitBe (wholemeal bread by Allied Mills)   The name undoubtedly derives from '*vit*amin *B*', since bread contains thiamine (vitamin B_1). There may also be a suggestion of '*vit*ality' or some similar 'health' word. The name is an old one.

Viva (car by *Vauxhall* Motors)   The name is a 'favourable association' one, as well as an alliterative name to go with *Vauxhall*. *Viva* suggests both English 'vivacious' and 'vivid' and Italian 'vivace' (the brisk, lively musical tempo). It also has a more limited but positive association with the Oxbridge oral examination called a 'viva'. This gives the name 'class'.

VIYELLA   **Viyella** (twill woven cloth by William Hollins & Co.)   The rather unusual name derives from a similarly unusual place name. The cloth was originally manufactured in the factory of William Hollins

185

in the valley called the Via Gellia, near Matlock in Derbyshire. The local inhabitants pronounced the name 'the Vi Jella', and this influenced the final form of the trade name, which was first registered in 1894. A spin-off (literally) from the name was that of *Clydella* (with which the fabric is sometimes confused). The Via Gellia itself has a mock Roman road name derived from that of the man who built it, Philip Gell of nearby Hopton Hall, Wirksworth. (The road is now a section of the A 5012 between Buxton and Nottingham.)

Volkswagen (car and manufacturer)   The famous 'people's car' (the meaning of the German name) ordered by Hitler. The original company to manufacture the car was set up in 1937 as the *Gesellschaft zur Vorbereitung des deutschen Volkswagens mbH* ('Company for the development of the German people's car'). The site for the works was 50 miles east of Hanover, near Fallersleben, and was named (1938) as the *Stadt des KdF-Wagens* ('Town of the Strength-through-Joy Car'). (The town that grew up was renamed Wolfsburg in 1945 by the British military government, and the Volkswagen Werk GmbH, as it had now become, was temporarily renamed the Wolfsburger Motorenwerke.) The prototype of the *Volkswagen*, called the 'Volksauto', was built by *NSU* in 1934 to a design by *Porsche* as a small, air-cooled, rear-engined vehicle. The previous year Hitler – who himself always had a *Mercedes* – had told Porsche that he wanted a 'car for the people', which was to be air-cooled and to cost under 1,000 marks (i.e. roughly £50). The first *Volkswagens* were manufactured in 1936, with a military version of the car ordered by Rommel for use in the desert. After subsequent mergers and take-overs *Volkswagen* came to produce not only the 'VW' but the *Audi* and the *NSU*.

Volvo (car and manufacturer)   The first *Volvo* car made its test run from Stockholm to Göteborg, in Sweden, in 1926. It was produced by a company set up by two engineers, Assar Gabrielsson and Gustaf Larson, who felt that there was a future for a car industry in Sweden. The name is Latin for 'I roll', but originally this did not apply to the car but to a subsidiary of the firm where the two men worked, SKF, which was a ball-bearing concern. The name, with its two 'Vs' and two 'Os' is visually and graphically memorable, and a good international name – but is its resemblance to an anatomical term a potential embarrassment? (Doubtless *Volvo* are aware of this – yet the logo on the cars shows the name in the centre of a circle with a top-right out-pointing arrow – the astronomical sign for Mars or the male!)

Vono (bedding and beds and manufacturer) There is some un-certainty about the name, but it is thought it may derive from the surname Vaughan – a family of this name founded the business around 1920. In its stylised form it is a successful name: easily written, easily spelled, easily pronounced, easily remembered, and international in appearance. It is also, with its two 'Os', aestheti-cally satisfying. Almost the perfect trade name, therefore!

Vosene (medicated shampoo by Beecham Products) The name is curiously difficult to track down. Is it entirely arbitrary? Perhaps not, since the product was first put on the market by a retired Billingsgate fishmonger who had moved to Bury, Lancashire, in 1946, and the company who originally manufactured *Vosene* was called Vosemar Ltd. (It was acquired by Beecham in 1955.) Pos-sibly the name of that fishmonger was Vos (there are thirteen in the London Telephone Directory), or Vose, or Voss?

Walpamur (paints by Crown Decorative Products) The name is a contraction of The *Wa*ll *Pa*per *M*anufact*ur*ers Ltd, formed in 1899. This company began to manufacture paints in 1906 as a subsidiary activity to producing wallpaper. With the success of the paint side of the business, the company name was changed to *Walpamur* in 1915. In 1975 the name was changed completely to Crown Decor-ative Products, since it was felt that the name *Walpamur* was as-sociated too closely with the original water-based wall paints, whereas the company was now producing emulsion paints. More-over, the company's prime name of 'Crown' had become widely familiar as a trade name for its paints. The name *Walpamur* is a rather awkward one, although its final syllable '-mur' also suggests the French word for 'wall', which was presumably a bonus.

Waverley (pen nib by Macniven and Cameron) see **Pickwick**.

Weldmesh (welded wire by The BRC Engineering Co.) The name is virtually self-descriptive – '*weld*ed *mesh*'. The company, now a subsidiary of The British Reinforced Concrete Engineering Co. (hence BRC), was manufacturing various kinds of fabric reinforce-ment in the early 1900s. Soon after 1930 they began specialising in welded wire mesh, producing this as a separate business. The name has shown a tendency to be used generically for any type of wire-

187

mesh reinforcement system, which of course the company vigorously resists.

Welgar (cereal products by *Nabisco*)   see **Shredded Wheat**.

Westclox (clocks and manufacturer)   The name was adopted by The Western Clock Co. of the United States, founded in the late nineteenth century (and subsequently a subsidiary of General Time Corporation). Presumably the company had its headquarters in the western part of a state or to the west of a town or city.

White Horse (whisky by *White Horse* Distillers)   The origin of the name is the White Horse Inn, in the Canongate, Edinburgh, where the whisky was first sold. It was originally known as 'Mackie's' after the family who produced it, and was named *White Horse* by Sir Peter Mackie in the late 1880s. The inn itself is believed to have been named after the white horse ridden by Mary Queen of Scots from her palace at Holyrood House to Edinburgh Castle. The company of *White Horse* Distillers acquired its name in 1924, the year of Peter Mackie's death.

Wimpy (hamburgers by *Wimpy* International)   The name applies both to the hamburger – allegedly having 'secret' spices added and sold in bread baked to a special recipe – and to the *Wimpy* Bars where they are sold. The *Wimpy* originated in Chicago apparently some time before the Second World War. It acquired its name from a hamburger-loving character in a *Popeye* comic strip – J. Wellington Wimpy. Britain's first *Wimpy* Bar opened in 1954 at what was then the Lyons Corner House in Oxford Street, London, and J. Lyons have had the monopoly of sales everywhere outside the United States (where *Wimpy* Bars are under franchise from the United Biscuits Group). For another famous American trade name of comic-strip provenance, see *Jeep*. The name *Wimpy* must not of course be confused with that of the builders and contractors, George Wimpey & Co.

Winalot (dog biscuits by Spillers Foods)   A fairly transparent name, and a prestige one: dogs fed on *Winalot* win a lot of awards! Yet the origin was not exactly that, since *Winalot* was initially formulated as a greyhound food. Thus the prizes were first specifically won, or intended to be won, for racing. The name was first used in 1927.

Wincarnis (tonic wine by Reckitt & Colman)   The product originated in the 1880s as 'Liebig's Extract of Meat and Malt Wine', which was sold by a William Coleman (*sic*) at his chemist's shop in Bury St Edmunds, Suffolk. After the First World War, when Coleman's business had passed into other hands, the name of the tonic wine was changed to *Wincarnis*, a blend of 'wine' (or perhaps Latin *vinum*, 'wine') and the Latin for 'flesh', *caro, carnis*. In 1969 Coleman & Co. Ltd were acquired by Reckitt & Colman. Liebig's 'Extract' also led to *Oxo*.

Windolene (window-cleaning fluid by Reckitt & Colman) The name was first registered in 1922. The first part of the name is obvious; the second would seem to be intended to suggest 'clean' rather than be simply a suffix '-olene' (or both '-ol' and '-ene'). Reckitt & Sons registered the product name 'Wyndol' simultaneously with *Windolene*.

Wolseley (car by Austin Morris) The name is of Australian origin, coming from the *Wolseley* Sheep Shearing Machine Co. (whose own name is only coincidentally suggestive of 'wool'). Herbert Austin, founder of Austin, worked for this firm in Australia, then in 1893 returned to his native England to join the recently formed *Wolseley* engineering company there. He began to design cars for them, so that in 1900 the first *Wolseley* car was produced. Six years later he left to make Austin cars under his own name, while *Wolseley* continued, gaining a reputation for solid family cars. The firm came under Morris in 1927 and later reunited with Austin in the British Motor Corporation which eventually became *BL*.

Wolsey (hosiery and manufacturer) Another name that only by chance appears to be associated with 'wool'. The origin this time is with Cardinal Wolsey, who was buried in Leicester Abbey, the ruins of which are not far from the present *Wolsey* factories in Leicester. *Wolsey* Ltd was formed in 1920 as the result of a merger between R. Walker & Sons and W. Tyler & Sons.

XEROX **Xerox** (xerographic process by Rank-*Xerox*) The name derives from the scientific word for the particular dry-copying process, itself based on Greek *xeros*, 'dry'. Unlike a conventional photographic process, xerography does not use liquids or chemical developers but an electrically charged surface. The word 'xerography', in turn based on 'photography', was coined in 1948, although the process itself was invented by an American scientist, Chester Carlson, in 1937. The trade name, like *Exxon*, is striking and memorable because of its two 'Xs'. It is also sometimes used generically for any type of photocopying process, much as Cyclostyle, Mimeograph and *Roneo* were earlier at times used for any process of duplicating. 'Please', the firm's lawyers exhort the public, 'don't say "I'll *Xerox* a copy for you". Say, "I'll make a duplicate for you on the *Xerox* copier".'

Xylonite (cellulose nitrate by BXL)   The company that is now BXL (*Bakelite Xylonite* Ltd) has its origins in the *Xylonite* Co. founded in about 1868 by an English scientist, Daniel Spill. The company produced cellulose nitrate, and took its name from the Greek for 'wood', *xulon* (as in 'xylophone'), cellulose being one of the main substances of which wood consists. The *Xylonite* Co. closed in 1874, but three years later Spill and four others formed the British *Xylonite* Co, which in 1885 began making *Xylonite* shirt collars and cuffs. *Xylonite* as a name still belongs to BXL but the product itself is manufactured by the Sheet and Film Division of British Industrial Plastics. Standard dictionaries that give the word *Xylonite* often define it simply as '*celluloid*'.

Yale (locks by *Yale* Locks & Hardware)   The name is that of an American locksmith, Linus Yale, who first developed his pin-tumbler lock in 1848, then progressing via the *Yale* Infallible Bank Lock (1851) to the combination lock (about 1862). In 1868 *Yale* founded the *Yale* Lock Manufacturing Co. at Stamford, Connecticut. He is not the Yale after whom Yale University in Connecticut is named: this was Elihu Yale (1648–1721), formerly an English government official in India (although himself American-born). There are a number of makes of cylinder lock, all based on the *Yale* lock and sometimes erroneously referred to as such.

Y-Front (underwear by Lyle & Scott)   The name is descriptive of the inverted Y-shaped tape on the front of underpants. *Y-Front* underwear – which includes vests, that obviously have no 'Y-Front' – were first manufactured by Lyle & Scott in about 1950. Since the registration of the *Y-Front* name, some time before 1940, many attempts have been made to manufacture or sell underwear under this name. All such attempts have been successfully contested by

Lyle & Scott, including one made by *Wolsey* to market underpants named 'X-Fronts'!

Yorkie (chocolate bars by Rowntree Mackintosh) The name alludes directly to the Rowntree Mackintosh headquarters at York. It also indirectly suggests the 'solid' characteristic of a Yorkshire-man or 'Yorkie', such suggestion being deliberately made to describe the chocolate's chunkiness.

Yo-Yo (toy consisting of a reel wound and unwound on a string, made by Louis Marx & Co.) The name is in fact a trade mark. It is exclusive to firms manufacturing it within the Dunbee Combex Marx Group. Manufacturers outside this group are bound by law to use an alternative name for the toy. According to the *Guinness Book of Records* the device originated from a Filipino jungle fighting weapon recorded in the sixteenth century, with the name for it allegedly meaning 'come-come'. The craze for playing with *Yo-Yo*s is said to have been started in Chicago by one Donald F. Duncan in 1926. The toy was first marketed in the United States by Louis Marx in 1929, and was introduced to Britain in 1932. Although true *Yo-Yo*s are Louis Marx ones, the word is sometimes used generically (as *yo-yo*) for any make of the toy.

Z

Zam-Buk (antiseptic ointment by Fisons) A former ingredient of the ointment was a substance known as 'Zambuci oil'. *Zam-Buk* was originally the formula of a medical officer in the Indian Civil Service, and first came on the market in 1903.

Zebrite (grate polish by Reckitt & Colman) The name suggests 'zebra', and this indeed was the animal chosen, because of its black-and-white stripes, for the original product. This was a 'black lead for polishing purposes' introduced by Reckitt & Sons in 1890, simply under the name 'Zebra'. The name was changed to *Zebrite* in 1952, partly because the new name reflected the 'black and white' concept of the earlier product (and which like it was packed in a black-and-white wrapper), and partly because the ending '-brite' indicated that the product was a polish.

Zephyr (cars by Ford Motor Co.) Cars named after winds have always had a certain popularity. A zephyr is a soft, gentle westerly breeze, and as such the word is a good name for a car that should run smoothly, gently, and warmly. Compare more exotic names such as *Scirocco* and *Passat*.

Zipper (slide fastener)   The word was once a trade mark. It was coined by the American company of B.F. Goodrich as a trade mark for its overshoes provided with such fasteners in 1925. (Slide fasteners themselves had been invented some time before this, with Whitcomb L. Judson patenting a 'Clasp Locker or Unlocker for Shoes' on 29 August 1893.) The name was chosen from the fact that operating the fasteners produced an audible sound 'zip'. The actual coining is said to have been the work of a Goodrich executive, who when first shown the new boots 'zipped' them up and down and said 'Zip 'er up!'. The name thus applied to the overshoes (which Britons know better as galoshes), which were known as '*Zipper* Boots'. From its use of overshoes, the fastener came to be widely used on other common articles, and predictably the name 'Zipper' was increasingly applied to the fastener itself. By 1928, as the *Oxford English Dictionary Supplement* shows, the word 'zipper' was taking on the aspect of a generic noun. This naturally alarmed Goodrich, who appealed to the courts to have their name protected. Their rights in the trade mark were sustained – but only with reference to their boots. The position now is therefore that *Zipper* Boots are boots with a zip manufactured by the B.F. Goodrich Co., but that 'zipper' has become a common noun for a zip fastener (which term itself derives from 'zipper').

Zodiac (cars by Ford Motor Co.)   The Ford Motor Co. at one time went in for names beginning with 'Z'; this and *Zephyr* are two of them. Apart from its astronomical and astrological significance, which give the name an exotic air, the general meaning of the word (cycle or circuit) is suitable for the name of a wheeled vehicle.

Zonophone see **gramophone**.

Zubes (throat lozenges by Roberts Laboratories)   The origin can only be guessed at. The name may be purely arbitrary, or have a specific derivation. It seems to have originated some time before the First World War, and has since been held by a number of companies, with Roberts Laboratories acquiring it in about 1971. (*Zub*, pronounced 'zoob', is the Russian word for 'tooth'; could it be that the lozenge is a toothsome or palatable one?)

Appendix I
Letters and suffixes

There seems little doubt that individual letters of the alphabet, and also particular suffixes, play a special role in the effectiveness of a trade name.

Of all the letters of the alphabet, one vowel, 'O', and one consonant, 'X', are specially favoured.

'O' has for many years been used in English as a terminal vowel of a word or element to fulfil a particular function.

1   It occurs as a final combining vowel in ethnic terms (Anglo-American, Sino-Soviet), in scientific and technical terms (cumulo-nimbus, partheno-genesis), and in more recent literary and critical expressions (serio-comic, politico-social).

2   It frequently occurs before the final element of a scientific word (photography, astronomy, thermometer, physiology).

3   Doubtless partly as a result of this usage, it comes as the final letter of many abbreviated words (photo, compo, hippo, demo, memo, video, disco).

4   From this in turn comes its use as a final vowel of several slang words, in some of which it is virtually meaningless (ammo, lingo, appro, blotto, doggo).

5   A special application is its use in spoken words designed to attract attention or to indicate a positive reaction or message. These range from the former cries of streetsellers ('Milko!', 'All-alive-o!', 'Pie-o!') via the commonest self-announcing word of all ('Hello!') to such responsive expressions as 'Goodo!', 'Righto!' and toasts and farewells such as 'Bung-ho!' and 'Cheerio!'

6   Finally, the vowel is used terminally to form an affectionate shortening of a masculine proper name (Jacko, Robbo, Timo, Micko).

In standard words and names, 'O' occurs as the final letter to give a number of associations.

1   *Foreign* generally, but particularly Italian and Spanish (amigo, bambino, tempo, magnifico).

2 *Exotic*, especially African or oriental (jumbo, Negro, macao, mikado).

3 *Musical*, from the Italian (soprano, piano, concerto, allegro, scherzo).

4 *Classical* (Milo, Sappho, Apollo, Scorpio, Leo, Virgo)

This considerable range of uses and associations means that the vowel 'O' has long been popular as a trade-name suffix (see below).

Considered purely visually, the letter has a considerable aesthetic appeal. It has a perfectly rounded form, and is complete and basic. As a circle, it has a 'targeting' effect, drawing the eye to its centre. Its shape is moreover associated with the human eye (for seeing and noting a trade name containing it) and mouth (for consuming a product!). On its own, too, it is a natural expression used to convey surprise, delight, and pleasure ('Oh, look!', 'Oh yes!'). In its more poetic form, 'O', it has a similar function, as in Whitman's, 'It's O for a manly life in the camp.'

Small wonder, then, that the letter is used not only as a suffix in trade names but frequently as a vowel in any position. Indeed, it can be effectively used twice or more in a name (*Bronco, Do-Do, Ferodo, Omo, Oxo, Polo, Volvo, Vono, Roneo, Odo-Ro-No*).

In many ways 'X' complements 'O', and not only from the combination of the two letters in noughts-and-crosses (or tic-tac-toe) and football pools!

Unlike 'O', however, it is not used extensively as a terminal or other letter in English, and its most common occurrence is in the affix '-ex-' with which prefix many English words begin (excellent, extract, expert, and so on) and which serves as a constantly popular suffix for trade names (see below).

Apart from its strong classical connotations – several Greek words and names begin with 'X' and even more Latin ones end with it – the letter has found one use in English, however. This is the commercial 'shorthand' form for '-cks' or a similar sound, as in sox (socks), chox (chocolates), snax (snacks), bix (biscuits) and pix (picks or pictures).

Whereas there are comparatively few words containing or ending in 'O' that relate directly to commercial products (except perhaps radio, dynamo and product itself), there are a number of standard words with 'X' that are closely linked with the advertising world and the marketing process. Among them are excellent, luxury, texture, extra, flexible, maximum, box, fix, mix, oxygen, extract, complex, flux, and, of course, sex. There are also several words having the sound of 'X' of this type, as accessory, electrics, access, prospects and the like.

As a letter in itself, 'X' is possibly even more 'charismatic' than 'O' since it has several symbolic associations favourable to the

194

trade-naming process. As a sign for a cross (and Christianity) it has great status value, either at a general ethical level or more personally. An 'X', after all, is a sign that 'marks the spot' where something desirable (treasure?) is to be found. It is also the mark made by a person when casting a vote as well as serving as a substitute for the name of a person who cannot write his signature. 'X', too, is the symbol for an unknown quantity (as the mathematical 'x') or identity (as 'Mr X', 'Brand X'). ('Brand X' was the anonymous washing powder unfavourably compared with Daz in early TV commercials in Britain. One result of this was that a Lancashire shopowner planned to market his own brand of powder actually named 'Brand X'.) Conventionally, it has come to be used as a symbol to denote the strength of an ale, from XX (medium strength) to XXX (very strong) and even XXXX (extra strong). Its uses as a category of film ('adults only') and as the personal sign for a kiss also help to give the letter a special impact. Oddly, its use as the sign for a wrong answer (the opposite of a tick) seems to have little adverse effect on its popularity in trade names. This is doubtless because its use to show a *right* answer, as the voting mark already mentioned, outweighs this other undesirable association.

In its visual appearance 'X', like 'O', is aesthetically satisfying, and its regular, uniform shape gives it a desirable balance and symmetry. Like 'O', too, 'X' is a 'target' letter, drawing the eye to its central point at the cross of the two diagonals. Unlike 'O', however, a trade name with more than one 'X' is rarely satisfactory. *Xerox* is reasonably balanced, but the double 'X' of *Exxon* is simply excessive. *Ex-Lax* is something of a mouthful but more acceptable.

The incisive sound of 'X' is also valuable for a trade name that needs to be businesslike, efficient, or 'snappy'.

Probably one of the most satisfying and memorable trade names of all is the one that combines both letters in perfect harmony and balance – *Oxo*.

'X' contains the sound of 'ks', and the letter 'K' itself is perhaps the third favourite of the trade name creators. In fact no less than four letters of the English alphabet have the sound 'k' and words containing these letters are frequently respelled with 'K' in trade names. The four letters are 'c' (when 'hard' before 'a', 'o' and 'u'), 'q', 'x', as we have seen, and of course 'k' itself. An initial 'c' is often turned into a 'k' in trade names, giving such names as *Kleenex*, Kleer, Krooklok, Kumfikut, and Kosi. An initial 'qu' is often similarly converted, as in *Kwells* and the many trade names starting Kwik-.

The popularity of 'K' seems mainly due to two factors. First, it occurs regularly in words having an exotic association (yashmak, sheikh, batik, karate, koala, krypton), and second, it is noticeably

more eye-catching, and thus memorable, than the rather commonplace 'c' for which it is so often a substitute.

It is not used to form any distinctive suffix, unlike 'O' and 'X',
and its visual appearance has nothing like the impact made by
these two other letters.

It makes up for this, though, by its sound, which is even more
'commercial' than that of 'X', whose initial 'k' sound is rather
dampened by the following soft 's'.

The classic example of a trade name making optimum use of 'K'
is, of course, *Kodak*. The appeal that the letter had for George
Eastman, who devised the name, is one that it must have for many
consumers and customers, since the sound of 'K' is associated with
many regular words expressing a quick, clean, or efficient action,
among them a number beginning cl- (clasp, clean, clever, click,
clinical, clip, clock, close, cluster).

The letter, or its sound, also commences several 'prestige' words,
such as cap, cup, client, class, cure, cute, cost, crystal, crown, king
and queen, making it even more valuable in a trade name.

The enormous popularity of *Kodak* itself, although meaningless,
must have increased the vogue for the letter in trade names. It is
very likely, for example, that the name *Kotex*, also apparently meaningless, was directly inspired by it.

Kodak and *Kotex* both have a double 'K' sound, and other names
also get double value from the letter, among them *Kit-Kat*, *Klaxon*,
Kleenex, *Konica*, *Contac*, *Cookeen*, *Cutex* and, most effectively, *Cuticura*
and *Coca-Cola* (this latter name having three 'K' sounds).

Apart from 'O', 'X' and 'K', most other letters of the alphabet
are not markedly favoured for trade names. (An exception is 'A'
used as a suffix – see below.) True, the 'soft' values of such letters
as 'L', 'M', 'N', 'R' and 'S' are exploited (see *Lenor*, which uses
three of them), but in many cases the presence of these letters in a
name is simply coincidental, even if appropriate (as in *Lilia*, *Marmite*, *Nestlé*, *Ribena*, and *Sensodyne*). The letter 'V', too, has certain
useful associations (victory, vital, virile), and names beginning with
this letter easily outnumber those beginning with 'W', which letter
seems curiously unpopular for trade names, doubtless because of its
cumbersome appearance and weak sound. (In the English language,
this position is reversed, and there are many more words starting
with 'W' than with 'V'.)

Let us now consider some of the most common trade-name
suffixes.

1   The suffix -*a*, sometimes appearing in the form -*ia* or -*ea*, is
probably the most common there is. It gives a name a foreign look,
and frequently an exotic one. At the same time the suffix is a
classical one and, as a grammatical consequence of this, a feminine

one. (Most Latin first declension nouns end in -a and are feminine, and the same ending is used for a Latin feminine adjective.) Not surprisingly, many trade names with the suffix -a actually are foreign in origin, as *Fiesta, Granada, Kia-Ora, Lambretta, Vespa* and *Viva*. In some names the final -a is not a true suffix but the last letter of a Latin element, as in *Ryvita* (Latin *vita*) and *Bournvita*. In others the suffix is really -ca standing for 'camera', as in *Fujica, Konica, Leica* and Praktica (a '*practi*cal *ca*mera'). In a very few cases the suffix seems to represent the English -er or -or, as in *Sifta* ('sifter') but not *Cuticura* ('curer').

The suffix -ola is a special one (see below).

2 A suffix denoting either a diminutive or a feminine association (and often both) is *-elle*, with the related *-ella, -etta* and *-ette*. (These suffixes are standard ones in French and Italian respectively.) Of these four, -ette has come to be used in standard English to denote a diminutive or female word or name, such as suffragette, novelette, drum majorette, Annette, Bernadette, Jeanette, Lynnette, Nanette. There are also a few words with -elle (bagatelle, mademoiselle) but these are more obviously direct French borrowings. The suffix -ella is even rarer in standard English, although it is seen in umbrella (from the Italian *ombrella*), tarantella (again from the Italian) and, of course, Cinderella, the little cinder girl. The latter name may well have influenced the names of the fabrics *Viyella* and *Clydella* and also the womenswear *Spirella*. All three products have homely, feminine associations. The other suffixes are seen in such names as the fabrics *Courtelle* and *Lirelle* and the curtain tapes *Rufflette*. Possibly, too, the ending of *Sarille* belongs in this group. (Further girls' names that strengthen the feminine association generally are Camille, Henrietta, Isabella, Loretta, Michelle, and that little plum of a name, Prunella.)

3 The suffixes *-ene* and *-ine* (or *-in*) are frequently used for trade names of medicines and chemical substances, as they are for standard English words of this type (benzene, quinine, gelatin, penicillin). Among familiar examples are *Anadin, aspirin, Crimplene, Dequadin, Dramamine, Germolene, Listerine, Marzine, Phosferine, Seccotine*, and *Terylene*. (See also -gen below.) In some cases, especially when in the form -lene, this suffix seems to stand for 'clean'. This is true of *Windolene*, and perhaps of *Germolene* above. It may even apply to *Drene* and *Vosene*, both being hair 'cleaning' products.

4 The famous *-ex* suffix seems to have two main connotations. First it is used simple as a classical element to give a name a prestige flavour but to have little if any meaning in itself. Probably this is its use in such names as *Dimplex, Durex, Kleenex* and *Lurex*. Second, it denotes some specific English word, such as *ex*cellent or, when preceded by 't', *t*exture. Unless so specified by the manufac-

turer or creator of the name, of course, it is difficult to know when 'excellent' is the intended meaning. The 'texture' sense, however, can be clearly appreciated in such names as *Aertex*, *Playtex*, and *Spontex*. The classical '-ex' can, though, have a meaning – that of 'out' or 'from' or 'derived from'. This is the significance of the element when used as a prefix in such standard English words as 'exclude', 'extract' and 'express'. In trade names this sense of the suffix is evident in such names as *Earex* (out with earache), *Hedex* (out with headaches), *Sweetex* (out with sugar) and perhaps *Kleenex* ('cleans out'). In other cases the '-ex' is actually part of a longer word or element, either Latin or English. Latin *rex*, 'king' and *lex*, 'law', can be suggested (even if coincidentally) in such names as *Pyrex* and *Triplex*. English '*tex*ture' we have mentioned, as well as other words containing 'x' when we considered this letter. Other names ending in -x need to be considered in the light of the nature of the product and the letters that precede the 'x'. The final three letters of *Copydex*, for example, may derive from 'index', while the '-ox' of *Radox* stands for 'oxygen'. In the case of *Electrolux* the suffix (-lux) not only suggests Latin *lux*, 'light', but English 'luxury' and even 'luck'. Three favourable associations for the price of one! (Other Latin words ending in -x with good marketing associations are *dux*, 'leader' and *vox*, 'voice'. The -ex suffix was specially in vogue in the 1920s.*)

5   The suffix *-gen* or *-gene* has a limited application but a distinct one. It is used almost exclusively for pharmaceutical products, and is doubtless based on *oxygen* while at the same time meaning 'producing', 'giving'. *Sanatogen*, for example, 'produces health', while *Stergene* has a sterilising effect. It is possible that the word 'hygiene' has also influenced the use of this suffix.

6   The suffix *-ite* has the general sense that it has in standard English, that is 'belonging to', 'connected with' (as Jacobite, socialite, Israelite, Pre-Raphaelite). It is also used, in a number of ways, to indicate a range of scientific substances or organisms (many of them fossils or minerals), and from this has come to be used in trade names simply to mean 'this is a manufactured commercial product'. Examples of it in this function are *Araldite*, *Bakelite*, *Coalite*, and *Xylonite*. In *Marmite* the -ite is not a true suffix, and in *Zebrite* it is part of a variant spelling of 'bright'.

7   The famous *-o* suffix has been popular since the nineteenth century in such names as *Rinso*, *Bisto*, *Brasso*, *Brillo*, Blanco, *Jell-O*, Silvo, *Mirro* and *Paxo*. From these examples it will be seen to be

* A correspondent in *American Speech* (July 1927) instanced *Pyrex*, Celotex, *Kleenex*, *Kotex*, Simplex, Footex, Kanotex, Duplex, Bendex, Laminex, Pointex, Pinex, and Cutex.

largely associated with domestic products, and will thus not have the exotic or scientific connotations mentioned earlier when we considered the letter 'O'. Indeed, *Jell-O* would seem to have been inspired, even if subconsciously, by the streetsellers' cries ('Milko!' and the like). With more recent trade names it can have any of the connotations mentioned, such as scientific (*Aero*, *Dymo*, *Flymo*), foreign or exotic (*Allegro*, *Denovo*, *Scirocco*), or classical (*Echo*, *Milo*). In a number of names the true suffix is -co, which will usually indicate '*co*mpany' (*Atco*, *Nabisco*, *Pifco*, *Deeko* – but not *Tesco*). In others the suffix is really -mo and means 'motor' or 'dynamo' (*Dymo*, *Flymo*). A change of consonant will produce other words, so that the -to of *Vimto* is 'tonic' and the -cro of *Velcro* is '*cro*chet'. The -co ('company') suffix is common in acronyms such as Conoco (*Co*ntinental *O*il *Co*mpany), Texaco (The *Texa*s *Co*mpany), and Amoco (*Am*erican *O*il *Co*mpany).

8   A specialised suffix is *-oid*. In English words this is normally used to mean 'having the form of', 'resembling'. Like -o it began as a nineteenth-century suffix, receiving a considerable impetus from 'celluloid', which dates from 1871, and 'tabloid', dating from 1898. The latter word is an interesting one, since it was originally devised (from 'tablet' with this very suffix) by Burroughs Wellcome & Co. in 1884 as a trade mark applied to chemical substances used in medicine and pharmacy and afterwards for other goods. (It was held by the Court of Appeal to be a 'fancy word' as applied to the goods for which it was registered and was restricted to the products of this company.) The suffix appears in a small but time-ranging selection of trade names, from *Iron Jelloids* (which are jelly-like) to *Polaroid* (which is to do with the polarising of light).

9   Another specialised suffix is *-ol*. This is used chiefly for scientific products or pharmaceuticals containing either oil (Latin *oleum*) or some derivative or compound of alco*hol*. The 'oil' sense appears in such names as *Castrol*, *Clairol*, *Humbrol*, and perhaps *Virol*, while the 'alcohol' indication is given in *Dettol* and perhaps in *Euthymol* (but not in *BiSoDol*, apparently, or *Oxydol*). The -ol of *Ibcol* is in fact the suffix -co ('company') plus the 'l' of 'Limited'.

10   An interesting suffix is *-ola*. It, too, can mean 'oil', as in Mazola ('maize oil') but otherwise seems to be a kind of quasi-Italian diminutive, as exemplified in *Pianola* – which name, together with *Victrola* (which was based on it), boosted other names with the suffix, such as *Farola*. (The suffix even came to be used for a standard word, 'payola', meaning a bribe offered in return for help in promoting a commercial product by unlawful means.) Possibly even *Coca-Cola* and *Pepsi-Cola* benefit from this suffix, too, as well as themselves reinforcing it.

11   One of the most popular suffixes to be used for a specific

application is -on or -lon. This is used almost exclusively for synthetic fabrics. The suffix originated from *rayon* (which in turn was, it seems, partly inspired by 'cotton'), but was widely and extensively popularised by *nylon*. It can be seen in such names as *Bri-Nylon*, *Dacron*, *Dralon*, *Fablon*, *Orlon*, and many more (see the entry *nylon*). Like *nylon* itself, many names with this suffix are purely arbitrary and have no meaning. A number of them have been devised by a computer, so that the letters before the suffix are random (although in a few cases apparently stand for the initials of the fabric's inventor).

12   The suffix -*um* is sometimes found. This is of classical origin (it is the ending of Latin second declension neuter nouns and neuter adjectives) but in trade names has no specific meaning except to indicate a manufactured product – as in some cases the suffix -ex is used. It can occur in arbitrary names such as *Librium* and *Valium*, or as the ending of a genuine Latin element, as in *Aquascutum* (*scutum*, 'shield') or *linoleum* (*oleum*, 'oil'). In *Postum* it is unusually appended to a personal name. It is difficult to know precisely what type of Latin word inspired the use of the suffix – whether a historical word such as colosse*um*, muse*um*, or for*um* or a scientific term such as alumini*um* (alumin*um*) or urani*um*. It is not currently used widely, and is mainly restricted to drugs (such as Diemalum and Somniferum).

Other suffixes exist, of course. Some of them are self-explanatory, such as the more modern -mat (-matic) meaning 'automatic' and -teria meaning 'self-service' (as in cafe*teria*). Others are more restricted in use, as the -id of *Cyanamid* or the -ade of *Lucozade*.

For interest, check lists follow for all the names in the Dictionary ending in each of the twelve suffix groups mentioned above. In some cases the names have a 'suffix' that is really simply a terminal letter or letter group, but such names are included since to some degree they capitalise on the true suffix that the endings resemble. *Gillette*, for example, suggests the feminine diminutive suffix seen in *Rufflette*. Names whose final letters are clearly not suffixes (as the -on of *Avon* or the -in of *Penguin*) are, however, omitted from the lists.

To supplement list 4 (the suffix -ex) a further list is given of all names in the Dictionary, without exception, that contain either the letter 'x' in any position or a letter group such as '-cks-' that *produces the sound* of 'x'. It will be seen that compared to the 24 names quoted in list 4, a total of 71 names in the Dictionary have an 'x factor', making just on 9 per cent of the overall total of 783 names treated.

1   -*a* : Aga, Agfa, Alfa-Laval, Ambrosia, Ascona, Atora, Atra, Avia, Banda, barathea, Bata, Biba, Bonjela, Bournvita, Bukta, Cessna,

Cinerama, Columbia, Cona, Corona, Cortina, Creda, Cuticura, Decca, Elida, Fanta, Fiesta, Flora, Formica, Fujica, Goya, Granada, Honda, Hygena, Innoxa, Kia-Ora, Konica, Lada, Lagonda, Lancia, Leica, Lilia, Lufthansa, Manta, Matsushita, Mazda, Mecca, Minolta, Nivea, Omega, Polyfilla, Procea, Ribena, Rizla, Rowenta, Ryvita, Sabena, Saxa, Scania, Sifta, Simca, Škoda, Slimcea, Strada, Tia Maria, Toshiba, Toyota, Valderma, Valpeda, Vent-Axia, Vespa, Vileda, Viva.

2 *-elle* (-ella, -etta, -ette) : Chevette, Courtelle, Clydella, Gillette, Giulietta, Lambretta, Lirelle, Rufflette, (Sarille), Spirella, Viyella.

3 *-ene* (-ine, -in) : Anadin, aspirin, Benzedrine, Bermaline, Crimplene, Dequadin, Dexedrine, Disprin, Dramamine, Drene, Duralumin, Germolene, Listerine, Loxene, Marzine, melamine, Methedrine, Ovaltine, Panadeine Co, Phosferine, Plasticine, Rexine, Saxin, Seccotine, Silvikrin, Terylene, Vaseline, Veganin, Vosene, Windolene.

4 *-ex* : Aertex, Ampex, Amplex, Andrex, Copydex, Cutex, Dimplex, Durex, Earex, Gannex, Halex, Hanimex, Hedex, Kleenex, Kotex, Lurex, Optrex, Perspex, Playtex, Pyrex, Rolex, Spontex, Sweetex, Timex, Triplex. (Also prefixes in Exide, Ex-Lax, Exxon, and see supplementary list of 'x' names below.)

5 *-gen* (-gene) : Energen, Sanatogen, Stergene.

6 *-ite* : Araldite, Arborite, Bakelite, Coalite, Dolomite, Marmite, Xylonite, Zebrite.

7 *-o* : Aero, Alfa-Romeo, Allegro, Aspro, Atco, Avro, Be-Ro, Biro, Bisto, Brasso, Brillo, Bronco, Burco, Cinzano, Day-Glo, Deeko, Denovo, Do-Do, Dymo, Echo, Ekco, Eno, Esso, Ferodo, Flymo, Glaxo, Jell-O, Kalamazoo, Li-Lo, Marlboro, Meccano, Milo, Mirro, Nabisco, Odo-Ro-No, Omo, Oxo, Panadeine Co, Paxo, Pifco, Polo, Roneo, Sanyo, Scirocco, Sorbo, Subbuteo, Tesco, Toldo Typhoo, Umbro, Veeto, Velcro, Veno, Vimto, Volvo, Vono, Yo-Yo.

8 *-oid*(s) : Altoids, celluloid, Iron Jelloids, Meloids, Osmiroid, Polaroid. (See also p.199 for Tabloid.)

9 *-ol* : Berol, BiSoDol, Bradosol, Castrol, Clairol, Cuprinol, Dettol, Ercol, Euthymol, Humbrol, Ibcol, Lysol, Oxydol, Skol, Virol.

10 *-ola* : Coca-Cola, Farola, Pepsi-Cola, Pianola, Victrola.

11 *-on* (-lon) : Ban-Lon, Bri-Nylon, Canon, Chinon, Dacron, Dralon, Enkalon, Exxon, Fablon, Klaxon, nylon, Mogadon, Mu-cron, Nikon, Orlon, rayon, Revlon, Savlon, Teflon.

12 *-um* : Aquascutum, carborundum, Librium, linoleum, Platignum, Postum, Solignum, Valium.

Names containing 'x' or sound of 'x': Aertex, Ajax, Ampex, Amplex, Andrex, Bantam Books, Bendix, Britax, Copydex, Corgi Books, Cutex, Cydrax, DAKS, Dexedrine, Dexion, Dimplex, Durex, Earex, Electrolux, Exide, Ex-Lax, Exxon, Felix, Gannex, Halex, Hanimex,

Horlicks, Innoxa, Klaxon, Kleenex, Kotex, Loxene, Lurex, Lux, Mandrax, Max Factor, Maxwell House, Minimax, Mothaks, Optrex, Oxo, Oxydol, Paxo, Perspex, Playtex, Pyrex, Quix, Radox, Rexine, Rolex, Saxa, Saxin, Saxone, Scalextric, Spontex, State Express, Sweetex, Tampax, Three Candlesticks, Timex, Triplex, Turtle Wax, Vauxhall, Velox, Vent-Axia, Vick (now Vicks) Volkswagen, Westclox, Xerox, Xylonite.

Appendix II
Computer-devised names

The names that follow* were devised by a computer that was programmed to fulfil certain conditions. Each name was to have four letters, with the first and third a consonant and the second and fourth a vowel. Further, C, Q and X were not admissible as the first consonant, nor C and Q as the second, while the vowels were restricted to A,I,O,U or Y (i.e. all vowels omitting E). In spite of these constraints, such conditions allow 14,400 possible combinations of letters. Of these, 260 are quoted. Readers may like to consider what, if any, 'free associations' some of them may have (how about SOXO, WAKU or PIXY?). Note also that very few of the names in this sample are ordinary words in the English language.

BABA	DAMY	FIGO
BAGY	DASU	FILI
BALU	DAXO	FIRA
BARO	DIFI	FIVY
BAWI	DIKA	FOBU
BIDA	DINY	FOHO
BIHY	DITU	FOMI
BIMU	DIZO	FOSA
BISO	DOGI	FOWY
BIXI	DOLA	FYVA
BOFA	DOPY	FYZY
BOJY	DYSY	GAGU
BONU	DYXU	GALO
BOTO	FAFO	GARI
BOZI	FAKI	GAWA
BUGA	FAPA	GIBY
DADI	FATY	GIHI
DAJA	FAZU	GIMO

* Quoted from Werkman, pp. 478–9.

GISI	KISA	NIMA
GIXA	KIWY	NUTY
GODY	KODU	NUZU
GOJU	KOJO	NYGO
GYLU	KYGU	NYLI
GYRO	KYLO	NYRA
GYWI	KYRI	NYVY
HADA	KYWA	PABU
HAHY	LABY	PAHO
HAMU	LAHU	PAMI
HASO	LAMO	PASA
HAXI	LASI	PAWY
HIFA	LAXA	PIDU
HIJY	LIDY	PIJO
HINU	LIJU	PINI
HITO	LINO	PITA
HIZI	LITI	PIXY
HOGA	LUWI	POFU
HOKY	LYDA	RANO
HOPU	LYHY	RATI
HYMY	LYMU	RAZA
HYSU	LYSO	RIFY
HYXO	LYXI	RIKU
JAFI	MAFA	RIPO
JAKA	MAJY	RIVI
JANY	MANU	ROBA
JATU	MATO	ROGY
JAZO	MAZI	ROLU
JIGI	MIGA	RORO
JILA	MIKY	ROWI
JIPY	MIPU	SAGA
JIVU	MIVO	SAKY
JOBO	MOBI	SAPU
JYFU	MOHA	SAVO
JYKI	MYFI	SIBI
JYPA	MYKA	SIHA
JYTY	MYNY	SILY
JYZU	MYTU	SIRU
KAGO	MYZO	SIWO
KALI	NAGI	SODI
KARA	NALA	SOJA
KAVY	NAPY	SOMY
KIBU	NAVU	SOSU
KIHO	NIBO	SOXO
KIMI	NIHI	SUFI

SUKA	VOLO	ZAHA
SUNY	VORI	ZALY
TAMA	VOWA	ZARU
TARY	VUBY	ZAWO
TAWU	VUHU	ZIDI
TIDO	VUMO	ZIJA
TIJI	WAKU	ZIMY
TINA	WAPO	ZISU
TISY	WAVI	ZIXO
TIXY	WIBA	ZOFI
TOFO	WIGY	ZOKA
TOKI	WILU	ZONY
TOPA	WIRO	ZOTU
TOTY	WIWI	ZOZO
VADU	WODA	ZUGI
VAJO	WOHY	ZULA
VANI	WOMU	ZUPY
VATA	WUTO	ZUVU
VAXY	WUZI	ZYBO
VIFU	WYGA	ZYHI
VIPI	WYKY	ZYMA
VIVA	WYPU	ZYRY
VIZY	WYVO	ZYWU
VOGU	ZABI	

Appendix III
Unexplained names

The names that follow could not be satisfactorily explained for lack of information. Each name basically needs, in addition to the name of manufacturer: (1) explanation of its origin or derivation; (2) date (year) of first use or of registration; (3) change of ownership; (4) legal involvement, if any; (5) forms to which changed in foreign countries. Readers possessing such information are asked to send it to me c/o the publishers, supporting their material with the appropriate references to printed sources, private documents, etc. Some of the names are no longer active.

Alexandre (womenswear shops)
Bolex (cameras)
Contax (cameras)
Conway Stewart (pens)
Cosina (cameras)
Craven 'A' (cigarettes)
Croid (adhesives)
Dry Fly (sherry)
Dry Sack (sherry)
Emu (wool)
Fynnon ('health salts')
Jacqmar (scarves)
Jokari (bat and ball game)
Kangol (berets and safety helmets)
K-Tel (records)
Mac (throat lozenges)

Mamiya (cameras)
Noilly Prat (aperitif)
Oil of Ulay (cosmetics)
Osram (electric lamps)
Pentax (cameras)
Philco (radio and TV sets)
Q-Tips (cotton swabs for babies)
Richard Shops (womenswear stores)
Rocola (shirts)
Sadia (water heaters)
San Toy (cigars)
Stork (margarine)
Tecalemit (garage equipment)
Tri-Ang (toys)
Yashica (cameras)

As mentioned in the Introduction, information will also be welcome for those names whose origins are indicated in their respective entries as being uncertain or unsubstantiated.

Addenda

Below are given brief origins of names originally included on p. 206, and supplied by various correspondents to whom I here express my sincere thanks. I hope to provide full entries and individual acknowledgments in a future edition of the book.

Achille Serre (dry cleaners)   Originated in a Manchester cleaning business run by one H. (Bill) Serre. New owners of the business dropped the 'B' of 'Bill' to give the French-looking name.

Butterfly (adhesive paper products)   The manufacturers, Samuel Jones & Co., had their premises in Peckham Grove, Camberwell, London, and used the Camberwell Beauty butterfly as their device and name.

Canon (cameras)   The name originates in *Kannon*, the Japanese Buddhist goddess of compassion and mercy, and this was the name first used (in the spelling *Kwannon*) for the camera in the 1930s.

Hanimex (cameras)   The name originates in that of the company's Australian founder, Jack Hannes, with the *Han*nes *Im*port and *Ex*port Company providing all the letters of the name.

Mazawattee (tea)   Not 'ma's awa' to tea' or 'master, what tea', and the like, but two Tamil (Indian) words meaning 'luscious garden'. The name was created in England in the 1880s.

Penguin (chocolate wafer biscuits)   Apparently simply the name of a friendly animal, with the biscuit marketed mainly for child consumers.

Tabasco (sauce)   From the name of the state in Mexico where the variety of capsicum grows from which the hot, red sauce is prepared.

Vat 69 (whisky)   Apparently from a vat so numbered selected out of a total of nearly a hundred by blenders as containing the best whisky for a new brand in 1882.

Veno (cough mixture)   Either from one W. H. Veno, who built a house in Altrincham (now Greater Manchester) in the 1880s, or perhaps from the address of the Veno's Drug Company's premises in Gros*veno*r Street, Manchester.

Bibliography

The Bibliography is in four parts. Part one lists the standard dictionaries consulted for trade-name entries; part two gives the encyclopedias similarly used. The third and main part lists all other books consulted. These vary from specialised reference works to more general publications. Some are company histories. The fourth and final part lists relevant articles in journals and newspapers. These, like the books, vary from specialised articles on trade marks and trade-mark law to consumer magazines and general features.

1   *Dictionaries* (authors' and editors' names in brackets)

Chambers Twentieth Century Dictionary (E. M. Kirkpatrick). Chambers, Edinburgh, 1983.

Collins Dictionary of the English Language (Patrick Hanks). Collins, London, 1979.

The Concise Oxford Dictionary (J. B. Sykes). OUP, 1982.

Encyclopedic World Dictionary (Patrick Hanks). Hamlyn, London, 1971.

The Oxford English Dictionary (James Murray and others). OUP, 1971.

Reverse Dictionary of Present-Day English (Martin Lehnert). VEB Verlag Enzyklopädie, Leipzig, 1973.

The Shorter Oxford English Dictionary (C. T. Onions). OUP, 1975.

A Supplement to the Oxford English Dictionary (R. W. Burchfield). OUP, Volume I, A–G, 1972; Volume II, H–N, 1976; Volume III, O–Scz, 1982.

The Universal Dictionary of the English Language (H. C. Wyld). Routledge & Kegan Paul, London, 1961.

Webster's Third New International Dictionary (Philip B. Gove). G. & C. Merriam, Springfield, Mass., 1971.

2   *Encyclopedias*

Encyclopaedia Britannica, 15th ed., Encyclopaedia Britannica, Chicago. 1976.
Everyman's Encyclopaedia, 6th ed., Dent, London, 1978.

3   *Books*

Adams Jr, Russell B., *King C. Gillette: The Man and His Wonderful Shaving Device*. Little, Brown & Co., Boston and Toronto, 1978.

Baglee, Chris and Morley, Andrew, *Street Jewellery: A History of Enamel Advertising Signs*. New Cavendish Books, London, 1978.

Baker, R., *New and Improved. . . : Inventors and Inventions That Have Changed The Modern World*. British Museum Publications, London, 1976.

Beeching, Cyril Leslie, *A Dictionary of Eponyms*. Clive Bingley, London, 1979.

Bragina, A. A., *Neologizmy v russkom yazyke* [Neologisms in Russian]. Prosveshcheniye, Moscow, 1973.

Button, Henry and Lampert, Andrew, *The Guinness Book of the Business World*. Guinness Superlatives, Enfield, 1976.

Campbell, Hannah, *Why Did They Name It. . .?* Ace Books, New York, 1964.

Carter, E. F. (ed.), *Dictionary of Inventions and Discoveries*. Robin Clark, Stevenage, 1978.

A Century of Trade Marks, 1876–1976. HMSO, London, 1976.

Chemist & Druggist Directory, 1975. Benn Brothers, London, 1975.

Croucher, Robert M., *The Observer's Book of Motor Cycles*. Warne, London, 1977.

Dorlay, J. S., *The Roneo Story*. Roneo Vickers Ltd, Croydon, 1978.

Dunkling, Leslie, *The Guinness Book of Names*. Guinness Superlatives, Enfield 1983.

The Food Makers: A History of General Foods, Ltd. General Foods, Ltd, Banbury, 1972.

Gable, Jo, *The Tuppenny Punch and Judy Show: 25 Years of TV Commercials*. Michael Joseph, London, 1980.

Games & Toys Year Book for 1978/1979. Games & Toys, London, 1978.

Gelatt, Roland, *The Fabulous Phonograph: 1877–1977*. Cassell, London, 1977.

Gregg, D. W. A., *Brand Names for the Investor: A Guide to Manufacturers' Trade and Brand Names*. London Business Publications, London, 1963.

Grenville Smith, R. and Barrie, Alexander, *Aspro: How a Family Business Grew Up*. Nicholas International, Melbourne, 1976.

Hardingham, Martin, *Illustrated Dictionary of Fabrics*. Studio Vista, London, 1978.

Havenhand, Greville, *Nation of Shopkeepers*. Eyre & Spottiswoode, London, 1970.

Hopfinger, K. B., *The Volkswagen Story*. G. T. Foulis, Henley-on-Thames, 1971.

Jacobson, Sven, *Unorthodox Spelling in American Trademarks*. Almqvist & Wiksell, Stockholm, 1966.

Kendal, Robert, *The Competitors Handbook*. Paul Elek, London, 1977.

Key British Enterprises, 1979/1980. Dun & Bradstreet, London, 1979.

Kleiner, Richard, *Index of Initials and Acronyms*. Auerbach, Princeton, 1971.

Kornilov, L. and Fil'chikova, N., *Ot glashataya do neona* [From Herald to Neon]. Znaniye, Moscow, 1978.

209

Krauschar, Peter M., *New Products and Diversification*. Business Books, London, 1977.

Ladbury, Ann, *Fabrics*. Sidgwick & Jackson, London, 1979.

Lazell, H. G., *From Pills to Penicillin: The Beecham Story*. Heinemann, London, 1975.

Liebesny, F. (ed.), *Mainly on Patents: The Use of Industrial Property and its Literature*. Butterworths, London, 1972.

Lingeman, Richard R., *Drugs from A to Z: A Dictionary*. Allen Lane/Penguin, London, 1970.

Louis, J. C. and Yazijian, Harvey, *The Cola Wars*. Everest House, New York, 1980.

Mencken, H. L., *The American Language*. Abridged edition with annotations and new material by Rowen I. McDavid, Jr, Routledge & Kegan Paul, London, 1963.

Millard, Patricia, *British Made?* Kenneth Mason, Havant, 1969.

Morley, John (ed.), *Launching a New Product*. Management in Action Series. Business Books, London, 1968.

Moskowitz, Milton, Katz, Michael and Levering, Robert (eds), *Everybody's Business: An Almanac*. Harper & Row, San Francisco, 1980.

Mullen, Chris, *Cigarette Pack Art*. Ventura Publishing, London, 1979.

Nicholson, Tim, *Car Badges of the World*. Cassell, London, 1970.

Payton, Geoffrey, *Payton's Proper Names*. Warne, London, 1969.

Petersen, Clarence, *The Bantam Story*. Bantam Books, New York, 1975.

Pilditch, James, *Communication by Design: A Study in Corporate Identity*. McGraw-Hill International, Maidenhead, 1970.

Potter, Stephen, *The Magic Number: The Story of '57'*. Max Reinhardt, London, 1959.

Praninskas, Jean, *Trade Name Creation: Processes and Patterns*. Mouton, The Hague, 1968.

Rimmer, Brenda M., *Trade Marks: A Guide to the Literature and Directory of Trade Names*. British Library Board, London, 1976.

Roberts, Peter, *Any Color So Long As It's Black: The first fifty years of automobile advertising*. David & Charles, Toronto, 1976.

Robinson, Patrick, *The Shell Book of Firsts*. Ebury Press and Michael Joseph, London, 1974.

Robson, Graham, *The Land-Rover: Workhorse of the World*. David & Charles, Newton Abbot, 1976.

The Royal Warrant Holders Who's Who. The Royal Warrant Holders Association, London, 1921.

Seidler, Edward, *Let's Call It Fiesta: The Auto-Biography of Ford's project Bobcat*. Patrick Stephens with Edita, Lausanne, 1976.

Stiling, Marjorie, *Famous Brand Names, Emblems and Trade-Marks*. David & Charles, Newton Abbot, 1980.

The Times 1000: Leading Companies in Britain and Overseas. Times Newspapers, London, 1979.

Trade Marks: Report on a Survey among Housewives. Confederation of British Industry, London, 1975.

UK Trade Names 1982/3. Kompass Publishers, East Grinstead, 1982.

Werkman, Casper J., *Trademarks: Their Creation, Psychology and Perception*. J. H. de Bussy, Amsterdam, 1974.

Wilson, Charles, *The Story of Unilever*. Cassell, London, 1970.

4 *Journals and Newspapers* (author and relevant article in brackets)

American Speech, July 1927 (Walter E. Myers, Trade-name suffixes).

Atlantic Monthly, August 1932 (Frank H. Vizetelly, Pillaging the language).

Dialect Notes, vol. IV, pt. 1, 1913 (Louise Pound, Word-coinage and modern trade-names).

Financial Times, 17 September 1970 (Tony Dakin, The perils of popularity).

Industrial and Engineering Chemistry, September 1937 (E. W. Leavenworth, Lost monopolies of names and things).

Journal of Applied Psychology, October 1959 (Harry A. Burdick, Edward J. Green, and Joseph W. Lovelace, Predicting trademark effectiveness).

The New York Times, 10 January 1960 (Robert Alden, Advertising: trademark feuding recalled).

The New York Times Magazine, 7 July 1957 (Edith Efron, Brand new brand names).

She, October 1979 (Marjorie Stiling, Symbols of success).

South Atlantic Quarterly, Winter 1959 (S. V. Baum, Trademarks: a capital tug of war).

Sunday Times, 19 October 1980 (Andrew Cornelius, How Metro almost met its Match).

Sunday Times Magazine, 14 September 1980, 12 October 1980, 2 November 1980, 9 November 1980 (Johnny Black, Branded).

Telegraph Sunday Magazine, 12 October 1980 (James Leasor, Marks of Distinction).

Time, 6 July 1962 (The Marketplace: That which we call a rose).

The Times, 22 November 1978 (Bernard Levin, Another unacceptable face of capitalism).

The Times, 25 November 1978 (Letter to the Editor: Terry Stancliffe, Household trade names).

U.K. Press Gazette, 9 July 1979 (A sub's guide to registered trade-names).

U.K. Press Gazette, 8 October 1979 (A journalists' guide to registered trade-names).

Which?, autumn 1957 onwards.

Acknowledgments

This book could never have been written without the help of very many manufacturing companies and other organisations. The list that follows is intended to convey my sincere thanks to the officers of the respective companies mentioned. There were other correspondents, to whom I am of course also grateful, but those below were, I felt, particularly helpful, either writing to give exceptionally detailed or important information (and sometimes writing several times) or sending useful background material in the form of company publications and the like. Some firms lent photographs and books, others telephoned to help. I was not expecting managing directors or chairmen to write, since my initial enquiry was always directed to the 'Publicity Manager'. Many did, however, and I am most appreciative of their personal assistance. A few firms even kindly sent samples of their products – unsolicited, of course – and one such consignment was of practical help in combating the effects of an English winter as I worked on the book.

A few people were specially helpful, and I list them separately, at the end of the main roll.

Richard Aldwinckle, public relations manager, RHM Foods
Allan Allbeury, public relations executive, The Nestlé Co.
Terry Allen, chief press officer (news), Vauxhall Motors
J. C. Bailey, manager, public relations, Lyons Maid
Shirley Barnett, PR Projects
Peter L.G. Bateman, director, Rentokil
L.F. Baxter, communications executive, Chloride Group
E.A. Bean, Sony (UK)
R.W. Bennett, managing director, Ardente
H.J. Beshaw, plant manager, Vanden Plas assembly plant, British Leyland UK
A. Biddlecombe, public relations officer, Colt International
S.C. Bland, tapestry buyer, Parker Knoll Furniture

T.A. Bolton, business affairs manager, public affairs, Jaguar Rover Triumph

R.T. Britton, group trade marks department, Reckitt & Colman

W.B. Cameron, managing director, Waverley Cameron

C.G. Campbell, company secretary, DAKS-Simpson

A.R.W. Carrington, group legal adviser, The Prestige Group

B.R. Caukwell, registration manager, International Chemical Co.

A.J. Chalmers, The Rank Organisation

P.J. Chinn, executive director, Bahco Tools

S.R. Chinn, managing director, Viscose Group

Dennise Choa, Helena Rubinstein

C.E. Clapham, company secretary, Optrex

D.E. Cookson, administrator, Kodak Museum, Kodak

R.E. Cooper, director of public affairs, Esso Petroleum Co.

C.D. Dane, director, Dane & Co.

J.G.M. Davis, Nicholas Laboratories

M. Davis, product manager – retail, Deeko

Jeremy del Strother, secretary, Nationwide Building Society

Mrs Eileen M. de Vletter, secretary to financial director, Hitachi Sales (UK)

Robin Dickeson, public relations and advertising manager, Scania (Great Britain)

W.T.S. Digby-Seymour, secretary and solicitor, 3M United Kingdom

L.J. Donald, publicity manager, Electrolux

D.D. Dunkley, design and display executive, Hovis

Elizabeth Ellett, public relations, Bowater Scott Corporation

Ian Elliott, product affairs manager, communications and public affairs, Austin Morris

Ms Lucia Ercolani, Ercol Furniture

Carol Evans, group publicity officer, DRG (UK)

L.W. Feltham, public relations department, Brooke Bond Oxo

Peggy Field, secretary to executive director, Trebor

D.W. Finney, general manager, Jakar International

Maureen Fortey, administrative co-ordinator to publicity manager, The Decca Record Co.

R.D. Foster, group advertising manager, Sirdar

E.G. Gadd, secretary, Jeyes Group

Ammes Gardner, advertising manager, Berlei (UK)

Helen J.A. Gibbons, product manager, Rowenta

Hazel Gicht, advertising and public relations department, El Al Israel Airlines

P. Giering, assistant advertising manager, Roneo Vickers

D. Goodman, public relations manager, Hoechst UK

Pamela M. Gray, public relations officer, Formica

D.G. Green, public relations manager, Carnation Foods Co.

Roslyn Greenaway, secretary to Sindy Brand manager, Pedigree Dolls & Toys

Mrs S.L. Greenwood, secretary to curator, Kodak Museum, Kodak

Michel Grinberg, délégué général, groupe Gillette, Paris

Kevin Halliden, Dunlop

P.J.C. Harbutt, director, Harbutt's Plasticine

A.W.J. Hart, marketing manager, United Rum Merchants

J.B. Hayes, chairman and managing director, Wolsey Division, Courtaulds Knitwear

R.T. Heatherill, advertising department, The Drambuie Liqueur Co.

T. Heywood, chairman and chief executive, Holt Lloyd International

A.W. Hill, deputy publicity manager, Ferodo

A.K. Hirst, managing director, Ex-Lax

John Hitchin, marketing director, Penguin Books

Tony Hobbs, press officer, Trusthouse Forte

J.P. Honan, managing director, Southon-Horton Laboratories

R.G. Horwood, advertising manager, John Dickinson Stationery

J.R. Hudson, manager, Energen Foods Bureau

Charles J. Humphreys, marketing department, Umbro International

Peter R. Hunt, director of external affairs, The Coca-Cola Export Corporation

Mrs J.L. Hussey, press officer, Marks & Spencer

Jean Hyett, public relations manager, Lilia-White

A.D. Jackson, commercial director, Newey Goodman

C.I. Jessop, product group manager, Sterling Health

David Johnson, publicity manager, Trubenised (Gt Britain)

Erik Johnson, Mercedes-Benz (United Kingdom)

M.H. Karslake, president, Lambretta Preservation Society

Malcolm Kelley, managing director, Ladybird Books

R.W. Kelly, marketing services manager, Sterling Industrial

Mr Kibblewhite, Vono

Lord Killearn, The Morgan Crucible Co.

Simone Klass, public relations executive, Goya International

R.A. Kujawski, brand manager, Plough (UK)

T.D.O. Lewis, managing director, Coffee HAG (UK)

Barrie Liss, director, Evode Holdings

Mr McLauchlan, publicity manager, Lotus Cars

B. Makin, associate director, International Laboratories

Keith Marchant, public relations, Rowntree Mackintosh

Paul Mathieu, Carl Byoir & Associates

Miss Chris M. Mellor, advertising and sales promotion executive, Aristoc Kayser Wolsey Hosiery

M.L. Mellor, secretary, Express Dairy Foods

James Moller, director, The Parker Pen Co.

L. Moon, administrative secretary, Cadbury Schweppes

Miss C. Morgan, marketing services department, Firestone Tyre & Rubber Co.

Mrs Rosamund Morley, public relations department, Gallaher

J.G. Moss, chairman, Kelsey Industries

P.G. Moss, head of trade marks and patents department, Allied Breweries

Kenneth J. Moyes, manager, press and public relations, General Motors

John Murphy, managing director, Novamark International

Miss Catherine Murphy-O'Connor, marketing services supervisor, Ampex

M.S. Naylor, Procter & Gamble

Jessica Nevard, personal assistant to group production manager – Marlboro, Philip Morris

R.W. Newman, assistant to company secretary, Nabisco

A.G. Noble, secretary, Chesebrough-Pond's

G.W. Nockolds, chairman and managing director, E.S. Perry

Mrs Valerie Noon, publicity and press officer, Lec Refrigeration

C.D. Nyberg, secretary and director of public relations, Geo. A. Hormel & Co., Austin, Minnesota

W.J. Ollett, trade marks department, Courtaulds

Arthur S.P. Orr, managing director, McCaw, Stevenson & Orr

B.E. Osborne, marketing controller, Manor Bakeries

C.E. Page, curator, Symington Museum of Period Corsetry, R. & W.H. Symington

A.F. Peters, Shell

Leonard Petts, historical research, EMI

Shirley Platzer, British Tissues

Mrs C.S. Pochciol, assistant marketing manager, own goods marketing (medicinal) department, The Boots Co.

K. Pollitt, managing director, Vessen

B.A. Pollock, information adviser, Mobil Oil Co.

Maria Potempski, public relations manager, Corah

M. Powers, advertising and sales promotion manager, Valor Heating

O.A. Proctor, managing director, Securon Manufacturing

C.J.R. Purdey, joint managing director, Merrydown Wine Co.

Jane Quail, assistant public relations manager, Spillers Foods

B.A. Ramage, group trade marks department, Reckitt & Colman

P. R. Ramage, public relations manager, Permutit-Boby

A.C. Reynolds, marketing services manager, Farley Health Products

A.E. Rhodie, R. Paterson & Sons

N.C. Robinson, managing director, Earex Products

T.J. Roper, Dimplex Heating

Miss B. Rosenbaum, head of information division, The Advertising Association

R. Ross-Turner, public relations services manager, LRC International

R.G. Russell, general manager, Mitsubishi Electric (UK)

Miss S.L. Savage, marketing assistant, Barker & Dobson

Patricia Schooling, Holt Schooling Public Relations

Mike Scott, public relations officer, Golden Wonder

T.J. Sellar, secretary, Lyle & Scott

P.A. Senn, director, Selectus

Richard Seth-Smith, public relations manager, Fiat Motor Co. (UK)

Maura Shackley, group commercial librarian, Berec Group

L. Shaw, divisional advertising and publicity manager, William Hollins & Co.

D.I. Sheppard, group trade marks department, Reckitt & Colman

Allan Shriver, technical editor, 'Amateur Photographer'

J.F. Silcox, secretarial assistant, Abbey National Building Society

Gwyneth Simmons, group communications, Beecham Group

J.R. Smith, communications, Caterpillar Tractor Co.

Maureen Staniforth, information library, Unilever

D. Startup, Mobyke-DKW (UK)

Dr. Storkebaum, Vize-Direktor, Ciba-Geigy AG, Basel

John F. Storrs, media relations manager, Berol

Roger Tamplin, Berger, Jenson & Nicholson

E. Telford, secretary, Corning

R.G. Thake, director and company secretary, The Rawlplug Co.

Molly Theobald, consumer services manager, Wander

D.H. Thomas, deputy managing director, Schreiber Furniture

J.A. Tolhurst, secretary, Ogden's

Bruce K. Turner, managing director, Bermaline

Peter E. Turner, marketing services manager, Bovis Construction

Robert C.J. Tuttle, patent attorney, Jeep Corporation, Southfield, Michigan

Miss Jane Twemlow, publicity department, Fodens

George Underwood, Subbuteo Sports Games

Ralph Vernon-Hunt, managing director, Pan Books

Peter Watts, public relations, H.J. Heinz Co.

B.D.P. Wetters, group patent agent, Turner & Newall

216

David T.G. White, conference services consultant, Tannoy Audio Communications

P. Whittaker, managing representative UK, Sanforized Services

J.A. Williams, group product manager, Thermos

Julia B.C. Williams, product manager, Timex Corporation

Miss Marion Wilson, secretary to divisional managing director, Alfa-Laval

Rosalind Woolfson, Opus Public Relations

Jennie Wormald, publicity department, BTR

I would particularly like to express my gratitude to Mr A.R. Reid, formerly chairman of LRC International, for telling me in person how he came to devise the name *Durex*, and to Mr R.A. Watson, formerly managing director of Associated Adhesives, for similarly giving me the background to *Gloy*.

I would also specially like to thank my father, R.G. Room, formerly personnel manager of the Avon Rubber Company, for obtaining essential information regarding the name behind *Avon* tyres.

For the actual typing of the manuscript, I am greatly indebted to Jan Chatfield, Kim Reseigh and Michelle Smith of Ace Secretarial Services ('Accurate, Confidential, Express'), Petersfield, Hampshire, who gamely and cheerfully coped with a sudden assignment and thereby enabled me to meet my deadline. They indeed were real aces.

For permission to quote from *Tono-Bungay* by H.G. Wells I am indebted to A.P. Watt Ltd, and for permission to quote the computerised names on pp.203–5, I acknowledge the kind consent of J.H. de Bussy bv of Amsterdam.

For advising on the legal aspect of the wording of the book at a number of points I am greatly indebted to the solicitor Mr Patten Bridge of the firm of Patten Bridge & Co., London.